NATIVE AMERICAN DANCE : CEREMONIES AND SOCIAL TRADITIONS

CHARLOTTE HETH
GENERAL EDITOR

NATIONAL MUSEUM OF
THE AMERICAN INDIAN
SMITHSONIAN INSTITUTION
WITH STARWOOD PUBLISHING, INC.
WASHINGTON, DC

THE MUSEUM AT WARM SP

Native American Dance: Ceremonies and Social Traditions has been made possible in part through the generous support of David Rockefeller.

Library of Congress Cataloging-in-Publication Data

Native American dance: ceremonies and social traditions / Charlotte Heth, general editor.

p.   cm.

Published in conjunction with an exhibition of the National Museum of the American Indian, held at the Alexander Hamilton U.S. Custom House, New York, Nov. 15, 1992 to Jan. 24, 1993.

Includes bibliographical references and index.

ISBN 1-56373-020-0: $45.00. — ISBN 1-56373-021-9 (pbk.): $24.95

1. Indians — Dance — Exhbitions. 2. Indians — Rites and ceremonies — Exhibitions. 3. Indians — Religion and mythology — Exhibitions. 4. National Museum of the American Indian (U.S.) — Exhibitions. I. Heth, Charlotte. II. National Museum of the American Indian (U.S.)

E59.D35N38   1992   92-34969

394.3'0897 — dc20   CIP

Fred Nahwooksy: Project Developer
Charlotte Heth: General Editor
Gaye Brown: Project Director
Terence Winch: Editor
Design by Grafik Communications, Ltd.
Typeset in Berkeley Book and Gill Sans Extra Bold Condensed and printed on Quintessence 80 lb. text
Printed by Peake Printers, Inc.

This book is published in conjunction with a series of Native American dance presentations accompanying the National Museum of the American Indian's exhibition *Pathways of Tradition: Indian Insights into Indian Worlds*, on view at the Alexander Hamilton U.S. Custom House, Bowling Green, New York City, 15 November 1992 to 24 January 1993.

The National Museum of the American Indian, Smithsonian Institution, is dedicated to working in collaboration with the indigenous peoples of the Americas to foster and protect native cultures throughout the Western Hemisphere. The museum's publishing program seeks to augment awareness of Native American beliefs and lifeways and to educate the public about the history and significance of native culture.

COVER: *Comanche* tosa coby *(white-face) dancer John Keel at the Vietnam Veterans Annual, Anadarko, Oklahoma, May 1992. His arrangement of eagle feathers, face-paint design, animal-skin headgear, and dance style are evidence of the individual expression that continues to change within the context of Native American ceremonial and social traditions. See "Southern Plains Dance: Tradition and Dynamics," figure 126.*

HALF-TITLE PAGE: *A Kodiak Alutiiq Dancer uses a "Whistling Mask" for his courting song. See "Contemporary Alaska Native Dance: The Spirit of Tradition," figure 166.*

FRONTISPIECE: *Oqwa Pi, or Red Cloud (also known as Abel Sánchez), ca. 1899-1902 –1972 (San Ildefonso Pueblo), Tewa "Comanche" Dance, graphite and watercolor on paper, 142.8 x 181.5 cm. National Museum of the American Indian, Smithsonian Institution, no. 22.8606. This social-parody dance—in which Tewas dress as Plains Indian warriors and dance to the accompaniment of songs containing a few Comanche words—is discussed in "The Beauty, Humor, and Power of Tewa Pueblo Dance."*

ILLUSTRATION p. vii: *San Carlos Apache dancers at the Gallup Ceremonial, New Mexico, 1990*

ILLUSTRATIONS pp. viii, xi: *A fancy dancer and dance regalia at the Keepers of the Western Door Powwow, St. Bonaventure University, New York, July 1992*

ILLUSTRATION p. 184: *Grass Dancer, Keepers of the Western Door Powwow, St. Bonaventure University, New York, July 1992*

C O N T E N T S

ix   FOREWORD

W. Richard West

1   INTRODUCTION

AMERICAN INDIAN DANCE: A CELEBRATION OF SURVIVAL AND ADAPTATION

Charlotte Heth

19   INSIDE THE LONGHOUSE: DANCES OF THE HAUDENOSAUNEE

Ron LaFrance

      Dancing the Cycles of Life

      Linley B. Logan

33   THE FIESTA: RHYTHM OF LIFE IN THE SIERRAS OF MEXICO AND THE

ALTIPLANO OF BOLIVIA

Nancy Rosoff and Olivia Cadaval

      Zapotec Dances and Music from the

      Northern Sierra of Oaxaca

      Manuel Ríos Morales

      The Music and Dance that Nourishes and Gladdens the

      Deities of the Tzotziles and Tzeltales

      Jaime Torres Burguete

      The Aymara Fiesta: Linking Community Realities

      Tomás Huanca Laura

65   WHITE MOUNTAIN APACHE DANCE: EXPRESSIONS OF SPIRITUALITY

Cécile R. Ganteaume

      The Crown Dance

      Edgar Perry

83   THE BEAUTY, HUMOR, AND POWER OF TEWA PUEBLO DANCE

Jill D. Sweet

      Shadeh

      Rina Swentzell and Dave Warren

105   SOUTHERN PLAINS DANCE: TRADITION AND DYNAMICS
       Thomas W. Kavanagh
           Tonkonga: The Kiowa Black Legs
           Military Society
           William C. Meadows and Gus Palmer, Sr.

125   NORTHERN PLAINS DANCE
       Lynn F. Huenemann
           The Sun Dance
           Arthur Amiotte
           Stoney
           Fred Nahwooksy

149   CONTEMPORARY ALASKA NATIVE DANCE:
       THE SPIRIT OF TRADITION
       Maria Williams
           Dance Rattles of the Northwest Coast
           Mary Jane Lenz

169   MODERN NATIVE DANCE: BEYOND TRIBE AND TRADITION
       Rosalie M. Jones
           Cherokee Stomp Dance: Laughter Rises Up
           Rayna Green

185   SELECT BIBLIOGRAPHY, DISCOGRAPHY, AND VIDEOGRAPHY

188   CONTRIBUTORS

192   INDEX

196   PHOTOGRAPHY CREDITS

F O R E W O R D

In my life as a Southern Cheyenne, dance has always occupied a very special place. When I was six years old, my father made for my younger brother and me our first dance ensembles, complete with feather bustles, moccasins, buffalo-bone breast plates, bells, and head roaches. Realizing, perhaps, that at the time I was more enamored of the colorful fluffs on the bustles and the sounds I could make with one-inch bells strapped at my knees, my father took considerable care to explain why certain materials were used in the dance outfits, what they meant, and what their importance was in the Cheyenne Way. When he taught us the dances them-selves—which included the Eagle, Shield, Buffalo, Round, Two-step, and War dances, among others—he paid equal attention to emphasizing the place of dance as ceremony rather than only as performance. As a result, I have always considered dance to be among the most profound cultural expressions—for me personally—of what it is to be Cheyenne.

Against this personal history, you will understand why I am especially pleased to introduce *Native American Dance: Ceremonies and Social Traditions,* the first scholarly publication of the Smithsonian Institution's National Museum of the American Indian. This collection of enlightening essays has grown out of the combined efforts of several of the leading scholars and practitioners of dance in the Indian community. It admirably serves the museum's commitment to honor and nurture native peoples and their cultures—a commitment that we intend to fulfill through publications, public programs, training, and community service, even before all the facilities for the new museum are complete. As an institution of living culture, we cannot act too quickly in preserving and recognizing Indian traditions and lifeways.

There is an irony in publishing *Native American Dance* on the occasion of the quincentenary of Columbus's first encounter with the native peoples of the Western Hemisphere, for the book treats an aspect of being Indian that has endured and, indeed, blossomed in the face of great cultural adversity. Dance is the very embodiment of indigenous values and represents the response of Native Americans to complex and sometimes difficult historical experiences. Music and dance combine with material culture, language, spirituality, and artistic expression in compelling and complex ways, and are definitive elements of native identity. Dance reflects the vast capacity of native peoples to endure culturally and to continue as a vital contemporary cultural phenomenon, notwithstanding historical oppression and a way of being that stands in stark contrast, if not rebuttal, to much that drives the current techno-logical age. The dance of native peoples is thus both a vital means of surviving culturally and a powerful expression of that survival.

We hope that this book will contribute to the knowledge of these vital traditions, whose documentation, analysis, and preservation have received significantly less attention than they deserve. The topics and themes that follow derive from the particular interests and experiences of the authors. Rather than offering a comprehensive overview of Native American dance, the book intends to suggest the breadth and diversity of form and meaning in native dance traditions. We hope that by revealing the richness of the field, the essays will motivate further research, documentation, and publication—not to mention appreciation.

The authors have approached their subjects from a variety of personal perspectives: native and non-native, male and female, observer and participant, academic and community scholars. What they share is an abiding interest in traditions that embody the human capacity to express ideas and feelings in movement while simultaneously suggesting cultural ethics and aesthetics shaped by unique historical experiences. Perhaps the most important theme that unites the authors' varied approaches is "motive": why do Native Americans dance? The reasons are as complex and manifold as the dances themselves: to assert cultural identity, to fulfill family and community obligations, to enjoy the sense of belonging to a group, to feel the sheer joy of movement. Whether it is ceremonial or social in nature, native dance is an essential part of being—it may be wonderfully entertaining, but it is never regarded as entertainment.

In addition to owing a debt to the authors for increasing our understanding of native dance, there are a number of people I wish to thank for making this book a reality. We owe a very special thanks to Dr. Charlotte Heth for assuming the responsibility of general editor. We greatly appreciate her taking time from her full schedule as a speaker, advisor, administrator, and teacher to lend her scholarly expertise and experience to this undertaking. Her guidance has helped make *Native American Dance* a significant contribution to the field. In addition, several other prominent scholars graciously agreed to serve anonymously as peer reviewers for the essays—to them we are likewise indebted.

The Public Programs staff of the National Museum of the American Indian, first under Acting Assistant Director James Volkert and then under newly appointed Assistant Director Richard Hill, worked quickly and efficiently to produce this book in time for the museum's complementary dance program. Exhibitions Coordinator Fred Nahwooksy developed the concept for *Native American Dance*, identified the authors, and advised on all aspects of the project. Gaye Brown, Director of Publications, guided the project through editing, photography research, and design and production, in addition to handling contract negotiations. Editor Terence Winch, with the museum's Publications Office, ushered the manuscripts through the complex editorial process and managed the myriad tasks required to produce a book of this scope. Lou Stancari, editorial assistant, brought energy and organization to the many details of production and editing.

The museum's curatorial staff provided learned assistance with fact-checking and photography research, and Sharon Dean, Karen Furth, Pamela Dewey, Laura Nash, and Janine Jones of the museum's Photography Department met many eleventh-hour requests for images from the collection. Richard Hamilton, Judy Kirpich, and Resa Scott of Grafik Communications pooled their considerable talent to create a handsome and sensitive design. Their work, along with the contemporary photography of Walter Bigbee, Jeffrey Jay Foxx, Fred Hirschmann, Mark Kelley, Kevin King, Scott Logan, Barbara Lau, Michael A. Moore, Izzy Seidman, Roger Sweet, and Harry Tonemah, brings the dance to life visually. Finally, Ruina Judd and Lynne Shaner of Starwood Publishing lent time and support to ensure that the book finds a wide readership.

As Director of the National Museum of the American Indian, I am proud to present *Native American Dance: Ceremonies and Social Traditions*. The authors have brought lively, yet serious, attention to an integral part of native life and culture, both past and present. It is precisely through these kinds of illuminating efforts that we are better able to understand and appreciate the immense contribution that is the art and culture of the native peoples of the Western Hemisphere.

W. RICHARD WEST, JR., DIRECTOR
Southern Cheyenne and member of the Cheyenne and Arapaho Tribes of Oklahoma

AMERICAN INDIAN DANCE: A CELEBRATION OF SURVIVAL AND ADAPTATION

CHARLOTTE HETH

American Indian dance exists everywhere in America and in every venue, from the most traditional and private spaces to those most public and accessible.[1] Thousands of dancers perform every day in out-of-the-way places — not to satisfy paying audiences or patrons, but to assure the continuation of ancient lifeways, to honor deities and each other, to associate with friends and kin, and to affirm their Indian identities. Others showcase Native American dance on the stage, using the worlds of ballet, modern dance, or abridged versions of traditional dance (fig. 1).

Most Indian dance events are non-commercial and succeed with nothing but word-of-mouth advertising. Since admission is rarely charged, and parking is often free, an audience from outside the local community is usually neither cultivated nor expected. The best performers and leaders (or choreographers) rely on time-tested notions of space, time, music, dress, adornment, and steps to create dance events. Most dancers learn by participating from childhood and continuing throughout their lives. Nowadays, a few enroll in classes, take private or group lessons, or complete apprenticeships with master Indian dancers. Most either make their own dance apparel or commission it from friends and family, and few make any money practicing their art (figs. 2, 3).

Who are these dancers? They are fortunate members of surviving, ancient lifeways in this hemisphere. As shown in the essays that follow, they organize and participate in powwows; social and seasonal dances; life-cycle ceremonies; feast days and fiestas; stomp dances; agricultural ceremonies; special tribal, religious, and honoring ceremonies; family and clan events; and medicine rites. Their collaborators and fellow dancers are Native American people who share common interests and ideologies. They are people living and changing in a modern world. They live everywhere — on reservations, in cities, villages, and rural communities from Tierra del Fuego to the Yucatán to Point Barrow (figs. 4, 5).

Although many dances and ceremonies are performed regularly by Indians living on or near reservations or in rural areas of the United States and Canada, new contexts — like urban Indian gatherings and powwows, for example — foster the composition, change, and continuation of certain traditions, primarily those from the Plains. Music and dance are frequently shared across tribal boundaries in an ever-expanding circle of tradition. Whether the songs and dances came originally from the Creator, another deity, a guardian spirit, a slain monster, or even an animal, human choreographers and composers have always played the most important part in creating and perpetuating the music and dance.

I FIRST ANNUAL INTERTRIBAL POWWOW, LEWISTON, NEW YORK, 1979. DANCER #6 IS THE LATE EARL MEDICINE.

2 MAKING A DANCER'S
SASH,
A CRAFTSMAN
DEMONSTRATES
FINGERWEAVING.

3 BRENDA WHITE EAGLE
READIES HER SON, LANCE
QUIVER WHITE EAGLE, FOR A
TRADITIONAL COYOTE DANCE
AT A NEW JERSEY POWWOW,
JULY 1992.

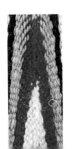

4 KUU JAW, A HAIDA
DRUMMER FROM
BRITISH COLUMBIA

5 A CELEBRATION
ORGANIZED BY THE
WEAVERS' COOPERATIVE,
SNA JOLOBIL, IN TENEJAPA,
MEXICO

When we speak of early historic times of Indians, we limit ourselves to the written words of others. When we speak of prehistoric times, we must rely on the work of archaeologists. What we, as scholars, need to include to create a more complete picture of Indian dance history are the oral histories and sacred narratives of native peoples themselves. To address this need, Indian people, in many of the articles that follow, have given personal accounts of dance history and intimate glimpses into their feelings about particular dances.[2]

Looking at the ancient art of the Americas, it is possible for one to imagine many dances dating back to prehistoric times. In the fall in North America, stately dancers in feather cloaks and engraved shell jewelry perform a Harvest Dance. In the winter, storytellers entertain young and old alike with legends of animals who can dance, talk, and sing. In the spring, dancers celebrate the cleansing of the earth and its waterways after a long winter. In the summer, children perform animal dances and games. All these activities existed when North America was inhabited only by native peoples. Some of these dances still exist today.

In Central and South America, similar activities occurred and continue to this day. Huge processionals and circle dances of pre-Columbian origin survive today alongside Catholic religious events (figs. 6, 7). Animal dances and other representational and mimetic forms also endure, featuring fish, mammals of earth and water, reptiles, and birds. Popular also are the European and African-derived dances that represent syncretism at its best.

After European contact, many Indians were dispersed from aboriginal lands to new homelands, cities, or reservations as a result of wars, inducements by treaty, and other economic and political forces. While some peoples disappeared altogether, other smaller groups intermarried with neighboring peoples, both Indian and

6 CERAMIC FIESTA SCENE, WITH THREE MUSICIANS PLAYING DRUMS AND RATTLES, SURROUNDED BY A CIRCLE OF DANCERS (SIX OF WHOM ARE ALSO WHISTLES), CA. 300 B.C.– A.D. 600, 20.5 CM (DIAM.). NAYARIT, WEST MEXICO. NATIONAL MUSEUM OF THE AMERICAN INDIAN, SMITHSONIAN INSTITUTION, NO. 23.2162

7 MAYAN CARNIVAL DANCERS BEFORE THE CHURCH IN CHIAPA DE CORZO, MEXICO

5

8 KEEPERS OF
THE WESTERN
DOOR POWWOW,
ST. BONAVENTURE
UNIVERSITY, NEW YORK,
JULY 1992

9 LEGENDARY
FLUTE PLAYER
COCOPELLI, A
PETROGLYPH IN
GALLISTEO, NEW
MEXICO

non-Indian, or were adopted by larger tribes. Often government agents grouped peoples together arbitrarily, or because of language, cultural similarities, or geographical proximity. This widespread destruction and dislocation of tribes and their cultures affected music and dance greatly.

Indian religious practices, the nexus for most dances, were often banned by the churches and colonial governments. When the Pueblo Indians of New Mexico and Arizona revolted in 1680 and forced the Spanish south to El Paso, they gained concessions regarding taxation, governance, and the moderation of religious persecution from the Europeans. After the revolt, native religions and dances were practiced, to some extent, alongside Catholic rituals. While the United States Government's ban on Indian religions in the nineteenth century targeted the Sun Dance and Ghost Dance in particular, it affected all other native religions as well. In Canada, the government seized many beautiful ceremonial objects and much dance regalia when Northwest Coast Indian potlatches (huge native giveaway celebrations) became illegal. In the twentieth century, economic necessity and a U.S. Government relocation program have compelled many Indians to migrate to cities. Their creative solution for surviving urban alienation has been to start powwow clubs with other Indian community members, with Plains Indian music and dance dominating, regardless of the multiplicity of heritages (fig. 8).

10 MOLD-MADE CERAMIC RATTLES, CA. A.D. 600–800, 14 CM LONG. JAINA ISLAND, CAMPECHE, MEXICO. NATIONAL MUSEUM OF THE AMERICAN INDIAN, SMITHSONIAN INSTITUTION, NOS. 24.3403, 23.3044, 22.5598

From prehistoric evidence, early contact drawings, paintings, and verbal descriptions from today's Indians (the keepers of tribal memory), we know something of early ceremonies, dances, and musical instruments (fig. 9). Dancers performed both to vocal and instrumental music featuring a variety of instruments. The musicians set the beat and marked the changes with both kettle and frame drums (with and without water); hand-held rattles of gourd, rawhide, horn, and turtle-shell; animal-tooth, turtle-shell, shell, and deer-hoof strung rattles (worn on various parts of the dancers' bodies); conch-shell trumpets; bird-bone whistles or trumpets; many cane and ceramic flutes and whistles; striking sticks; struck logs (hollow or otherwise); rasps; musical bows; and other similar instruments. The various rattles enriched the sound by underscoring important words, keeping the beat, and adding sonic layers to the texture of the music.

Many of these instruments have survived — the drums; the hand-held rattles; the strung rattles worn on the dancers' arms, legs, and torsos; the flutes; conch-shell trumpets; whistles; hollow logs; rasps; and striking sticks among them (figs. 10–12). Some important new additions to the catalogue of instruments and dance regalia involve the substitutions of metal rattles and bells for ones formerly made of natural materials. Tin-can leg rattles, for example, have substituted for turtle shells and metal saltshakers for the hollow-gourd rattles used in the Gourd Dance. Sequins, trade beads, plastic bones, and other mass-manufactured items adorn today's dance outfits. Popular Latin American musicians now use *claves, guiros, teponaztles,* and other rhythm instruments based on the striking sticks, rasps, and hollow logs of the past.

Dance still occupies an important position within many Indian groups that continue to practice the old religions and dances vital to their way of life. Because many dances and songs have spiritual and supernatural sources, they retain their original significance and value. These traditional dances, often tied

to seasonal or life-cycle events, are regionally or tribally specific; the singers usually perform in native languages and the ceremonies unfold according to ancient calendars and belief systems. Few traditional dances offer individual freedom of expression. Rather, each dancer embodies the unique opportunity to express himself or herself in physical action. In addition to public dances, there are private and semi-public dances for curing, prayer, initiation, storytelling, performing magic, playing games, courting, hunting, and influencing nature (fig. 13). In performing these songs, dances, and rituals, the Indians of today reaffirm their ties to a living culture.

Dance forms vary because Native Americans are different not only from other peoples, but from each other as well. One finds few solos, yet many ensemble forms. Many of the latter have a leader and chorus; some are unison groups, others groups with featured soloists; a few have dancers with individualistic styles. Sometimes one finds multi-part dances, with the dancers occupying a variety of roles. Not all Indian people dance to a drum. Often the dancers themselves, activating the rattles and bells that adorn their dance clothes, set their own beat.

11 DOUBLE BLACK-WARE FLUTE WITH EIGHT HOLES AND THREE MODELED BIRDS, CA. 300 B.C – A.D. 600, 46 CM LONG. COLIMA, WEST MEXICO. NATIONAL MUSEUM OF THE AMERICAN INDIAN, SMITHSONIAN INSTITUTION, NO. 24.7525

12 DRUM OR TWO-TONED WOODEN GONG (*TEPONAZTLI*), WITH GLYPH BEARING DATE, CA. A.D. 1493, 44.6 CM LONG. AZTEC, TLAXCALA. MEXICO. NATIONAL MUSEUM OF THE AMERICAN INDIAN, SMITHSONIAN INSTITUTION, NO. 16.3373

ndian dance is not particularly acrobatic in terms of leaps, but somewhat restrained, with the dancers staying close to the earth, both for philosophical and practical reasons. Dancers usually take small steps — because of space, number of participants, or the need to conserve strength in order to dance for long periods of time (sometimes all day or night). Some dancers mimic animals or birds (figs. 14, 15), or the work of hunting, fishing, planting, harvesting, and preparing food, or other occupations, or warfare. The largest motions are in the torso and head, with very few twists of the dancer's body. When they are extended, feet act as a unit with the legs, and hands with the arms. Small movements of the forearms and wrists occur when the dancer shakes an implement such as a rattle, stick, or branch. Some expressions in dance require crouching or bent-over postures, which are not usually quick movements, and the dancer usually stays in the bent-over position for a musical phrase or longer section of the dance (fig. 16). While individual expression is allowed in most North American Plains dances, Pueblo dances require unison and strict rules of motion, broken up from time to time by the relatively free movements of the clowns. The Hoop Dance, a "show dance" of many tribes, is one of the most individual — it features a dancer's manipulation of a dozen or more hoops over and around his torso, legs,

14 JULIAN MARTINEZ (1879–1943),
HUNTER AND TWO DEER DANCERS,
CA. 1924, WATERCOLOR AND
GRAPHITE ON BOARD,
29.5 X 69.8 CM. NATIONAL MUSEUM
OF THE AMERICAN INDIAN,
SMITHSONIAN INSTITUTION,
NO. 24.7983

16 DANCER AT COMANCHE
HOMECOMING, WALTERS,
OKLAHOMA, JULY 1992

15 EAGLE DANCE
DEMONSTRATION,
SAN ILDEFONSO PUEBLO,
1989

and arms to form a variety of geometric shapes. Customarily, Indian dances require communal interaction, cooperation, compliance with group norms, and, not accidentally, several generations of participants (fig. 17).

The dance space is often conceived in terms of circles, with the dancers moving either clockwise or counterclockwise, as determined by their cosmology and worldview. Other dance orientations involve line dancers moving forward or backward in unison, or dancing in place, and dancers moving in a processional into and out of larger dance areas. In the far northern and southern latitudes, the familiar lines and circles often become almost stationary or dissolve into purposeful meanderings in order to use all of the available space, particularly when dances are performed indoors.

Because dance is tied to belief systems, often the directions of the dances, the words to the music, the number of repetitions, the choice and manufacture of instruments, the dress and bodily adornment, and the interaction of performers are symbolic in nature and cannot be properly observed without knowing something about theology. Indeed, in Indian life, the dance is not possible without the belief systems and the music, and the belief systems and the music can hardly exist without the dance.

On the whole, Indian music in North America is mostly vocal and monophonic with rattle and/or drum accompaniment. It comprises vocal and instrumental solo pieces, leader-chorus responsorial songs, unison chorus songs, and multipart songs (some of which are without instrumental accompaniment, although multipart songs are rare outside of California and the Northwest Coast). Most Indian music accompanies dance. While many singers use a drum to set the beat and signal repetitions and changes in dance movements, rattles are the most widespread instruments.

Many songs have a wide range, testing the stamina and artistry of the singers. Others — such as the Bird Dance songs of Southern California Indians, lullabies, and hand-game songs — are usually narrow in range and easier to sing. Although most songs are performed, for the most part, in native languages, some include vocables (non-translatable syllables) used to carry the melody in the same way that "fa-la-la" and other vocables do in European folk songs. These vocables are fixed and are indeed the words to the songs. Many of the melodies start high and descend throughout the rendition; others undulate from beginning to end. Variations in vocal style identify tribal and regional differences and genres of songs. A few songs sound like recitations on one or two pitches. Besides the sounds of the drum, bells, and an occasional whistle, the "pulsation," or intentional quavering of the voices, enhances the texture — especially in Plains, Pueblo, Apache, and Navajo music. Shouts and animal cries are important markers in defining musical form and in signalling dancers. In North America it is rare to find melodic instruments accompanying singing and dancing.

Ceramic, wooden, and cane flutes are, however, widespread in the Americas; they are double, single, and multiple, like panpipes. Some are anthropomorphic or zoomorphic, and some contain water in order to make birdlike sounds. A few flutes are extremely long and played in concert. In Venezuela, rattles and hollow, struck idiophones serve as a shaman's musical implements for curing.

The Apache fiddle in North America (made from a mescal stalk) and musical bows from both hemispheres are examples of early stringed instruments, although pre-Columbian evidence is difficult to find for these. Given the rapid adoption and adaptation of stringed instruments such as guitars, fiddles, and the like, either a few strings existed in the past, or the novelty was too appealing to resist. In contrast to North American Indian practices, one finds many varieties of stringed instruments in Central and South America, played by Indians to accompany dance.[3]

With American Indian dance, unlike most Euro-American classical and folk dance, it is often not possible to predict certain elements: the exact length of a dance, the number of beats before a turn, the number of dancers required, the exact time of the performance, or even whether a rehearsal will be held. Although many Indian communities offer songs and dances from ancient times, even some of these old ceremonies require new compositions each season — such as the Turtle (*Okushare*), Cloud (*Pogonshare*), and Basket (*Tunshare*) dances of San Juan Pueblo.[4] While the ancient standards and beliefs are upheld, new words and tunes appear within that framework, and the dancers must rehearse anew with the singers.

Other forms — like the Stomp Dance of the Cherokees, Creeks, Yuchis, and other formerly Southeastern United States tribes — have infinite variation within a set framework. No two stomp dances would ever be identical. The song/dance leader begins with a standardized introduction, with his chorus echoing him in call-and-response fashion. Then he chooses from among the many songs in his repertoire, stringing them together in a cycle. Each song and each section in the song vary in length and number of beats from time to time because of inspiration, introduction of words, or individual artistry. Since the dancers, singers, and instrumentalists (women dancers wearing turtle-shell leg rattles) all dance with and follow the leader, the improvisatory style is exhilarating, not problematic. The leader gives a hand signal for a subtle change of beat, the dancers slow or stop, and all make the transition to the next song, sometimes marking it with a group shout. These two examples of freedom and constraint illustrate one reason why "traditional" dance and music have not only survived, but thrived.

17 A YOUNG DANCER RECEIVES GUIDANCE DURING A DANCE AT THE EIGHT NORTHERN INDIAN ARTS AND CRAFT FAIR, 1989.

Because Indians in the twentieth century live differently from their ancestors, occasions for the per-formance of music and dance have expanded to non-traditional settings. Since the first time Indians performed for others — perhaps other Indians or Europeans — outside of their native habitats, aboriginal dance has often existed out of context. In the 1990s, Indian traditional singers and dancers can be found at Indian and county fairs, public receptions honoring dignitaries (Indian or otherwise), national Indian conferences, political rallies, crafts fairs, public programs of museums and colleges, demonstrations by Indian political activists, graduation ceremonies of Indian students, tourist attractions, amusement parks, and in various Indian education programs. Indian traditional dance can now be studied formally from the preschool to the university levels.

A few professional dancers and musicians have arisen from these unusual circumstances. Some are retired and wish to share their knowledge and culture; some believe they have a duty to educate the general public in order to abolish negative stereotypes; others teach children to carry on their traditions. Customarily these singers and dancers make extra money by consulting and performing in public. In these contexts, the leaders are usually very careful to stick to proper presentation of the songs and dances, to perform only the more secular selections from their repertoires, and to explain briefly the original context of the dance. The American Indian Dance Theatre, the most visible professional troupe, asks formal permission of tribal elders and governments before adapting native dances for the stage. In their extensive program notes they also strive to educate the audience while presenting a visual and aural feast.

An early trend in social-science research tended to freeze Indian groups into ancient categories, with no recognition of the native capacity for change. Many researchers sought out the oldest dancers and singers hoping to find "pure" art forms. This search for ostensible purity disallowed the fact that Indian people had the creativity and ability to change their music and dance — qualities associated with the Western world's definition of "art." While repeating ancient songs, dances, and ceremonies is necessary to maintain certain social, religious, and curing ceremonies, the creation and performance of new songs and dances is equally necessary to ensure sustained interest and continuity (fig. 18). It is commendable to re-enact a dance about a war expedition from the nineteenth century, but it is equally important to compose a new song and dance for the 1991 Operation Desert Storm, as some Kiowas have done.

Literacy is a tool that can mitigate against change — except, it seems, in Indian dance. Written documentation of Indian dance has been limited, partially by the constraints of dance notation, which is still evolving. A few scholars, such as Gertrude P. Kurath and Joanne W. Kealiinohomoku, have presented schemes for dealing with Indian dance, but most studies have focused on ethnography and ground plans.[5] With the advent of video documentation, dancers can now study past performances both for scholarly and perform-ance purposes. When these captured dances are re-created, they will probably be varied to suit the voices and styles of today's singers and dancers. New dances and genres are still being composed with new words, melodies, steps, and dress. For example, the women's Fancy-Shawl and Jingle-Dress competitions feature many innovations, particularly in freedom of movement (figs. 19, 20). The contemporary revival of many Indian

19 JINGLE-DRESS DANCE
COMPETITION, KEEPERS
OF THE WESTERN DOOR
POWWOW, ST. BONAVENTURE
UNIVERSITY, NEW YORK,
JULY 1992

18 CONTEMPORARY
INFLUENCES ARE
CLEARLY EVIDENT IN
THE DANCE DRESS OF
THIS SAN CARLOS
APACHE CLOWN AT THE
GALLUP CEREMONIAL,
1990.

20 FANCY-SHAWL
DANCE COMPETITION,
KEEPERS OF THE WESTERN
DOOR POWWOW,
ST. BONAVENTURE
UNIVERSITY, NEW YORK,
JULY 1992

dances has also fostered healthy controversy over authenticity of versions, proper instrumentation and dress, suitable venues, ownership of songs, dances, and ceremonies, and even whether some dances should be revived or not. But, in the end, the dynamics of change, stressing an appreciation of the creative process, and of tradition are not antithetical — they are complementary.

Social dance, the most communal and most easily learned dance, is likely to survive longer than other forms. The least communal and most specialized dances — ceremonial dances and curing ceremonies — may not outlast their specialist practitioners, particularly when knowledge of the ceremony is bound by fluency in Indian languages. Newer hybrid forms — such as "Chicken Scratch" or *waila* (from *baile*, the Spanish word for dance), based on Norteño styles of the Mexican border — defy prognosis. Music and dance are still vital in locations where Indians are concentrated — in certain rural areas and cities, and on the reservations.

If the leaders of our hemisphere allow people to continue living out of the mainstream in rural pockets, then native people will persevere in carrying on their language, music, dance, and ceremonies. If community life disintegrates further because of economic or political necessity, then music and dance may also perish.

The value of this music and dance to the peoples who created them and still use them cannot be overestimated. Indian music and dance pervade all aspects of life, from creation stories to death and remembrance of death. The importance of American Indian dance is found not only in its impact on modern society, but also in the traditions and values it expresses to and for the Indian peoples. This oral tradition has survived solely because the music and dance were too important to be allowed to die. Native peoples' relationships to their creators, their fellow humans, and to nature is what American Indian dance really celebrates.

1   "Traditional," as used by many Indian people and scholars, can be an overarching term with varying meanings. Sometimes it refers to the oldest norms: languages, religions, artistic forms, everyday customs, and individual behavior. At other times it refers to modern practices based on those norms. Again, it may refer to a time period before technological advances. It may even refer to categories of dance, music, and dress that draw most closely on ancient, established practices. Here I am referring to accepted and accustomed places for performances in reservation or rural communities — "dance places."
    To allow flexibility for the individual authors in this book, the term American Indian or Indian is used along with Native American, Native Alaskan, Native Canadian, and various other indigenous terms to refer to the original inhabitants of the Americas. A recent survey of 107 U.S. colleges and universities found these institutions evenly split between Native American and American Indian when it came to naming their Indian studies programs. See Charlotte Heth and Susan Guyette, *Issues for the Future of American Indian Studies: A Needs Assessment and Program Guide* (Los Angeles: American Indian Studies Center, UCLA, 1985).

2   See also Charlotte Heth, "Oklahoma's Indian Music: A Framework for Understanding," in *Songs of Indian Territory: Native American Music Traditions of Oklahoma*, Willie Smyth, ed. (Oklahoma City: Center of the American Indian, 1989), pp. 11–17.

3   The pan-Indian, pan-tribal, and urban movements of the past century have caused some diffusion of Indian styles and have created a commercial musical interest among the Indian record-buying public. One finds taped music played by Indian people at work, in automobiles, and as background at many gatherings. Some listen to show pride and reinforce identity, others to learn new songs or just enjoy themselves, and many make their own recordings of powwows, stomp dances, and other Indian gatherings for their listening pleasure. The Indian market for this dance music has spawned several commercial record companies.

4   See also Nora Yeh, "The Pogonshare Ceremony of the Tewa San Juan, New Mexico," *Selected Reports in Ethnomusicology* (UCLA Program in Ethnomusicology, Charlotte Heth, ed.) 3, no. 2 (1980): 102.

5   Gertrude Prokosch Kurath's *Half a Century of Dance Research* (Flagstaff, Ariz.: Cross-Cultural Dance Resources, 1986), is a compendium of Kurath's works on dance ethnology, many of which are devoted to American Indian dance. As founder in 1981 of Cross-Cultural Dance Resources, Joanne W. Kealiinohomoku publishes a newsletter on dance ethnology with many articles on American Indian dance.

INSIDE THE LONGHOUSE: DANCES OF THE HAUDENOSAUNEE

RON LAFRANCE

People, listen with your most careful ear, for today we have a new face among us." So begins the name-giving speech of the Haudenosaunee, as we Iroquois call ourselves, with the introduction of a new member of the nation — his or her introduction to the community at large. The newborn or infant will be given a gender-appropriate name that has been carefully selected from among the clan names, that is not taken by any other member of that particular clan, and that doesn't sound similar to other clan names. What is important about this particular ceremony and name is that we don't know what gift we have been given by the Creator at the time of our birth. It may be that the gift we are born with is the ability to sing the songs of our people.

As within most societies, the songs and dances of the Haudenosaunee (People of the Longhouse) fall into two major categories, social and ceremonial (fig. 21). The social dances, approximately nineteen in number, vary in length, verses, and tempo. There is a dance to suit every person's taste, from the very young to the very elderly. Most important, these dances are held for many reasons, one being to amuse the people as they spend their time on earth. The literal translation of *o-wen-tsia-ke on-wa-te-re-wa-tohn-te*, the term for social dance, is "the dances for the celebration of things that happen on the earth that are not of a spiritual significance." During ceremonies throughout the year, there are commonly a couple of social dances to amuse the people (fig. 22). The social dance is also one of the Haudenosaunees' subtle socialization

21 THE TONAWANDA LONGHOUSE, ON THE TONAWANDA INDIAN RESERVATION IN WESTERN NEW YORK STATE. THE LONGHOUSE, THE CENTER OF TRADITIONAL COMMUNITY LIFE AMONG THE IROQUOIS, IS CONSIDERED SACRED AND PHOTOGRAPHY IS NEVER ALLOWED WITHIN. THE DINING HALL IS AT THE LEFT.

processes, helping to prepare youngsters for leadership and responsibility and giving them the public legitimization of individual skills (fig. 23). Not everyone can sing, dance, or run a full ceremony or social by themselves—the dance teaches this lesson as it reinforces cooperation among the people.

The start of a social dance begins with the opening address, which acknowledges all of life, beginning with the people, and takes the people on a verbal journey that is very descriptive of every aspect of the world (Turtle Island) or Mother Earth and all the gifts that she has given us to sustain ourselves for the length of time we are here. Each aspect of our natural surroundings is mentioned: the earth we walk upon, the grasses we see, the bushes that may be used as medicines, the waters that quench our thirst, and all living things that require water. The entire universe — and our relationship to it — is taken into consideration. Usually at the end of the address the speaker will mention how fortunate we are to have among the people the singers who have been given the gift of song and memory. Equal mention is made of the beautiful sounds of the drum and rattles that accompany the singers and of the craftspeople who made these instruments, so important to the dance.

22 THE MOCCASIN DANCE, A SOCIAL DANCE IN WHICH MALE AND FEMALE PARTNERS ROTATE DANCE POSITIONS, PERFORMED AT THE ANNUAL BORDER CROSSING EVENT, NIAGARA FALLS, NEW YORK, JULY 1992

23 ADULTS LEAD CHILDREN IN A DANCE AT THE KEEPERS OF THE WESTERN DOOR POWWOW, ST. BONAVENTURE UNIVERSITY, NEW YORK, JULY 1992

24 A SMALL
WATER DRUM

25 FRANKLYN E.
MCNAUGHTON, AN
ONONDAGA OF THE
BEAVER CLAN, HOLDS
A HORN RATTLE USED
IN SINGING

26 THE AKWESASNE
SINGERS PERFORMING
SOCIAL DANCE SONGS
AT THE SMITHSONIAN'S
FESTIVAL OF AMERICAN
FOLKLIFE, JULY 1992

The small water drum is tuned to the individual singer's voice rather than being set in a particular pitch or key (fig. 24). The rattles are cow-horn rattles partially filled with BBs or cherry pits (fig. 25). The turtle rattle, never used during the socials, is used only during the ceremonials (and only by men). Similarly, the elm-bark and gourd rattles are rarely, if ever, used in a social dance.

Usually, a person is chosen to be the "House Keeper" or "Pusher." His responsibility is to find songs, singers, and individuals who will lead the dance once it is announced. When he has all the information he will go to the speaker for the evening and the speaker will announce, "People, listen, we are again lucky, the singers are in abundance and are ready to sing for our enjoyment this evening." Then he will introduce the dance, the name or names of the singers and the leaders, and invite all to participate. The House Keeper's role is important because he must have knowledge of the singers, the songs they can sing, the head dancers present that evening, and the skill to maintain a balance of tempo, time, and pace given the mood of the crowd. He must even be aware of the weather.

When the singers take to the bench, a different learning process occurs (fig. 26). The Head Singer and his helper or second drummer are announced as the lead singers. The helper is often a young man who is just starting out and may still be somewhat shy and modest. Recently, more women's singing societies are being formed than during previous times — in the last three decades, Haudenosaunee communities have seen the emergence of women singers. There are "sings" that take place throughout the year at various times when singing societies gather at different Haudenosaunee communities. The societies are also usually the social benefit societies in the communities, observing and helping those in need.

What happens at the bench is also fun to observe — children try to make their presence known and attempt to find room on the bench, and a little game ensues. The little ones gently push for space, while the singers are humorously reluctant to make room. The game tests the commitment the children have to sit at the singers' bench. After a brief time, room is made and they sit as long as their patience and concentration allow. Often the children will look for cousins or uncles, and sometimes for their fathers and grandfathers, to sit next to. In a very loose and informal way, the people thus begin to see the emergence of a generation of singers (fig. 27).

The Head Singer has a particular set of songs or verses that he or she has learned from the person with whom they sang as second drummer. Once they are confident, they too will compose new verses. When a singer begins, the people can tell with whom he or she has sung and where and when a particular set of verses or songs was developed and composed. Usually the Head Singer will try a very difficult verse to see if his helpers can sing with him. This practice — always done with a sense of humor — is not to make any one feel ashamed or intimidated, but to advance the music and the melodies. It is a way to build and enhance the music's vocabulary.

28 ERNEST SMITH
(1907–1975),
*HANDSOME LAKE
PREACHING,* 1936,
WATERCOLOR,
38.5 X 51 CM.
ROCHESTER MUSEUM
AND SCIENCE
CENTER, ROCHESTER,
NEW YORK

DANCING THE CYCLES OF LIFE

Within the traditional communities of adherents to the "Code of Handsome Lake" religion (named for the early eighteenth-century Iroquois prophet), dance remains an integral aspect of the ceremonial expression of gratitude for the gifts of life from the Creator (fig. 28). Pockets of traditional followers remain throughout the Iroquois Six Nations Confederacy Reservations in what is now New York State. In our language, we are first the Ongweh-oh-weh-ney (the Real People). The Ongweh-oh-weh-ney once lived in long bark houses and later became known as the Haudenosaunee (People of the Longhouse). Today the Haudenosaunee continue to practice their ceremonies in contemporary Longhouse structures.

The world is an environment of continuous renewal, a balance of life and death, positive and negative energy. Traditional Longhouse people acknowledge the balance in the cycles of life and the importance of a tribute that expresses their thanks for them. Within the Longhouse culture, ceremonial dances are carried out in ritual respect for the positive energies of nature. Ceremonial observances are accompanied by prayer, song, and dance. The combination of these three elements reinforces the significance of the people's expression of gratitude for the gifts from the Creator. When the Ongweh-oh-weh-ney dance ceremonially, they are expressing their thanks and happiness

for the sustaining gifts of life, as the Creator instructed. The Great Feather Dance is one of the dances that accompanies many religious observances in the Longhouse (figs. 29, 30). Upon engaging in the Great Feather Dance, young men and women are instructed, "When you dance, dance real hard and yell out in happiness so the Creator will hear you and know your joy."

The Haudenosaunee, recognizing the inherent power women possess regarding the cycles of life, dedicate dances specifically to women and their life-sustaining gifts. A matriarchal society, as reflected in their understanding of cycles, the Haudenosaunee reserve for women a predominant role in the world out of reverence for the gifts of life they possess. The Haudenosaunee believe that the origin of this world began with Sky Woman. We exist here on Mother Earth, which bears all that supports us. The sustainers of life, "the three sisters" (corn, beans, and squash), flourished from the body of the daughter of Sky Woman (fig. 31). As human beings, the Ongweh-oh-weh-ney were formed from the flesh of the Mother Earth and return to her womb at the end of their time, thus completing the cycle of life.

In the ceremonial Women's Shuffle Dance, a young woman carrying a basket containing the three sisters leads the procession of "Givers of Life." In this dance they massage Mother Earth in an expression of oneness, comfort, and fertility. When

29 ERNEST SMITH
(1907–1975),
GREAT FEATHER DANCE,
WATERCOLOR,
32 X 42. 3 CM.
ROCHESTER MUSEUM
AND SCIENCE CENTER,
ROCHESTER, NEW YORK

30 A TRADITIONAL HEADPIECE
WORN BY A HAUDENOSAUNEE
MAN; LEATHER WITH SILVER
BAND, WAMPUM BEADS AND
FEATHERS ATTACHED. GRAND
RIVER RESERVATION,
ONTARIO, CANADA. NATIONAL
MUSEUM OF THE AMERICAN
INDIAN, SMITHSONIAN
INSTITUTION, NO. 6.354

31 ERNEST SMITH (1907–1975),
THREE SISTERS, 1937,
WATERCOLOR, 38.5 X 51 CM.
ROCHESTER MUSEUM AND
SCIENCE CENTER, ROCHESTER,
NEW YORK

ceremonial or social dances are held within the Longhouse, the Women's Shuffle Dance is one of the dances performed first, in an acknowledgment of the beginning of a cycle (fig. 32).

Introduction to dance begins at an early age. The cycle starts with infants and continues into old age. Children who are raised within the traditional Longhouse community are indoctrinated into the realm of dance before they can walk. When children are infants they are carried in the arms of their parents and passed from mothers to fathers and to any extended family member during the dancing. One of the instructions in the Code of Handsome Lake states, "Let the little children and old folks come and give thanks." It is beautiful to see our elderly assisted to the dance circle to acknowledge with a smile all who pass, and listen to a few songs to show their respect.

The future of the Confederacy's social, political, and religious existence for the "seventh generation" (i.e., seven generations into the future), depends on nurturing the children of today. The concerns and decisions made by the Confederacy have always been determined by evaluating their effect on the seventh generation. The present generation of Native American youth is the seed to an integral cycle of cultural renewal and growth. In increasing numbers, young Iroquois women and men are embracing the responsibility to learn, and participate in, their ceremonies and dances.

The continuation of religious practices is marked by the pervasive and dominant role that

young people have assumed in ceremonies today. During my most recent visit home to participate in annual ceremonies, I was more aware than ever of our elders' eyes fixed on the youth. There was a pleasant glow, a color of life and rejuvenation in the wisdom of their expression, a sureness that their concerns are being taken up by the next generation for the seventh generation. Indeed, the fate of the seventh generation is being left in good hands. In all of the traditional communities, the strong young voices of singers can be heard. Young voices — sometimes slightly wavering in delivery, struggling to find rhythm, slightly out of pitch — are beautifully powerful in their heartfelt determination to keep tradition alive and well. Here, once more, the cycle of renewal is being strengthened by strong young hearts and minds.

There is a morning prayer song that is sung in the Longhouse to welcome in the day during our mid-winter ceremonies. This song manifests the reverence we hold for the cycles of life and the future existence of this world for the seventh generation.

I love my world
I love my time
I love my growing children
I love my old people
I love my ceremonies

Linley B. Logan

3 3 ALLIGATOR DANCE,
JIM SKYE DANCERS,
IROQUOIS INDIAN
MUSEUM, HOWE CAVE,
NEW YORK, MAY 1992

The same process happens with the dancers; the little ones attempt to "get in front" to show their agility and amuse not only themselves, but all the people. The teenagers are engaged in the same process, for someday they too will be chosen to lead the social dance. They also know they may be called upon to lead the ceremonial dances, which sometimes causes a slight trauma. Leading a social dance can be intimidating at times, but the sacred ceremonial dances are even more intimidating for some.

The dances are a locus for social interplay, a way for the teenagers to meet new friends and link up with visitors from other communities. They are also a good place to meet members of the opposite sex.

Usually, the first dance that is announced is the Stomp Dance, sometimes referred to as the Old Man's Cane or the Standing Quiver Dance. This dance is a slow-paced Shuffle Dance with the Head and Second Singer often singing short melodious syllables that require a response. The response sounds may or may not be different from the initial, leading sound. These sounds or verses are normally short and the dance usually lasts about ten to fifteen minutes. The song itself can be sung for as long as an hour, depending on the singer and from which Haudenosaunee communities he or she has collected verses. In some cases, the language of the verses will reveal where the singer or the delegation has been.

Once, at an education conference, four elders in attendance wanted to have an informal singing session. One singer sang the Stomp Dance for approximately two hours and remarked, "Gee, there are a lot of verses I forgot!" One of the other elders sang a song that hadn't been sung in twenty-five years. For the observers, this was a rare opportunity to see masters sing songs rich in their own history and origins.

Some of the Haudenosaunee dances and songs have been borrowed from other Indian nations throughout the course of time. The Alligator Dance, brought back from down south among the Seminoles and Miccasukees, is one such borrowing (fig. 33). Another is the Delaware Skin Dance, taken from the Delaware people (fig. 34). The Rabbit Dance, introduced in the last four decades, was brought back from the western tribes. One of the first times the dance and song were heard occurred in the late 1950s. The pitch and sounds were changed somewhat to fit the levels of the Haudenosaunee singers, and a new dance was acquired. The western singers are able to sing in very high pitches, whereas the Haudenosaunee singers generally do not train their voices to sing such high notes or sounds. During the last two decades many Haudenosaunee singers have been exposed to high sounds and as a result have been attempting to carry off the powwow style of singing, which is characterized by high pitch. It is amusing to hear new singers as they train, for often their voices will crack when they attempt to reach a very high pitch.

During the Six Nations meetings, or when the delegates from various communities travel to selected Haudenosaunee Longhouses to deliver the *Gaiwiio* or the "good word," the first Stomp Dance is led by one of the delegates, who will sometimes mention where the delegation has been. On the last evening of the meetings (which usually last five days), they will sing a verse that tells the people the next community to which they are traveling. The next dance is usually the Women's Dance, of which there are two basic styles (fig. 35). The one mostly sung at the social is the New Women's Shuffle Dance; the other is the Older Ladies' Dance, a slower dance in which many of the verses have words that evoke certain times and events. Each year different new verses are added to the "song bag," or repertoire, of the singers. The song bag includes basic songs a Head

Singer performs and new ones that he or she has composed. Often when the songs are sung, you can see tears trickle down the cheeks of the elderly women or feel the warmth the song generates in the smiles on peoples' faces. Such signs reveal that a very important part of the Haudenosaunee culture is still alive.

The rest of the dances are named after animals, not as an act of worship, but rather to honor their contributions to the society. The structure of the dances is also different, requiring a different line-up of the participants. Some dances are partner dances — a man and a woman, two men and two women, women only, men and women in separate lines (or, in some cases, in separate circles, depending on the dance). If a ladies' choice is called at a Haudenosaunee social dance, the announcer may go on to say that the social dance is for our amusement and we should not be jealous or possessive of each other. Should a single woman or man ask a married person to dance, the married person should feel honored, not jealous. Humor is a very important aspect of the social and ceremonial dances — if a ladies' choice is called, for example, the speaker will often remark in jest that if the man doesn't honor the request a fine may be levied on him. It is important that everyone feel good during the dance.

In the Alligator Dance, the elbows are hooked together, and at a certain point in the dance, the man swings his partner around in counterclockwise motion, in similar fashion to a square dance or Virginia Reel. Sometimes the man will get carried away with excitement and lift the woman off her feet. Other dances include the Fish Dance, a very fast dance with partners changing places at prescribed times in the verse. The Robin Dance, the Snake Dance, the Corn Dance, the Shaking Bottle or Pine Tree Dance, and the Shaking the Bush Dance are all partner dances (fig. 36). It is almost impossible to do all the dances in one evening. As a result, it is important that the Pushers bear in mind what dances and songs have not been sung recently at previous dances, so that they can call them and ensure that these songs will continue to be heard, sung, and danced for the coming generations.

Throughout the social, speakers will get up and encourage the people to participate, to praise the singers and dancers. By showing that they are having a good time and are sharing their individual gifts with the community, the people demonstrate that they are keeping their word to the Creator. Usually halfway through the social, the House Keeper, announcing the community's good fortune in having caring and accomplished cooks who are happy to share their gifts with the people, will call for a brief break. When the break is over and the Longhouse cleaned up, the dance resumes. Before the next dance is announced, the speaker will get up and publicly thank all those who prepared food for the people. Often individuals are identified by name for their fine cooking and are encouraged to continue their efforts in the future. The importance of these kinds of announcements is to acknowledge everyone who has made a contribution and let them know how much their work is appreciated. In the winter, the fire tenders are mentioned, as are the water haulers, woodcutters, and the cleaners who help make the Longhouse cozy and warm for the people. The point is that each person has a gift and skill to share.

The other important socialization process occurs among the young people, who begin at an early age to interact linguistically and socially with others in the community. They sit with their clans during ceremonies at the social, becoming keenly aware of their clan and blood relatives. From very early on, they enjoy the benefit of having the elders to talk to. They are able to hear different members' names repeated, dances described, and sometimes stories told. When there are people at the social from other communities, the visitors are introduced and politely asked if they have any "words" or messages they want to convey. Visitors are offered hospitality, including food and housing should they require it. Sometimes bonds between the community and people of another nation will be made in one night that will last for many years. This process, which reinforces community bonds at a personal and social/political level, has characterized the Haudenosaunee people for centuries.

3 5 WOMEN'S DANCE,
JIM SKYE DANCERS,
IROQUOIS INDIAN MUSEUM, HOWE
CAVE, NEW YORK, MAY 1992

3 6 ROBIN DANCE,
KEEPERS OF THE
WESTERN DOOR
POWWOW,
ST. BONAVENTURE
UNIVERSITY, NEW YORK,
JULY 1992

THE FIESTA: RHYTHM OF LIFE IN THE SIERRAS OF MEXICO AND THE ALTIPLANO OF BOLIVIA

NANCY ROSOFF AND OLIVIA CADAVAL

Among the Zapotec of Oaxaca, Mexico, the Maya of Chiapas, Mexico, and the Aymara of the Bolivian Altiplano, music and dance are part of a larger ceremonial context called the fiesta (fig. 37).[1] Fiestas, shared events that people prepare for and participate in, assume a traditional form and are generally invested with sacred meaning. Fiestas define and reaffirm complex relationships that relate to other community activities. These relationships involve members of a community, their environment, and their deities. Each group has its distinct cultural traditions and language. But there are commonalities in the role of music and dance, and in the function of the fiesta system as a whole. Music and dance are significant in defining the group's identity and are used by all three groups as a means of preserving their culture. Music and dance are inextricably tied to the performance of sacred ceremonies in the fiestas that are derived from both indigenous and European cultures. All three groups base their fiestas on a combination of two calendars—one that is determined by agricultural activities and rites of passage, and the other by the cycle of Catholic holy days and saints' days. Finally, it is through these fiestas that social relationships are reinforced, not only among community members, but also between them and their deities and their natural environment.

Among all three groups, fiestas are supported by complex systems of sponsorship. A fiesta sponsor pays all the expenses associated with the celebration, such as flowers and candles for the mass and food and drink for the musicians, dancers, and celebrants. Because of the great expense of sponsoring a fiesta, a sponsor depends on a network of reciprocal obligations in which he receives aid in the form of money, liquor, and food from relatives and friends, and from individuals who wish to sponsor a fiesta in the future. In return for this aid, the sponsor will be expected to reciprocate with gifts in kind when these individuals sponsor their own fiestas. Although the terms and rules vary for each group, the goal is always cooperation in financing a fiesta. The role of sponsorship, however, does not end with the fiesta itself. Rather, sponsorship brings with it social prestige that may eventually lead to political office.[2]

THE ZAPOTECS OF OAXACA

Mexico, with a total population of more than eighty million, is home to between five and twelve million indigenous people. There are over fifty-six different ethnic groups, the largest of which are the Nahuas, the Mayas, and the Zapotecs. The Zapotecs number roughly 400,000 individuals, most of whom live in the state of Oaxaca. All speak the Zapotec language, but there may be as many as nine different regional dialects.[3] The Zapotecs, who make up the largest ethnic group in the state, are divided into four different subgroups inhabiting distinct geographical zones: the Valley, the Southern Sierra, the Northern Sierra, and the Isthmus of Tehuantepec. The Zapotecs of the Northern Sierra are the focus here.

The Zapotecs of the Northern Sierra live in small, isolated villages in the most remote section of the Sierra Madre Oriental, a massive mountain chain that runs through northeastern Oaxaca (fig. 38). The region is dominated by a group of twenty mountains called *Zempoaltépetl* in Nahua or *Ya.a Galgr* in Zapotec. Subsistence crops such as corn, beans, squash, chiles, sugar cane, and coffee are usually cultivated on the hillsides.

The Zapotecs of the Northern Sierra refer to themselves in their native language as *béné xo.n*, which means "people of the Northern Sierra." They are primarily farmers, although they engage in some cattle ranching. Other domesticated animals include donkeys, chickens, turkeys, goats, and pigs.

Each community specializes in a particular industry. For example, Zoochila is known for its bread, Tavehua for its pottery, and San Pedro Cojonos for its merchants, who bring goods from the city of Oaxaca. The many communities of the Northern Sierra region are therefore economically interdependent (fig. 39).

According to Manual Ríos Morales, Zapotec dance and music cannot be understood outside of the ceremonial context of the fiesta.[4] The large number of fiestas celebrated throughout the year forms part of what the Zapotec refer to as their ritual universe, which informs their everyday as well as ceremonial life. This ritual universe of the fiesta includes not only the rites themselves, but also the accompanying dances, music, songs, food, clothing, masks, and ornaments. These elements constitute a fiesta, during which the Zapotec are able to communicate with their gods and the natural environment and fulfill reciprocal obligations between one another.

The Zapotec base many of their fiestas on two different kinds of calendars: agricultural and Catholic liturgical. Fiestas based upon the agricultural calendar mark the initiation and termination of certain agricultural activities, while those based on the Catholic liturgical calendar are connected to the cycle of holy days and patron saints' days. In Mexico, the long period of colonization resulted in the imposition of the Catholic religion onto

38 NORTHERN SIERRA OF OAXACA, 1992

Mexico

STATE OF CHIAPAS

STATE OF OAXACA

South America

BOLIVIA

LAKE TITICACA

■ Northern Sierra region
■ Central Highland region
■ Altiplano region

37 THE COMMUNITIES IN MEXICO AND BOLIVIA THAT ARE DISCUSSED IN THIS ESSAY ARE LOCATED WITHIN THE REGIONS HIGHLIGHTED.

39 MARKET DAY, ZOOGOCHO, OAXACA, 1992

40 DANCE OF THE CHINAS
OF OAXACA, FIESTA OF
ST. ANTHONY OF PADUA.
YALÁLAG, OAXACA,
JUNE 1992

41 MALINCHE
DANCERS.
ZOOCHILA,
OAXACA, JUNE
1992

indigenous belief systems. Throughout the colonial period, pre-Columbian temples and ceremonial centers were destroyed and Catholic churches were constructed on the ruins. The names of Catholic saints were imposed on the place-names of villages and their populations. This period of intense evangelization succeeded in fragmenting indigenous identities and creating new ones, so that ritual and ceremonial life began to gravitate around the "patron saint" of each village. The Zapotec, for example, began to dedicate their fiestas to the patron saints, but they also continued to perform their traditional dances, music, and rituals—thereby keeping many pre-Hispanic elements alive (fig. 40).

Although contemporary Zapotec dances cannot be traced directly to pre-colonial ones, Manuel Ríos Morales maintains that "these dances *re-create* the whole mythological past; they *preserve* their own conception about the unity of man, the universe and God that keeps alive the hope of group continuity."[5] However strong European influence may seem to be, the underlying meaning of the dances is still Zapotec and expresses gratitude to the gods for enabling the Zapotec people to live in peaceful coexistence with nature. The dancers and musicians have the privilege of carrying this message to the supernatural world because this gift of communication is only possible through the performance of dance and music in a ritual context.

Most of the dance groups are composed entirely of children. According to Ríos, this is the way in which cultural traditions are passed down from generation to generation. The future of the Zapotec people is in their children. By teaching them the dances and having the students perform them during fiestas and ceremonies, the Zapotec are ensuring the survival of their culture (fig. 41).

Zapotec traditional dances are divided into two categories: *danzas tradicionales* and *bailes tradicionales*. Since both terms translate as "traditional dance," we will use the Spanish terms to help differentiate the two. The *danza tradicional* is situated within a ceremonial context and the choreography has prescribed forms regarding use of space, steps, styles, costumes, themes, and number of participants. The *baile tradicional*, on the other hand, occurs only in a social context. While the choreography of the *bailes* follows certain standards of movement and defined musical forms, variations in steps and interpretation are possible. These social dances are usually performed by couples. The fortieth anniversary celebration of the founding of Zoogocho's elementary school, celebrated in June 1992, included both types of dances.

The *danzas tradicionales* best illustrate the variety of dance themes present in Zapotec ceremonial life. There are four types of *danzas tradicionales*: drama dances, ethnic group dances, animal dances, and satirical dances. Each dance has its own choreography, costume, mask, and music. They are usually performed outdoors, in large plazas with the band sitting or standing to the side.

The drama dances are about the Conquest or other events pertaining to combat. The Malinche Dance, for example, depicts the betrayal of the Aztec people by an Indian woman called La Malinche, the interpreter for the Spanish conqueror Cortés, who is thought to have betrayed her people by going off with him. The Malinche Dance is performed by sixteen dancers—eight boys and eight girls. The dancers wear beautiful velvet costumes and straw or felt hats, both elaborately decorated with beads, sequins, ribbons, and mirrors. The characters of Moctezuma (the Aztec king) and Malinche are represented by male and female dancers wearing elaborate feather headdresses. The two-part dance begins with eight girls dancing together in two rows. The rows face one another and, as the dancers move forward and backward from one another, they swing different colored scarves at their sides. The rows of dancers move away from each other toward opposite ends of the plaza, then back again toward the center. All movements are repeated at least two times. Four of the dancers wear long scarves around their waists, which they then untie, handing an end to the dancers in the opposite row. The two rows of dancers continue to move in place while they hold the long scarves between them. The dancers then crisscross their positions, so that the scarves become crossed and twisted and a circle is formed. Moving in place, the girls

ZAPOTEC DANCES AND MUSIC FROM THE NORTHERN SIERRA OF OAXACA

Today, there are more than 800,000 Zapotecs living in Mexico. We, the fifty-thousand Zapotecs from the Northern Sierra of Oaxaca, are an agricultural people living primarily in small rural towns. The center of our lives is our community and family. The foundation of our socio-economic organization is based on the legacy of two traditional institutions: *gozona* and *tequio*. *Gozona*, a Zapotec word, refers to the exchange of personal services, including obligations of reciprocity and similar types of help. *Tequio* is a Nahua word that refers to the voluntary and mandatory work performed to meet a community's needs. These traditions — together with our beliefs, music, dances, language, and teachings from our ancestors — form our Zapotecan identity.

Our ancestors taught us to respect nature in its diverse forms: water, land, mountains, valleys, wind, and people. Their message to us has always been: "All things, just like man, feel, speak, and have their own soul and God; all things are closely related." In Zapotec culture it is consequently very difficult to establish boundaries between ritual and daily activities, between the profane and the sacred, or between that which belongs to God and that which belongs to humanity.

There are sacred times and spaces that we all respect, and in which we partake as members of a community. We participate as representatives of traditional, religious, and municipal authorities, or as constituents of commissions or traditional institutions like *mayordomia* (fiesta sponsorship) and *gozona*. The culmination of these activities is expressed in our traditional fiestas, where music and dance are the most important elements. During these events, we thank our gods for all that we have received and for all we hope to obtain. Music and dance have a very profound meaning for us. Through them we reflect our particular ways of understanding life, the universe, and society. If music expresses our feelings, dance expresses our gratitude (figs. 42, 43).

Our contemporary music and dance are enriched by the native traditions of our ancestors, as well as by African and European contributions. Some of the steps, rhythms, songs, sounds, and costumes belong to the Zapotec tradition, while other elements are recent contributions that we have adopted, at the same time adapting them to our particular approach. Therefore, besides expressing ritual symbolism, our dances and music also reflect the transformation of our thought and the realities of our history.

In the same way that our traditional dances have changed, our pre-Hispanic music performed by simple instruments—rattles (*sonajas*), horns (*cuernos*), bamboo flutes (*flautas de carrizo*), and drums (*tambores*)—has been enriched by the integration of brass instruments in our musical bands, which are the soul of our communities (fig. 44).

In the Zapotec region, each town has its own band, whether large or small, and regional music is characterized by groups of melodies called *sones*, *jarabes*, and *marchas*. In this context, band and dance form an inseparable duality among the Zapotecs, as they do for our neighbors the Mixes and Chinantecs.

Manuel Ríos Morales

42 A DANCE DURING THE FORTIETH ANNIVERSARY CELEBRATION OF THE FOUNDING OF THE GENERAL LAZARO CADENAS SCHOOL, ZOOGOCHO, OAXACA, JUNE 1992

43 TIGER DANCE.
ZOOGOCHO,
OAXACA,
JUNE 1992

44 A ZAPOTEC BRASS BAND MARCHES THROUGH ZOOGOCHO, OAXACA, JUNE 1992.

continue to crisscross their positions in both a clockwise and counterclockwise direction, so that the circle gets smaller as the the scarves become more twisted. Following this, the whole circle moves in a clockwise, then counterclockwise, direction. The whole dance is reversed until the dancers end up where they started.

Ríos points out that all dancers perform movements of attraction and separation that represent the union and separation of terrestrial and celestial forces, of human beings and nature, and of community members and God. As the girls finish their dance, the boys enter the dance area. The girls walk away and the boys start dancing. The boys' dance is faster in pace. They skip and spin toward and away from one another, shaking rattles. The boys and girls then dance together, using the same hop-skip step. The dance begins in two rows, with the boys on one side and the girls on the other. They weave in and out and spin around one another, forming and unforming pairs of dancers. The dancers then form two rows again. The dance resembles a quadrille because each couple eventually takes a turn moving down the center of the two rows.

45 MALINCHE DANCE AROUND A RIBBONED POLE (*PALO DE LISTONES*). ZOOCHILA, OAXACA, 1992

The second part of the Malinche Dance requires sixteen people, who dance around a *palo de listones* (ribboned pole), which resembles a maypole (fig. 45). Each dancer holds a ribbon as they slowly walk around the pole, first counterclockwise, then clockwise, pausing after every step to point a toe and drag it along the ground. The tempo of the music speeds up and the dancers move more quickly around the pole, weaving in and out of one another, so that the resulting ribbon pattern on top of the pole resembles a multicolored braided design. The boys continue to shake their rattles in time to the music. For the Zapotec, the pole represents the sun and the ribbons are its rays, while for other groups, the pole represents the earth and the ribbons its fruits. There are several pre-Hispanic elements in the Malinche Dance. For example, the rattle symbolizes fertility and the feathers, worn by Moctezuma and Malinche, symbolize power, authority, and wisdom.

Ethnic dances are about other ethnic groups and they are usually identified by the costumes the dancers wear. One of the more popular ethnic dances is the Dance of the Black Men (*Danza de los Negritos*; fig. 46). According-ing to Ríos, this dance originated in Guatemala during colonial times when the native people came in contact with African slaves. The dance is usually performed by eight boys, who wear

46 NEGRITO DANCE. ZOOGOCHO, OAXACA, JUNE 1992

elaborate black-velvet jackets, pants, hats, and brightly painted wild-boar masks. The outfits are decorated with colorful scarves, ribbons, and pompons; each hat has a toucan beak protruding from the top. As a boy dances, he clicks castanets in one hand and holds a staff in the other. The symbolism in this dance is quite rich and harkens back to pre-Hispanic times. The toucan beak, for example, is a symbol for the bird that represents the sun in most Mesoamerican cultures. The staff is a symbol of authority and the wild boar represents strength.

The two other types of dances, animal and satiric, serve different purposes. Animal dances—such as those depicting tigers, rats, and bulls—allude to mythological beings or their characteristics. The satiric dances are intended to ridicule the conduct of particular people.

Masks, usually worn only by men, are an important element in Zapotec dances (fig. 47). Like the elaborate

47 ZAPOTEC MASK USED
FOR A VARIETY OF DANCES,
CA. 1940. YALÁLAG,
OAXACA, MEXICO.
NATIONAL MUSEUM OF
THE AMERICAN INDIAN,
SMITHSONIAN
INSTITUTION, NO. 20.3444

costumes that represent mythological personages and deities, masks and the other dance accoutrements commemorate the pre-Hispanic Zapotecs.

Masks contain profound meanings that often reflect the way the Zapotec view the transformation of their culture as a result of the Conquest. Some transformations can be clearly seen—normally beardless Indian faces, for example, become bearded, while the bearded Spanish faces are represented as clean-shaven. These facial transformations, along with the depiction of grotesque facial expressions, reflect the violence between, and the separation of, the Spanish and the Indians produced by the process of colonization.[6]

Music is an integral part of Zapotec culture. Music and dance are inseparable. They are the center of educational and ceremonial life, which are so important for defining Zapotec identity. Every community has its own band, of which it is very proud (fig. 48). Music is so important that the Zapotec have an expression: "With music we are born, with it we grow and with it we have to die." Children are taught how to play instruments when they are very young, and most community bands include students of elementary and high-school age. As with dance, children are introduced to music at an early age so that they will learn the values of Zapotec culture

Zapotec music has also been transformed into new forms since colonial times. The pre-Hispanic instruments—such as bamboo flutes, drums, rattles, animal horns, and conch shells—have been replaced by large brass bands, referred to as *bandas de música* (music bands). The influence of European musical styles, including liturgical music, combined with the ethnic diversity of the Northern Sierra region, has produced an equally diverse musical tradition.

There are basically three types of music played during fiestas: *sones*, *jarabes*, and *alabanzas*. A *son* is an up-tempo piece that is played for the *danzas tradicionales*. Each dance has its own *son* that determines the rhythm and type of movement performed (e.g. lateral, forward, backward, on tiptoe, or any combination). The *jarabe* is a potpourri of dance tune excerpts that accompany the *bailes tradicionales*. The *alabanzas* are sacred hymns performed for occasions like funerals.

48 GENERAL LAZARO CADENAS SCHOOL BAND. ZOOGOCHO, OAXACA, JUNE 1992

THE TZOTZIL AND TZELTAL MAYA OF HIGHLAND CHIAPAS

The Maya Tzotzil and Tzeltal live in the highlands of Chiapas near the city of San Cristóbal de las Casas. This rough, mountainous region, which is accessible only by dirt roads, varies in altitude and climate from temperate foothills and valleys to the cool, high mountains, and then becomes warm in the northern lower region (fig. 49). Both groups live in widely dispersed *parajes* (hamlets) that form part of twenty-four *municipios* (townships). The focus here is on four of the largest *municipios*: Chamula, San Pedro Chenalhó, Tenejapa, and Zinacantán. The Tzotzil population consists of 226,681 inhabitants and the Tzeltal approximately 258,153. The people speak a variety of dialects of the Tzotzil and Tzeltal languages, which form part of the Maya Totonac group of Mayance.

The Tzotzil and Tzeltal are primarily agriculturalists who cultivate corn and beans for family consumption and to feed their pigs, chickens, and turkeys. They also cultivate coffee, bananas, and pineapples. Some families have orchards where they grow a variety of fruits — such as apples, peaches, plums, and pears — that are often sold. The women herd sheep, primarily for the animals' wool. Communities supplement their income selling crafts — such as baskets, leather work, furniture, and pottery. The Chamula are well known for their musical instruments. Ironically, while the market grows for traditional weavings among tourists and collectors, Tzotzils and Tzeltals more and more purchase commercial fabric to sew their everyday wear.[7]

49 CHIAPAS HIGHLANDS, 1986

Lack of land has become a major problem that has forced men to migrate to lower lands and the rain forest. Evangelism, which sometimes leads to the expulsion of converts from communities, has also caused forced migration. Members of some communities, like the Chamula, have become adept merchants who sell traditional and commercial goods to other rural communities and to buyers in the city.

Each *municipio* has a *cabecera municipal* (ceremonial and political center) called *hteklum*, where principal churches, the town hall, school, medical center, and small shops are located. *Municipios* may be divided into *parajes* (hamlets) or *barrios* (wards), each represented by civic and religious authorities. While corn is at the center of their cosmology, the sun is the supreme deity for the Tzotzil and the Tzeltal and is represented by the authorities who wear ceremonial hats with colored ribbons representing the solar rays. According to Jaime Torres Burguete, "Their form of organization and conception of the world has served these societies as the secret weapon of resistance against the imposition of foreign cultures."[8]

Each Tzotzil and Tzeltal community is recognized by the distinctive colors, designs, and weaving techniques of their dress. The women weave the finest garments with wool or cotton on the traditional backstrap loom. Designs are preserved through the dreams of weavers, through the memory and devotion to ancestors, and in the old weavings worn by the patron saints depicted in the churches. A design not only identifies the weaver's community but the community's mythical history. Textiles reflect both the roots and development of culture — its cosmology and syncretic elements. For example, the similarity between the brocade technique and "spiny star" design used in textiles in the town of Venustiano Carranza and the embroidery depicted in the ancient Mayan murals at Bonampak suggests pre-Columbian influence. After the first century of colonization, influences from other Indian groups appear — for example, the feathered wedding *huipil* of Zinacantán where the technique of weaving with feathers is adopted from the Aztecs. The cross stitch and some animal designs are of European influence. In more recent years, communities have borrowed techniques from each other. Weavers from Tenejapa visited San Andrés Larrainzar and San Pedro Chenalhó to learn the art of brocade and then adapted it to their own style.[9]

For the Tzotzil and Tzeltal, the fiesta is at the center of ritual and social organization (fig. 50). The fiesta integrates and transforms European festival elements into pre-Columbian organization of prayer and offerings to reaffirm the complex relationship with the natural and spiritual worlds of the Mayas. In their conception of the sacred, sun, sky, land, and deities are interwoven with the Judeo-Christian God and the saints. While the fiesta provides for the continuity and renewal of relationships between community and the natural and spiritual worlds, it depends on the cooperation and interaction between communities and community members. The civil and religious authorities also constantly interact. Tzotzil musician Mauro Hernández Bautista from Magdalenas, Chenalhó, explains that the religious authorities seek the support of the civil authorities to lead some rituals, to give emotive speeches at ceremonies, and to bless the

50 CARNIVAL CELEBRATIONS IN AMATENANGO, CHIAPAS, 1986

food with their prayer. Each participant depends on the others.[10]

Fiestas include dramatic performances, prayers, clowns and ritual humorists, dance, music, song, eating, drinking, and revelry. Food, candles, incense, fireworks, refreshments, and locally made hard liquor (called *pox*) abound. In Zinacantán, a horn is used to carry the *pox* (fig. 51).

There are basically two types of fiestas. The first are based on the Catholic liturgical calendar, which celebrates Carnival, Holy Week, and the patron saints of each community. Major figures of Carnival, dedicated to Jesus of Nazareth, include Saint Michael the Archangel, men masquerading as women, and ritual humorists who appear in Zinacantán and San Pedro Chenalhó as costumed figures with blackened faces, known as black men, or, in Chamula, as monkeys.[11]

The second type are agricultural fiestas which, according to Tzotzil musician Agustín García Gómez of San Pablo Chalchihuitán, are only celebrated in some communities on the Day of the Cross, and in others three times a year during the planting, growing, and harvest seasons. Musicians lead processions to sacred sites, such as springs (*ojos de agua*), hills, caves, and churches, where the fiestas are celebrated. Music insures abundance of crops and protects against illness and natural disasters.[12] In an agricultural dance in Tenejapa, for example, the dancers thank and petition the earth and deities for rain and a good crop. They also ask that the animals from the hills not destroy their crops. The dancers wear the skins of animals on their arms, which they raise to the sky during the dance to show the deities the animals that destroy the crops (such as the badger, raccoon, armadillo, and squirrel).

The musicians and dancers are the intermediaries between the community and the deities. Some *municipios* have an official group of dancers whose members are replaced only when they die. The group is known by a different name in each community. In Chenalhó they are called *jtoy kinetik*, or "the extollers" of the fiesta. In most communities, the principal sponsors and their wives take on the role of dancers. According to Burguete, these dancers bring passion and heat, energy and strength, enjoyment and happiness to the fiesta; in turn, the Nazarene, the sky, and the earth are happy to see their children venerate and adore them through the fiesta.[13]

The different types of dances include Carnival, dance dramas, animal dances, and the dance of the *negritos*.

51 TZOTZIL CEREMONIAL DRINKING HORN USED TO CARRY *POX* DURING FIESTAS, CA. 1949, ZINACANTÁN, CHIAPAS. NATIONAL MUSEUM OF THE AMERICAN INDIAN, SMITHSONIAN INSTITUTION, NO. 21.3538

52 CARNIVAL CELEBRATION, ZINACANTÁN, CHIAPAS, 1978

This last dance is found all over Mexico. For Carnival, dancers dramatize and ridicule acts that go against Indian life in order to teach moral lessons and proper behavior while making people laugh (fig. 52). For example, in San Pedro Chenalhó, Carnival celebrations, which usually begin on February twentieth and last five days, include games, tricks, and the performance of ceremonial scenes or acts (*actos*) that lend a degree of solemnity to the atmosphere of play, comedy, drama, and theater.[14]

The fiesta consists of approximately eighty to ninety participants, including the various sponsors, musicians, dancers, and cooks. The principal actors include the *pasiones* (the religious authorities), in ceremonial dress and brightly ribboned hats, and the black-men personages, whose faces are painted with black soot and who wear hats of monkey skin (fig. 53). The acts performed throughout the five days, which also include dances, are highly symbolic and contain multiple meanings. For example, an act performed on the Sunday of Carnival involving sacrificed turkeys includes elements of comedy, fear, and eroticism. In another act, performed on Monday and Tuesday, a bull made of straw mats attacks the participants and audience while cowboys pretend to control it and two black men lasso it because the latter are its owners (fig. 54). The bull represents evil and the attacks cause sickness in the soul of the people. Two of the participants then perform a curing ceremony with humor by saying the following: "What has made you sick? Do you have a headache, a stomach ache, or fright sickness? I will cure you. Here, take this medicine" (fig. 55).[15]

53 BLACK-MEN PERSONAGES (*IK'ALETIK*) WEARING MONKEY-FUR HATS AT THE TZOTZIL MUSIC AND DANCE FESTIVAL, SAN PEDRO CHENALHÓ, CHIAPAS, 1992

In Chamula, the dominant theme of Carnival is war and conquest. Although this fiesta is ostensibly a commemoration of the passion of Christ, all of the conflicts in which the Chamulas have participated are telescoped into this one celebration: the conquest by Cortés, the French intervention of 1861 to 1867, the invasion of Chamula during the Caste War from 1867 to 1870, the nineteenth-century Chiapas and Guatemala border dispute, and the Mexican Revolution of 1910 to 1917. Themes that involve the armed conqueror, the conqueror's mistress, and the battle are dramatized in this fiesta. The *pasiones*, or religious sponsors of the fiesta, impersonate the Indian Christ. Some of the costumes worn during this fiesta — black frock coats with a red cross on the back — resemble the military uniforms worn by the French grenadiers during the period of the French intervention.[16]

The musicians are farmers who become full-time musicians for a fiesta only when petitioned to play by the sponsors. Tzotzil musician Pascual López Ruiz, from San Juan del Bosque, recites a formal petition that a sponsor would use to request the leader of the band to play for a fiesta:

> *With your music and your* sones, *we remember and bring alive the customs and teachings of our first fathers-mothers. We need the harp, the guitar and the violin to praise and celebrate the* fiesta *of the patron saint.*[17]

In return for their participation, the musicians receive *pox* and other refreshments.

The musicians fulfill two obligations: first, their social obligation to assist sponsors in the celebration of the fiesta and to provide entertainment for the community; second, their spiritual obligation to dedicate the music to the saints and to the God of heaven and earth. Before playing, they light candles and incense and offer prayers. Even as they begin to tune their instruments, they hope the presence of the saint is with them.[18] Musicians feel they owe their skill to divine grace, God, and their patron saint (fig. 56).

54 CARNIVAL
PARTICIPANTS
DRESSED AS BULLS
AND SURROUNDED
BY FEMALE
IMPERSONATORS AND
A COWBOY, TENEJAPA,
CHIAPAS, 1986

55 CURING CEREMONY
PERFORMED ON FESTIVAL
PARTICIPANTS AFTER
THEY HAVE BEEN
"ATTACKED" BY A BULL.
SAN PEDRO CHENALHÓ,
CHIAPAS, 1992

Chamula musician Salvador Bautista López explains how musical instrument-makers observe ritual practices of gratitude and make offerings to the saints in order to contribute to the enhancement of the community's values.[19] Each community has its own patron saint of the instruments, and Chamulas are known as the best instrument-makers. Instruments vary in size. The smaller ones are carried on pilgrimages to sacred places and the larger ones are played in the homes of sponsors, at city hall, and in the church.

There are two groups of instrumentation: wind and percussion instruments and stringed instruments. The wind and percussion instruments, used only for ceremonies or fiestas, include the bamboo flute (with two or six holes), the cornet, the drum, and the rattle. These instruments are played, for example, during Carnival for the oath ceremonies involving participating fiesta sponsors and for the processions to and from the church and to and from the authorities' homes. The musicians are petitioned by the civil authorities, although the religious authorities will also ask for their services. Once the musicians agree to participate in a fiesta, they are responsible for announcing the fiesta a few days before it begins. In Chenalhó they walk the main streets playing their instruments to let the community know that a fiesta is coming. This music accompanies the authorities as they take the flags from the church to the house of the fiesta where the oath is taken. They also play in the house. Music also accompanies the *capitan* of the fiesta as he races on horseback around the plaza. The musicians lead processions in honor of saints and play for petitioning masses at sacred sites.[20]

The strings, harp, guitar, and violin make up the second type of instrumentation. They are of European origin and can be played for both formal and informal gatherings. The accordion has recently been added to the class of stringed instruments by Chamulas and the Tzotzil of Magadalenas, in the *municipio* of Chenalhó.

In Chenalhó, string musicians play for the *mixa*, a ceremony celebrated in each one of the sacred sites or homes of the gods in return for protection from hunger, sickness, and calamity for the whole community. The gods are also asked for plenty of rain for the corn and bean crops, and for the well-being of domestic animals. This ceremony is either the large *mixa* for all the inhabitants of a *municipio* or a small *mixa* for a community.[21] Some of the *sones*, or music pieces, refer to the holy Mother Earth, Heaven, the saints, and God of Heaven. Tzotzil musician José Pérez López, from Zinacantán, explains that most of the music pieces carry the names of the saints because they are dedicated to them.[22] Some songs are dedicated to nature. In Pantelhó, Chenalhó, and Mitontik, songs are dedicated to the saints, women, wealth, and the authorities. In Tenejapa, songs and *sones* are composed for saints, authorities, people from other communities, and for nature. Tenejapa musicians play for ceremonies called *jel a'tel* (change of authority), petitioning blessings for all the inhabitants of the *municipio*. Musicians play an initial song that asks the dancers to get up and sacrifice themselves and move their bodies to celebrate the saint.[23]

56 MUSICIANS PERFORMING DURING A CARNIVAL CELEBRATION IN CHAMULA, CHIAPAS, 1979

THE MUSIC AND DANCE THAT NOURISHES AND GLADDENS THE DEITIES OF THE TZOTZILES AND TZELTALES

In the state of Chiapas, Mexico, the native groups have kept their traditions and customs by means of a rigid religious organization — expressed in a system of traditional duties — that has engendered social cohesion and the preservation of their cultural identity.

The permanence and harmonic preservation of these communities is diligently guarded through the carrying out of duties that are called *abtel patan* (an office of the civil authorities) and *nichimal abtel* (an office of the religious authorities). By giving service to the community for one-year periods, eminent men and women are responsible for safeguarding the integrity of the group. In this way the Mayans — who call themselves "real men" — ensure that as long as the sun shines their lives are protected by the gods.

In gratitude to the divine beings for their labor that sustains human existence, festive celebrations with offerings of music and dance are organized by those whose turn it is to care for their communities and the universe.

The religious authorities in charge of "flower" or divinity duties (*los portadores de los cargos floridos*) serve and please the saints with great obligation and sacrifice.[1] Among the preparations they must make to appropriately celebrate the feast of the saint whom they are assigned to serve is the selection of musicians (fig. 57). They petition the musicians they consider the most skilled with gifts consisting of two bottles of *pox* (sugarcane liquor) and refreshments (fig. 58). With reverence and supplications, the petitioners address the musicians in the following way:

57 MUSICIANS IN A CARNIVAL PROCESSION AT TENEJAPA, CHIAPAS, 1986

I came to chat with you
I came to converse with you
I am going to choose your body
I am going to choose your person

Because I found my duty
I found my post
It was my turn to serve
It was my turn to be useful.

I will take charge
I will be responsible
For the feast
For the pascua
Of Saint—[name of saint served].

That is why now
I am going to choose your body
I am going to choose your flesh
Because you know
How to cheer
How to bring alive
The Sacred Feast
The sacred pascua

Because only with tunes
Only with the harp
Guitar
And violin
Is the feast happy
And enlivened.

The musicians do not resist the pleas of the servants of the festival, because they believe they have dreamt about the calling before they receive it. Once they have been spoken to, the musicians ask the saints to protect them, guide them, and intercede for them so that their specially prepared instruments and they themselves can adequately fulfill their mission. They have faith that the divine will give them the ability to play and interpret the music (fig. 59).

These artists participate at various moments of the celebration, playing *sones* (fast-tempo pieces) that accompany the people who dance in honor of the saints. The Chamulas, for example, dance up to eighteen *sones* in one act (with a performance consisting of several acts), be it in the house of the host, in the church, or in any other sacred place. All the Chamulas' tunes are devoted to the saints and to the Lord of Heaven and Earth. The tune devoted to Saint John says:

59 VILLAGERS IN
A CARNIVAL
PROCESSION
CARRY THE
STATUE OF A
SAINT FROM A
CHURCH,
TENEJAPA,
CHIAPAS, 1981

60 THE *ALFERECES* (FLAG-BEARERS) LEAD THE CARNIVAL PROCESSION IN TENEJAPA, CHIAPAS, 1981

Great Saint John
Great patron
Staff of my Holy Father
You are celebrated
You are consecrated
You are venerated.

We enjoy your celebration
We delight in your consecration
We are happy with your
veneration
Lord of heaven
Lord of glory.

In other communities it is customary to hold prayer and music ceremonies to ask for rain, good harvest, health, and happiness for all the population. It is believed that these fiestas will open the heart and mind to better understand and help others. In this way, the mandate of the primeval mothers and fathers who speak the same language as the gods is fulfilled.

Music — along with material items such as candles, incense, and *pox* — serves as food and nourishment to the gods. The *sones* produced with the harp, guitar, violin, flute, drum, trumpet, and rattle please the gods.

On certain occasions the dancers are few, in others many, and they are known by different names in the communities. In the case of Chenalhó, they are called *jtoy k'inetik* or *jpas k'inetik* (the ones who cheer up the feast or the ones who do the feast). There are also the *antzil ak'ot*, dancers dressed as women. The latter and the *jtoy k'inetik* appear only in the feast of Carnival, the time when the largest number of participants take part. In some aspects, the dancers personify the gods and therefore may wear masks or costumes. The *pasiones* (the primary sponsors), *alfereces* (the flag-bearers; fig. 60), and majordomos in their role as *encargados* (those in charge) play the main role as dancers because that is the way the feast of the divine beings is enhanced. The lords of heaven and earth are happy to see that their children venerate and adore them through the feast, re-creating a harmonic unity that sustains the continuity of the universe.

Jaime Torres Burguete

1   The Tzotzil terms for flowers and divinity are the same.

THE AYMARA OF THE ALTIPLANO

Bolivia has a total population of more than six and a half million people, of whom fifty to sixty percent are American Indians. The Aymara and Quechua are the two main groups, but there are other smaller ethnic groups scattered throughout the country. The Aymara (or Qulla) are a highland people who live in the Altiplano or "high plain" region of western Bolivia (fig. 61). The Altiplano region runs from the Peruvian border north of Lake Titicaca southward to the Argentine border. Elevations in this cold, windy, treeless zone range from 11,500 (La Paz) to over 21,000 feet. Lake Titicaca (12,500 feet), one of the highest navigable lakes in the world, lies at the northern extremity of the Altiplano region. The Aymara communities live in the vicinity of Lake Titicaca. The landscape is one of rolling, scrub-covered hills interrupted occasionally by volcanic outcroppings.

There are approximately three million Aymaras living within an area that includes the Lake Titicaca region of Peru and Bolivia and the northern sections of Chile and Argentina.[24] The Aymara are primarily agriculturalists and pastoralists. They cultivate a number of crops, including many varieties of potato, quinoa, barley, maize, beans, and onions. Domesticated animals include llamas, alpacas, sheep, pigs, cattle, donkeys, and guinea pigs. Fish is a common source of protein for communities living near rivers and lakes.

To the Aymara, life depends on the generosity of their deities, represented primarily by Pachamama (Mother Earth) and Achachila (the lake and mountain spirit). The gods reside in both the natural and supernatural worlds and the Aymara implore them daily for help and protection. Dance and music are two of the ways in which the Aymara express gratitude to the gods. Dance is an expression of cultural identity as well as a means of communicating with the natural and supernatural realms (fig. 62).

According to Tomás Huanca Laura, dance and music have great importance in family and community life, in the Aymaras' interactions with nature, and in their political struggles. Every occasion has a special type of dance that serves to renew and update cultural traditions.

There are basically two types of dances: those of colonial origin, which are centered on the patron saint of each community, and those based on the cycles of agriculture and herding and on the stages of life.

The patronal dances occur once a year during the patron saint's fiesta in each community. In the colonial period, these dances were obligatory but now they are an accepted tradition. The dancers generally wear elaborate

costumes and are accompanied by brass bands. The symbolism contained in these dances usually reflects the communities' conflicts with colonialism and political domination. The Carnival celebrations in the city of Oruro, although very much an urban phenomenon, clearly illustrate this type of dance.

Carnival, the Latin American equivalent to Mardi Gras, is very popular in Bolivia, and the city of Oruro has the most dramatic celebration with a spectacular parade called the *Entrada* (Entrance; fig. 63). The parade, which includes floats, dance groups, and bands, is rich in symbolism that combines pre-Hispanic, colonial, and contemporary elements. Over forty different dance groups participate in the parade, most organized expressly for this purpose. Each dance group is accompanied by two or more bands who either walk behind them or in a line beside them. The majority of the bands are brass bands, although some of the smaller, more "ethnic" dance groups are accompanied by the music of traditional Andean instruments. According to Huanca, most of the band members are Aymara. The parade participants are primarily students from diverse economic and ethnic backgrounds. Each dance group is preceded by a banner with the group's insignia and a float covered with textiles, silver objects, and the image of the Virgin of Socavón, the patron of Oruro.

63 *MORENADA* DANCERS PERFORM IN THE CARNIVAL PARADE OF ORURO, BOLIVIA, FEBRUARY 1992.

One of the most popular and spectacular dances is the *diablada* or Devil Dance (fig. 64). The *diablada* represents the victory of good over evil. In one version, the Devil Dance depicts evil spirits being conquered by the Archangel Michael, while in another version the devils represent the old mountain deities and Michael is a Spanish conquistador. The devil dancers wear elaborate costumes that are usually red and lavishly decorated with embroidery and appliqué work. Their grotesque, brightly colored masks have bulging eyes, snarling mouths with large teeth, protruding horns, and sculpted forms of condors, bulls, and double-headed serpents. Today, these masks are made out of plaster and cardboard and have light-bulb eyes, while those in the early 1920s were made of a gesso-plaster mixture over felt and had bottle-glass eyes (fig. 65). Each dancer wears a spur on his right foot and a wig of long, white hair — elements that harken back to the conquistadors. Some of the dancers wear silver coins on their belts representing the wealth of the local silver mines and alluding to the enslavement and exploitation of Indian people, who were forced to work in the mines by the Spanish colonists. The dancer representing the Archangel Michael wears a silver costume with wings, and a Mercury helmet, and he carries a sword. The dance has its own music, and the dancers move with quick, long-jump steps.

The dances related to agricultural and herding activities and life-cycle events are quite different. First, they predate the arrival of the Spanish, and second, they are more purely Aymara because they are related to basic subsistence activities and major life-events. Colonial influences are still present. But even though many of the fiestas coincide with the cycle of Catholic saints' days, the values and sentiments expressed in the celebrations are Aymara.

According to Huanca, agricultural and herding activities are very important to the Aymara because they are

> …*the organizing framework of the rhythm of a community and its values. The norms and customs established by generations are strictly observed and each thing has its place and time. In the same way that dance, music or the instruments are inseparable, none of them can be exempt from the rhythm of the agricultural and herding activities.*[25]

Many Aymara fiestas coincide with the agricultural calendar, which is divided into rainy and dry seasons. Some fiestas are scheduled to mark major events in the agricultural cycle, while others are scheduled so that they will not conflict too severely with agricultural activities.[26]

64 *A DIABLADA DANCER PERFORMS IN THE CARNIVAL PARADE OF ORURO, BOLIVIA, FEBRUARY 1992*

65 *DIABLADA* DANCE
MASK, CA. 1924. ORURO,
BOLIVIA. NATIONAL
MUSEUM OF THE
AMERICAN INDIAN,
SMITHSONIAN
INSTITUTION, NO. 13.4485

THE AYMARA FIESTA: LINKING COMMUNITY REALITIES

The celebration of the Aymara fiesta synthesizes the community's concept of life, which is defined by the interaction between everyday reality and nature. The fiesta preserves the multiple links between human life and the earth; between seed, sowing, and harvest; and between individual, family, community, and deities. Everything about the fiesta takes place within a framework of symbolic-ritual behavior—marked by mutual respect, thanksgiving, and petition—through which members of the community and the spirits

66 BONIFACIA
QUISPE FERNÁNDEZ
PAYS TRIBUTE TO
THE AUTHORITIES
OF HER COMMUNITY
DURING THE
CARNIVAL
CELEBRATION IN
LACAYA BAJA,
BOLIVIA, MARCH,
1992.

of their ancestors strengthen their ties to one another (fig. 66).

For the Aymara, the fiesta is a special time that interrupts daily life with ritual and pervades the social and spiritual life of the community. In general, fiestas have three stages: the beginning or reception, the *jach'a uru* (great day), and the *kacharpaya* (farewell). The faithful observance of the rites from beginning to end is strictly followed. The fiesta begins with three months of preparation before the actual event. The musicians rehearse and select the dancers, a process through which every individual demonstrates his or her place in the community. During this initial stage, the community invites their ancestral spirits to participate in the fiesta.

On the day named *jach'a uru*, food and drink play a central role. Displays of costumes and physical strength—accompanied by shouting, laughing, and mimicry—contribute to the day's atmosphere of friendship, openness, and ritual.

The fiesta concludes with the *kacharpaya*, during which the participants dance in groups, play instruments competitively, and eat and drink until sated (figs. 67, 68). Ultimately, inertia and fatigue bring the fiesta to an end. On this day, marked by moments of intense effusiveness, the celebrants' energies overflow as they bid farewell to the "personage of the fiesta," who will return next year. Once the fiesta is over, order resumes in the community and everyone returns to daily activities; memories and special moments remain that will accompany the annual cycle of work.

Fiestas and dances involve three forms of ritual offerings. The first one, the fiesta itself along with the dancers' participation, is an offering of the individual to the community. The second aspect is that food is offered to the spirits who protect home and crops and defend against the threats of sickness and natural phenomena, such

as hail storms. Finally, dance historically involved human sacrifice to expiate the collective faults of the community, as in the dance performed by the *Danzante*. In brief, the sense of the offerings means, on the one hand, that the spirits feed themselves, and on the other, that humans expect material rewards in terms of the well-being of the family and the community.

In Aymara communities, every social, cultural, economic, and political event is marked by religious-ritual behavior. The fiesta is a social event that

provides solutions. Cultural markers that regulate behavior and reaffirm customs—e.g., directional movements toward right and left—are strictly observed during the dance. The cultural heroes of the dances, symbols that play off against the traumatic results of the Conquest, are associated with negative and positive omens.

Finally, the fiesta and dance are not static, but are in constant flux. Mass communication, education, development programs, and forced migration are all factors that influence dance and

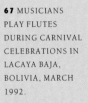

67 MUSICIANS PLAY FLUTES DURING CARNIVAL CELEBRATIONS IN LACAYA BAJA, BOLIVIA, MARCH 1992.

68 COMMUNITY MEMBERS DANCE DURING CARNIVAL CELEBRATIONS IN LACAYA BAJA, BOLIVIA, MARCH 1992.

mobilizes and energizes the community and "gives the Indian much more than pleasure: for him it means a reason to live, it focuses his thoughts in space and time."[1] It is the moment beyond societal boundaries, in which the community makes time its own and lives according to its own rhythm. In that sense the dance is a rebellion that integrates and re-creates the community's values. The fiesta also generates communal solidarity that reaffirms and renews the reciprocal relationships expressed during the celebration in the form of economic aids such as *ayni*, *apxata*, and *yanapa*.[2]

Dance is an encounter with the past and present, a foretelling of the future of the community and a display of ritual-symbolic practices—toward the gods, aggressors, nature, and the community's own members. In these relations, the powerful symbols of the dance emerge as the elements around which the community negotiates, accuses, and

music. These forces of change require the objective participation of community members in order to maintain the conduct and identity of the group through collective, conscious action—such as dance and the persistence of communal behavior during the fiesta as a whole.

Tomás Huanca Laura

1   Jacques Monast, *Los Indios Aimaraes* (Buenos Aires: Cuadernos Latinoamericanos, 1972), p. 203.
2   *Ayni* is a reciprocated exchange of goods or services, *apxata* is a voluntary contribution of goods for a special social event in which a moral obligation exists, and *yanapa* is a form of aid between real or ritual kin that does not have to be reciprocated.

During the rainy season, for example, there is a fiesta period that marks the time when the crops are maturing and that also coincides with a pause in agricultural activities. Referred to as the period of ripening (*maduración*), this fiesta period is an important ritual and social time during which kinship ties are strengthened, powers of authority are recognized, and offerings are made to the fertility gods in order to insure the success of the crops (fig. 69).[27]

The ritual cycle of the period of ripening begins on February second with the fiesta of the Virgin of Candelaria (Candlemas) and ends with Carnival at the end of the month. Because the Aymara broadened the meaning of the Catholic Virgin to connote Pachamama (Mother Earth), the fiesta of Candlemas, although

69 PEOPLE GATHER FOR THE CARNIVAL FIESTA IN LACAYA BAJA, BOLIVIA, MARCH 1992.

initially a Catholic feast day, is now an agricultural celebration dedicated to the maturing crops and the earth. During this fiesta, prayers and ritual offerings are made to the potato spirits and Pachamama so that the crops will be abundant.

The ripening ritual cycle ends with Carnival, an event that has its own internal structure of celebrations and includes much dancing. The dances performed at this time of year are called *anata* (encounter). The Carnival celebrations in rural areas are very different from those in the cities. In the rural context, the celebrations last a week and more clearly demonstrate the reciprocal relationship between community members and their environment. During the first two days of Carnival there is no dancing because ritual activity is restricted to the home and family. After two days, the community celebrations begin with visits to the houses of the community's leaders. Gifts of food, drink, flowers, and paper streamers are given to them as symbols of humility, respect, and honor. Dancing starts at this time, and community members are expected to dance for the leaders as a sign of greeting and respect. These dances are called *aruntaña* (welcome).

The next day, the whole community goes to the communal agricultural fields, accompanied by the music of cane flutes and drums, where they dance, feast, and perform an agricultural ritual. The dance performed during this time of year is called *Qhashwa* (fig. 70). The *Qhashwa* is performed to honor the potato spirits and to keep the freezing temperatures and hail away, both of which can destroy the crops during this time of year. The dance by men and women is performed in a tight circle with intertwined hands to reinforce the unity among members of the community. While they are moving round in a circle, the dancers step inward and then outward, singing *jawilla, jawilla*, which means "act of inviting," to the potato spirits. The circle then opens

7 1 AUTHORITIES BESEECH THE POTATO SPIRITS DURING THE *QUWACHIRI* RITUAL. LACAYA BAJA, BOLIVIA, MARCH 1992

7 2 A RITUAL SPECIALIST EXAMINES POTATOES FROM THE COMMUNITY'S AGRICULTURAL FIELDS. LACAYA BAJA, BOLIVIA, MARCH 1992

7 0 QHASHWA DANCE, LACAYA BAJA, BOLIVIA, MARCH 1992

up, and the dancers move in a snaking line until they form another circle. The singing is done a capella with the women singing the main chorus and the men responding.

After the dance, a potato ritual called *Quwachiri* is performed in which the leaders of the community summon the potato spirits and make offerings to them (fig. 71). While the men are praying to the spirits, the women go into the fields and dig up some potato plants. In the holes they place coca leaves and a quince so that the potatoes will mature to that size. The pulled potato plants are then examined by a ritual specialist who predicts the results of the crop (fig. 72).[28] After the ritual, the dancing continues for the rest of the day and throughout the night.

Because the danger of crop destruction due to hail and freezing temperatures is so real, the community allows the young people to perform the *Qhashwa* Dance on the coldest nights, to minimize agricultural risks and prevent strong frosts.[29] The young people dance and sing around a bonfire accompanied by cane flutes (*pinkillus*), panpipes (*sikus*), and bass drums (*wankaras*) until dawn the following day. The sounds of the drums, besides marking the tempo and rhythm of the dance, are associated with the thunder that heralds a rainstorm or hailstorm. In addition to preventing agricultural disasters, the dance promotes social interaction among young people and gives them an opportunity to learn how to do the dances and play the musical instruments.

Unlike the elaborate, and frequently rented Carnival costumes worn in Oruro and La Paz, the Carnival dress worn in rural communities generally consists of a person's best daily clothes. The men usually wear a poncho, a knitted cap with ear flaps (*lluchu*), and a sash; women wear multiple skirts (*pollera*), a blouse, sash, shawl (*manta*), and carrying cloth (*aguayo*). Ornaments of flowers, however, are always present because the important role of nature must always be acknowledged. The musical instruments played in rural areas also differ from those encountered in the cities. For example, the instruments usually played during Carnival are cane flutes, panpipes, and drums because the music they produce is most pleasing to the plants (fig. 73).

There are a variety of dances that are related to rites of passage. For example, the *Achuqalla tiwtiña* (which roughly translates as "the first fruits of the new family") is performed during the dry season when a couple builds their first house. Among the Aymara, newlyweds first go to live with the husband's parents and within three years, the couple moves into their own house.[30]

The construction of a house, one of the principal rites of passage, is usually accomplished in one day, primarily with the help of the couple's parents, although the rest of the community assists in building the roof. When the construction is completed, ritual offerings of food and drink are made to the deity of the home, Condór Mamani, in order to ward off evil spirits and protect the people who live in the house. A big fiesta is held, to which friends, relatives, and neighbors bring food, drink, and other gifts. Dancing starts in the evening and goes on all night, accompanied by songs and the music of flutes and drums. During the dances, it is customary to symbolically whip the owner of the new house while singing choruses that describe the house and rules of conduct for taking care of it. The house-building ceremony, therefore, acknowledges the relationship between the couple and their parents and their newly acquired status as household heads.[31]

In addition to the human voice, Aymara dance is accompanied by two kinds of musical instruments: wind and percussion. The wind instruments are associated with the sky, while the drums are symbols of Mother Earth. When played together, they represent cosmic wholeness. The wind instruments include a variety of cane-duct flutes (*pinkillus*) and panpipes (*sikus*) and a wooden flute (*tarka*). The percussion instruments, known collectively as *wankara*, include a variety of drums of different sizes and names. The wind instruments are always played in families of instruments of various sizes—reflecting the families of communities, which consist of individuals of varying ages.[32] Panpipes, for example, are always played in pairs, *arka* and *ira*. An ensemble is

generally comprised of several wind instruments and one or two drums. Frequently the same musician plays a wind instrument and bass drum simultaneously. This communal and complementary approach to music is characteristic of Andean music and dance in general.

D ance and music are central to the Zapotec, Maya, and Aymara cultures. On the one hand, they serve to reinforce the social and political structure of each society; and on the other, they connect the natural and supernatural worlds with the day-to-day activities of human life. Dance and music reaffirm fundamental values intrinsic to each group. They are a reaffirmation of tradition that has been able to transform historical encounters and foster continuous change. Dance and music are a means by which a community maintains its identity and values through collective, conscientious actions in an ever-changing world, no matter whether individuals live in rural or urban areas, or in other parts of the world. Despite the migration of many rural inhabitants to urban areas and to cities in the United States, dance and music traditions remain alive and viable in these new homes.

To be a dancer or a musician is an honor. Participants are allowed to focus their complete attention on these activities because participation is considered the result of divine inspiration and a responsibility equivalent to contributing time and labor to build a school or construct a road. Music and dance, passed on within families, are not just a calling. Growing consciousness about the importance of music and dance for the preservation of society and cultural identity is reflected in the way these activities have been integrated into the education of young people. The success of this process is seen in the participation of both elementary school-age children and university students in many fiestas.

The festivals that complement fiestas by bringing communities together to show off their dances are also important to this education process. These festivals are generally sponsored by governmental agencies and cultural institutions. In Chiapas, for example, the festivals present the music and dance of the most important fiesta of each participating community, but without all the ritual and sacred discourse that occurs during the fiesta. According to Burguete, the purpose of bringing dance and music groups together in one place

> is to unite them as one family … in order to re-encounter and become reconciled with their own
> roots, and for them to develop ties between indigenous people and to appreciate the diversity of
> cultures. Only then will they be able to respond to the cultural elements that are not their own,
> and therefore strengthen ethnic loyalty and their own identity.[33]

Dance and music—an inseparable part of a larger cultural and spiritual complex—are a key to a deeper understanding of the Indian world.

The information contained in this essay is based upon fieldwork research conducted by Tzotzil Maya ethnolinguist Jaime Torres Burguete (Instituto Chiapaneco de Cultura, Chiapas); Aymara anthropologist Tomás Huanca Laura (Centro Andino Desarollo Agropecuario, La Paz); and Zapotec ethnologist Manuel Ríos Morales (Centro de Investigaciones y Estudios Superiores en Antropología Social, Mexico). This essay, the result of collaborative research, would not have been possible without their excellent anthropological work. Other data utilized is the result of survey fieldwork conducted in Bolivia (25 February – 8 March 1992) and Oaxaca, Mexico (6 – 14 June 1992) by Olivia Cadaval (Smithsonian) and Nancy Rosoff (Smithsonian).

We are also indebted to the following individuals for their assistance. In Bolivia: María and Tiburcio Bautista of Qalaqi, Cristóbal Condoreno Cano of THOA, Agustín and Simone Choque of Kumana, Virginia Cirpa of CADA, Bonificia Quispe Fernández of Lacaya Baja, Téofilo Ricardo Mendoza of Kumana, Evaristo Espejo Quispe of Canal 7—Televisión Nacional, and Nicolás Villca Quispe of Teleart Communicaciones. In Chiapas, Mexico: Jacinto Arias of the Instituto Chiapaneco de Cultura. In Oaxaca, Mexico: María Morales Aquino of Yalálag, José Antonio Fuentes Chávez of Mexico City, Pedro Ríos Hernández, Damiana Morales, Alberta Martínez Marcial, Angela Marcial Mendoza, and Francisco Siguenza Yescas of Zoogocho, and Heriberto Ríos Morales of Oaxaca.

We would also like to thank David Bosserman and Michael Morrow for their emotional support and their assistance in the field, Lidya Montes and José Montaño for their help throughout the project, and George Arevalo for assembling the discography.

Finally, we are grateful to all the American Indian communities we visited for their hospitality and for their invaluable contribution to our research.

1   William Mangin, in Stanley Brandes, *Power and Persuasion: Fiestas and Social Control in Rural Mexico* (Philadelphia: University of Pennsylvania Press, 1988), p.8. A fiesta, according to Mangin, is:

> *...any event marking the ritual observance of particular occasions which has as its feature an organized personnel, a systematic and traditional structure and content, and a complex of ritual obligations. Eating and the drinking of alcoholic beverages are always part of the fiesta while music and dancing are often included. Any fiesta has a ritual character, in the sense that the fiesta and the event it marks are clearly, systematically and inseparably associated, and that supernatural aid is expected as a result of the performance of transcribed behavior patterns.*

2   Hans C. Buechler, *The Masked Media: Aymara Fiestas and Social Interaction in the Bolivian Highlands* (The Hague: Mouton Publishers, 1980), pp. 5–6.

3   Laura Nader, "The Zapotec of Oaxaca," in *Handbook of Middle American Indians*, vol. 7, Robert Wauchope, ed. (Austin: University of Texas Press, 1969), p. 331.

4   Manuel Ríos Morales, "Las danzas ceremoniales entre los zapotecos de la Sierra Norte de Oaxaca" (unpublished manuscript, 1992), p. 1. Much of the information on the Zapotecs in this essay is based on this manuscript.

5   Ibid., p. 20.

6   It is interesting that the dances depicting the Conquest—e.g., the Malinche—do not include one of the main characters, Cortés. Instead, the personage of Moctezuma is central, thus subverting any commemoration or glorification of the Conquest event.

7   Jaime Torres Burguete, "Ubicación de los tzeltales y tzotziles y su entorno geográfico" (unpublished manuscript, 1992), pp. 1–2.

8   Ibid., p. 3.

9   Walter F. Morris, Jr., *Mil años del tejido en Chiapas* (Chiapas: Instituto de la Artesanía Chiapaneca, 1984), pp. 8–9, 18–44.

10 Mauro Hernández Bautista, interview with Jaime Torres Burguete, 18 May 1992.

11 Victoria Reifler Bricker, *Ritual Humor in Highland Chiapas* (Austin: University of Texas Press, 1973), p. 9.

12 Agustín García Gómez, interview with Jaime Torres Burguete, 17 May 1992.

13 Burguete, "Ubicación," p. 16.

14 Burguete, "Nombre de la danza: carnaval de San Pedro Chenalhó" (unpublished manuscript, 1992), p. 4.

15 Burguete, "Ubicación," pp. 5–6.

16 Bricker, *Ritual Humor*, pp. 84–89.

17 Pascual López Ruiz, interview with Jaime Torres Burguete, 16 May 1992.

18 Burguete, "Ubicación," pp. 7–9.

19 Salvador Bautista López, interview with Jaime Torres Burguete, 17 May 1992.

20 Burguete, "Ubicación," pp. 14–15.

21 Ibid., p. 12.

22 José Pérez López, interview with Jaime Torres Burguete, 18 May 1992.

23 Burguete, "Ubicación," p. 11.

24 Tomás Huanca Laura, "La danza en las comunidades aymaras" (unpublished manuscript, 1992), p. 1. Much of the information on the Aymara in this essay is based on this manuscript.

25 Ibid., p. 3.

26 Buechler, *The Masked Media*, p. 39.

27 Huanca, "La danza," p. 7.

28 Ibid., p. 8.

29 Ibid., p. 11.

30 Ibid.; see also Hans C. Buechler and Judith-Maria Buechler, *The Bolivian Aymara* (New York: Holt, Rinehart and Winston, 1971), p. 80.

31 Ibid.; also, Huanca, "La danza," p. 12.

32 José Montaño, liner notes for *Aliriña*, Grupo Aymara (Chicago: Flying Fish Records, 1988).

33 Burguete, "Los encuentros regionales de musica y danza tzotzil, en contraste con las fiestas propias de las comunidades" (unpublished manuscript, 1992), p. 7.

WHITE MOUNTAIN APACHE DANCE : EXPRESSIONS OF SPIRITUALITY

CÉCILE R. GANTEAUME

Dance is one of the earliest and most enduring forms of communal expression. It allows people to come together and express feelings that lie deep within themselves. Among the White Mountain Apache dance is, above all, a spiritual experience. For through their dances, and the religious ceremonies in which they take place, the White Mountain Apache come into real contact with the natural world— that is, with the spiritual powers that created the universe and are manifest in nature. This is as true for White Mountain Apache people today as it was in the past.

Unlike so many Native American tribes and nations who were forcibly removed from their historic lands, the White Mountain Apache continue to live on land located within their traditional territory, in east-central Arizona. Yet, like other tribes, they have endured profound social and political upheaval. In 1870 the United States Army established a military post in the heart of their territory. With the army came the United States Indian Service, Christian missionaries, and, eventually, Bureau of Indian Affairs schools. Almost immediately, outsiders tried to interfere with the White Mountain Apache's traditional religious practices.[1] Today, knowledge of many of their ceremonies has been lost. Yet the ceremonies that have survived continue to hold profound social as well as religious meaning. In many ways, these ceremonies have evolved into extremely important rituals of cultural affirmation. But clearly, the idea that nature points to a divine saving power has remained paramount.

For the most part, White Mountain Apache dance and religious ceremonies have always been oriented toward healing.[2] In the past, the healing power of dance focused on an ailing individual who had broken a taboo, who had inadvertently behaved disrespectfully toward a supernatural power.[3] Today, while modern medicine has replaced much of the White Mountain Apache's earlier reliance on traditional curing ceremonies, dance continues to retain its strong spiritual significance. And dance still involves healing — a healing that takes place deep within oneself and that is turned outward toward others. Ronnie Lupe, chairman of the White Mountain Apache Tribe, speaks of dancing as "a communication with your inner self, [with your] whole world and surroundings. It opens you up," he says, "and makes you aware. [It makes you understand that] there is need in this world and that there is someone with greater power, [and that one day] that need will be answered."[4]

While the theme of healing can be said to run through every White Mountain Apache religious ceremony performed today, the purpose of an individual ceremony is articulated through its songs and prayers. Each ceremony has a corpus of songs and prayers that are associated with it, or rather with the specific power that is invoked during a ceremony.[5] In traditional White Mountain Apache religious belief, the different spiritual powers that are manifested in nature (in plants, animals, minerals, and meteorological phenomena) and in supernatural beings can be invoked and controlled through specific chants or songs. These songs are special invocations directed toward supernatural powers. Sung by medicine men and those who assist them, they reveal that the healing power at work among the White Mountain Apache today is the power of the *gaan*, mountain spirits who drive away evil. It is the power of *istənadleze*, Changing Woman, who endows young girls with the strength and ability to live as full and as long a life as possible. And it is the power of *nayenezgane*, Slayer of Monsters, who protects soldiers in war and brings them home safely. It is divine power.

The songs associated with White Mountain Apache religious ceremonies have always been considered sacred. Revealed to certain individuals in dreams, they provide those people with direct knowledge of the spiritual reality and power around them. Those who receive songs almost always become medicine men.[6] Edgar Perry, director of the White Mountain Apache Cultural Center, puts it this way: "In order to know that he's going to be a medicine man, he would have a dream, and that dream would be a beautiful song that was given to him. And so he heard that song. That's his song. Medicine man's song."[7] These songs are eventually revealed and taught to others in a ritual context. Most of the songs being sung today are thought to be generations old, passed down from time immemorial.[8]

In White Mountain Apache religious ceremonies, both music and dance are inextricably intertwined with fundamental beliefs concerning the profound reality of divine power. While they are invocations to specific powers, almost all sacred songs recall the very fact of creation and the design of the universe, most notably through repeated references to the four cardinal directions. In traditional White Mountain Apache religious thought, the east, south, west, and north are holy, and the colors associated with them (black, blue or green, yellow, and white, respectively) and the number four and its multiples have sacred connotations. Emphasized throughout sacred songs, these references invoke an awareness of the divine origin of the universe and the spiritual powers that sustain all life. The following verse, from a Crown Dance song transcribed and published by the ethnologist Pliny Goddard in 1916, is illustrative:

> *Earth was holy,*
> *Sky was made,*
> *Earth was made,*
> *The Gan young people lighted on the sky four times.*
> *Their lives, four directions they heard me.*
> *With pollen speech,*
> *With my mouth speech,*
> *It moves within me.*
> *The holy Gans were in line four times with me.*[9]

76 ACCOMPANIED BY HER
FRIEND, CARLA DAN GOSEYUN
(L.) PERFORMS HER SUNRISE
DANCE. STEPPING LIGHTLY
FROM FOOT TO FOOT, SHE
LISTENS TO SONGS THAT TELL
OF THE CREATION OF THE EARTH
AND OF CHANGING WOMAN. HER
CANE SYMBOLIZES HER LONG
LIFE TO COME.

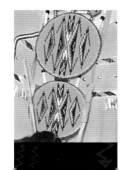

77 THE SUNRISE CEREMONY CONSISTS OF SEVERAL PHASES. DURING THIS PHASE, CARLA DAN GOSEYUN KNEELS ON THE BUCKSKIN AND, AS SHE SWAYS, RE-CREATES THE MOMENT WHEN CHANGING WOMAN WAS IMPREGNATED BY THE SUN.

78 DURING THIS PHASE OF THE CEREMONY, THE GIRL IS MASSAGED BY HER GODMOTHER, PHOEBE CROMWELL, AND "MOLDED" INTO A STRONG, HEALTHY ADULT.

80 TOWARD THE END OF HER SUNRISE CEREMONY, CARLA DAN GOSEYUN IS BLESSED BY HER MOTHER, ANNA GOSEYUN, WITH *HADNTIN* (SACRED CATTAIL POLLEN).

79 DURING THE CEREMONY, A GIRL MUST RUN AROUND HER CANE A TOTAL OF EIGHT TIMES. THE FIRST FOUR TIMES, HER CANE IS PLACED FARTHER AND FARTHER AWAY FROM HER. THE NEXT FOUR TIMES, THE CANE IS PLACED AT EACH OF THE CARDINAL DIRECTIONS. EACH OF THE FIRST FOUR RUNS SYMBOLIZES A STAGE OF LIFE THROUGH WHICH THE GIRL WILL PASS.

old White Mountain Apache great-grandmother, "or the baby has trouble or something. So that young girl, that one that danced, she gives her cane stick to her godmother and then she holds the baby, and the medicine man stands near and prays for the little baby and talks to this young girl and tells her what to do, so she holds the little baby this way and this way, to the four directions, and this way the baby gets better. See, a lot of sick people come,…and they line up and that little girl blesses them."[12]

The Sunrise Ceremony will continue for two more days. Sunday the girl will dance again. She will be accompanied, at different times, by a friend, her godfather, and crown dancers (fig. 81). Throughout the entire ceremony, it is the special power of Changing Woman that encourages the girl to endure her dance. Dance serves to strengthen her, to bring her to maturity, and to help her share in the faith of her community.

Crown dancing (sometimes called Mountain Spirit dancing) is performed when people want to invoke the power of the *gaan*, powerful spiritual beings who once lived among the White Mountain Apache and whose spirits now dwell in mountains. The power of the *gaan* is believed to be manifested in the wind. It is invoked by masked dancers who wear elaborate headdresses or crowns. During the religious ceremonies in which they perform, these dancers have the power to drive away evil, bestow blessings, or heal the sick. In the past, crown dancing may have occurred exclusively during healing ceremonies. Today, crown dancing is almost always performed at Sunrise Ceremonies and may also be performed during healing ceremonies. *Gaan* are invoked at Sunrise Ceremonies in order to bestow blessings. At healing ceremonies, *gaan* are invoked to cure an individual with a particularly serious or lingering illness.

Crown dancing is performed on the second night of the Sunrise Ceremony and again the following day. There are usually four male dancers personifying the *gaan*, and a fifth who is a clown (fig. 82). Saturday, late in the evening, people gather around a bonfire at the same dance ground where the young girl performed her Sunrise Dance. The medicine man who is officiating, and who has prepared the dancers, stands on the east, with the singers and drummers. "The clown always comes in first," says Edgar Perry, "He enters from the east. He is the chief. He has the power and he is the leader of the group. Even though he may be funny, but yet he has the power and he is directing the dancing."[13] Whirling his bull-roarer over head, the clown blesses each of the four cardinal directions. (A bull-roarer is a piece of wood, about eight inches long and two inches wide, tied at the end of a thong. Whirling the wood causes a roaring sound associated with the wind and power of the *gaan*.) The clown blesses the east first, then the south, west, and north. He then leaves the dance ground. This introductory rite lets the people know that the crown dancers are coming.

Today, the Sunrise Ceremony begins on a Friday. Sometime around midday the ritual items that will be worn or used by the girl throughout her ceremony are assembled and blessed by a medicine man.[11] These items include a drinking tube and scratching stick, an abalone-shell pendant, an eagle feather, and a special cane decorated with sacred objects — including yellow ochre, eagle and oriole feathers, bells, a turquoise bead, and four ribbons. The cane symbolizes long life, and the young girl will dance with it throughout her ceremony. Around five o'clock, the girl is ceremonially dressed by her godmother, as the medicine man

75 HERE, LINKED ARM IN ARM, THREE LINES OF MEN, WOMEN, AND CHILDREN PARTICIPATE IN A SOCIAL DANCE. THE WOMEN ARE WEARING TRADITIONAL CAMP DRESSES. 1984

directs the placement of each special object. After she is dressed, the medicine man speaks to all the people assembled, calling to mind the purpose of the ceremony and the need for reverence. He then sings four songs from the Sunrise Ceremony corpus, officially beginning the ceremony.

Early Saturday morning, when the Sunrise Dance takes place, at least four blankets covered with a buckskin are placed on a specially prepared dance ground. Cartons or burden baskets filled with candy, fruit, and coins have been placed to the east of the blankets, while to the west is placed a basket or abalone shell filled with *hadntin*, sacred yellow pollen. The medicine man, singers, and drummers stand behind the buckskin, facing east. The girl, accompanied by a girl friend, stands before them, in front of the buckskin. The two girls also face east. When the singing begins, the girls dance in place, stepping gently from one foot to the other (fig. 76). Together, the girls dance to a prescribed number of Sunrise Ceremony songs, usually thirty-two. These songs tell of the creation of the universe and of Changing Woman. It is during this dance, while these sacred songs are sung, that the girl receives the power of Changing Woman and becomes holy. She will remain holy for the next four days.

The Sunrise Dance is only one of several phases of the Sunrise Ceremony, which unites a girl personally and spiritually with Changing Woman (figs. 77–79). But while the entire ceremony is intended to bestow the gifts of Changing Woman (longevity, physical endurance, a good temperament, and prosperity most important among them) on an adolescent girl, the effective presence of Changing Woman is directed toward the whole community. After her Sunrise Dance, while the girl is invested with special spiritual powers, people line up to bless her with yellow pollen and pray for her (fig. 80). She too blesses and prays for them. In this prayerful atmosphere, healing takes place. "Maybe the baby's sick," explains Marie Quintero Perry, a seventy-seven-year-

These ideas concerning creation are reiterated visually in dance, through the placement of sacred objects, the position of key individuals, and the movement and action of dancers. Medicine men, singers, and drummers, for example, always face the east, the most holy of the four directions. Traditionally, four drummers accompanied an officiating medicine man, and dances (as well as songs) are performed in sets or multiples of four. In addition, dancers enter dance areas from the east, bless each of the four cardinal directions, and then, beginning at the east, dance clockwise around the arena or bonfire. This symbolism, always pointing to a deeper and greater reality, permeates all White Mountain Apache religious ceremonies.

The knowledge that their ceremonies, their dances and songs, belong to them — and that they are rooted in their collective past, having been passed down from generation to generation — is of great importance to the White Mountain Apache. And there is a growing sense today that while many of their ceremonies have been lost, those that do survive will go on forever, that they are to be passed down to the next generation, with reverence and respect.

he Sunrise Dance is part of the Sunrise or *Na-ih-es* (preparing her, getting her ready) Ceremony, one of the most sacred White Mountain Apache religious ceremonies performed today (fig. 74).[10] Held the summer after a girl's first menstrual cycle, this ceremony prepares her for adult life by calling upon the spiritual presence of Changing Woman. During the Sunrise Dance, Changing Woman transforms a young girl, making her spiritually strong and endowing her with a long and healthy life. While the actual ceremony lasts four days, planning often begins six months to a year in advance. Preparations, especially as the ceremony nears, involve numerous ritual procedures, including the gathering and making of ritual paraphernalia, blessings, purification rites, special prayers and songs. The family chooses the campsite and moves there about a week before the ceremony begins. During that week, final preparations —feasting, visiting, and social dancing —take place (fig. 75).

74 DRESSED IN CEREMONIAL CLOTHING AND FACING THE SUNRISE, A YOUNG GIRL, CARLA DAN GOSEYUN (L.), STANDS READY TO BEGIN HER SUNRISE DANCE. TO HER LEFT IS HER FRIEND CARMIN GOSEYUN. BEHIND HER STAND THE SINGERS, DRUMMERS, AND MEDICINE MAN. UNLESS OTHERWISE NOTED, THE PHOTOGRAPHS ACCOMPANYING THIS ESSAY WERE TAKEN AT THE WHITE MOUNTAIN APACHE RESERVATION, ARIZONA, 1991.

82 THE FIRST DANCER ON THE RIGHT IS *L'UBAIYÉ* (GRAY ONE), THE CLOWN. HE IS HOLDING A BULL-ROARER IN HIS RIGHT HAND AND A WAND IN HIS LEFT. WHIRLING THE BULL-ROARER OVERHEAD CAUSES A SOUND ASSOCIATED WITH THE WIND AND THE POWER OF THE *GAAN*. 1991

83 THE FIRST
CROWN DANCER,
DISTINGUISHED
BY HIS WIDE,
FAN-SHAPED
HEADDRESS, IS
ASSOCIATED WITH
THE EAST AND THUS
REPRESENTS THE
MOST IMPORTANT
GAAN. 1963

84 WHITE MOUNTAIN APACHE
DRUMS ARE USUALLY MADE
FROM HEAVY IRON
CONTAINERS OR POTS THAT
ARE FILLED WITH A SMALL
AMOUNT OF WATER. A PIECE OF
HIDE IS STRETCHED OVER THE
CONTAINER AND TIED TIGHTLY
IN PLACE. TO MAINTAIN THE
DESIRED TONE, THE DRUMMER
OCCASIONALLY TURNS HIS
DRUM TO KEEP THE HIDE
MOISTENED. 1984

Shortly thereafter, the crown dancers appear. They too enter from the east and are followed by the clown. Each crown dancer is carrying a pair of swordlike wands made from yucca or sotol wood (fig. 83).[14] They are wearing calf-high moccasins, buck-skin skirts decorated with metal cone tinklers, and wide leather belts with bells attached. Their torsos and arms are painted with black-and-white designs representing thunder, clouds, and rain.[15] Long strips of red cotton cloth, with four eagle feathers attached, hang from each arm. The crown dancers' headdresses consist of black cloth hoods, oak head frames, and sotol slat crowns. The crowns are painted with sacred images, which are prescribed by the medicine man and are specific to the ceremony in which they are used. After they have been assembled and painted, each dancer attaches his personal eagle feather and turquoise stone. As a rule, these sacred headdresses are worn only once. After the ceremony, feathers and turquoise are removed and the masks are put away forever in mountain crevices or caves.[16]

Upon entering the dance ground, the crown dancers bless the four cardinal directions and the medicine man begins to sing. From the very first measure of his song, the drummers, singers, and dancers know exactly when to join in. "Well, the medicine man would start singing, you know, just like a cappella and then after that the drums, all the drums, will come in. It's beautiful, everything just goes up," explains Edgar Perry, "everybody comes in, the drums and the rest of the singers. They know exactly when."[17] Most Crown Dance songs are slow in tempo, with an even four-beat rhythm. The words and vocables are accompanied by the steady beat of water drums, while the bells on the crown dancers' clothing accent the rhythm of the drums (fig. 84). The *gaan's* hoots ("oooohhhhh, oooohhhhh") are interjected spontaneously throughout the songs.

The dancers take their lead from the first crown dancer. Associated with the east, he represents the most important *gaan*. First, the dancers follow each other, dancing in a snakelike formation around the fire; then they dance with the girl and her friends; next, each crown dancer takes a turn dancing alone, one trying to outdo the other. Their moves are bold and dynamic; their steps, quick and agile. As they circle the dance ground they lunge and bob, twisting and turning their bodies sharply from side to side, tipping their headdresses back and forth (figs. 85, 86). Extending their arms, they thrust their wands toward the ground or overhead, all the while striking dramatic poses in quick, rapid succession (fig. 87). Sometimes, they stop suddenly and look around like a deer. Once they have danced, gradually circling the fire clockwise four times, the dancers leave the dance ground, exiting toward the east. After they have rested, they come back in to dance four more dances. And after they have danced for the last time, the clown once again blesses the four corners with his bull-roarer. This final blessing concludes the dance.

If the presence of the *gaan* is to be invoked during a healing ceremony, the person for whom the dance is being performed sits in the center of a dance area, facing east. Starting from the east, the crown dancers dance toward the sick person, touching him with their wands, thereby "throwing off the sickness." The crown dancers then line up

86 CROWN DANCERS
PERFORMING IN FRONT
OF NOTRE DAME
CATHEDRAL, PARIS,
1979. THE ARIZONA
HISTORICAL SOCIETY

87 A MEDICINE MAN
DECIDES WHAT
DESIGNS WILL BE
PAINTED ON THE
CROWN DANCERS'
BODIES,
REPRESENTING
SOURCES OF HOLY
POWER, THEY MAY
SYMBOLIZE THUNDER,
LIGHTNING, RAIN, OR
CLOUDS. 1984

at the south and again dance toward the sick person, touching him with their wands. They then approach the sick person in the same way from the west and the north sides. Sometimes the sick person is tied with strips of yucca leaves and, during their dance, the crown dancers will cut the yucca with their wands, symbolically relieving the sickness or pain.

Crown dancers are trained from childhood. "Not everybody dances," explains Ramon Riley, who works in the White Mountain Apache Tribal Employment Office and is himself a crown dancer. "You have to be trained from a little kid, be taught the prayers and know the songs. I guess anyone can dance, but you have to know what you're doing. You have to know the prayers and be purified. You have to go to sweat lodge. That's how I see that a select crown dancer knows what he's doing."[18] Usually, if a boy or young man is training to be a crown dancer, his father will ask a medicine man to pray for him. (He will offer the medicine man an eagle feather and piece of turquoise when he asks.) If the young man is considered sincere, the medicine man will teach him the prayers and songs that go with the dance and the connections between them.

When men who know how to dance, who know the proper prayers and songs, are selected for a Sunrise or healing ceremony, they are taken up into the mountains and are blessed by the medicine man who will perform

This story was told to Billy Crane by David Susan, a medicine man from Cedar Creek, Arizona, about the origin of the Crown Dance (figs. 88, 89). The events in this story happened many, many years ago.

+ + +

There was no rain and the land was dry. So the chief gathered the people and said, "People are getting hungry and we haven't any food to feed ourselves. We must go hunt. We'll leave in the morning so go and get yourselves ready." For some reason, the chief's daughter did not go. There was

88 CROWN DANCERS REPRESENT *GAANS*, BENEVOLENT BEINGS SENT TO THE APACHE PEOPLE BY THE GIVER OF LIFE. THE DANCER ON THE EXTREME LEFT IN THIS 1925 PHOTOGRAPH IS *L'UBAIYÉ*, A CLOWN. THE ARIZONA HISTORICAL SOCIETY

also a young boy who stayed behind. Looking around and seeing the chief's daughter, the boy asked her, "Why didn't you go hunting?" "I don't know, for some reason I just stayed home," she said. "Something told me to stay home too," said the boy, "and I was also told that I'm to lead the next hunt." "You see that butte?" he went on, "I'm going to climb that mountain and I'm going to play my flute." "How come you're saying all kinds of things when you should have gone hunting?" the girl asked. "Anyway," she told him, "you're too young to say that you're going to lead the hunt."

When the people returned from the hunt—tired, thirsty, and still hungry—the girl ran to her father shouting, "Hey Dad! This boy said he was going to lead the hunt. And he said he was going to play his flute up on the cliff. Did you see him?"

The next day, the chief gathered the people,

telling them, "We're going to have one more hunt, and there's a young man that's going to lead it." The boy explained, "I was told that I was to lead the next hunt. I was told to pick one hunter, hide him in the bush, and pick four boys who will go around the deer and chase it toward the boy in the bush so he can shoot it with a single arrow." Then he added, "But don't shoot any deer except the one-horned deer." This was mysterious, but they agreed and went out to hunt.

Eventually, a one-horned deer came along, and the boy who was picked to kill the deer did so. The hunters brought the deer home and had a big feast.

On the second and third days, the boy again instructed the hunters, telling them not to butcher the deer until he was present. "Don't touch the deer until I come there and instruct you how to butcher the deer." They followed his instructions the first three days and were successful. But on the fourth day, the hunters got impatient. "Let's go ahead and butcher the deer," they said. "We've butchered three deer before. We know what to do." But one hunter said, "No, let's follow the boy's instructions." "No," argued the others, "let's go ahead and butcher the deer." They butchered the deer and as they did, the boy came along. "I told you not to do this," he said. "This is a sacred hunt and you have ruined it. So, take the deer to the village and feed the people. I'll go back to where I found the deer tracks and see if our blessing, our luck, is still with us."

The boy re-traced the deer tracks with his dog. Going up the mountain side, he found a cave and heard a strange "ooooooohhhhh" sound and singing. He had never heard those sounds before. Curious, he entered the cave and saw the sacred Crown Dance. We had never known the dance before the boy went in there. But he shouldn't have entered the cave, because it was a sacred place. The boy was caught by the crown dancers. The dog ran home.

Meanwhile, the boy's grandmother was worrying. She went to the chief and he formed a search party. Everybody joined, including the

stood on the south side. Then a third group came. They were all in yellow and they had the upside-down "E" headgear. They stood on the west side. And then the clowns came out and stood on the north side. They wore white cross-shaped headgear. These dancers represented the colors and the cardinal directions that they stood in.

The crown dancers that were made by the people were all standing in the center. The crown dancers from the cave told each one of them to go to a different group and learn the dance because they're going to be dancing from this day forth. It was a sacred and holy dance. So the people began to bless the group of black crown dancers with yellow pollen and eagle feathers. Then they blessed the blue dancers. And then the yellow and white dancers.

Grandmother was blessing the dancers when her dog jumped on one. The dancer patted the dog's head and the grandmother realized that the dancer was her grandson. "Grandma," he said to her, "if you stayed at the mouth of the cave four days and four nights, I would have come back to you. But now I'm going to the spirit world. I'll be representing you, and you are to do this from this day forth — to heal and bless the people, and for the puberty ceremony and for all the good things. This is what I'll do for you and you'll be doing this dance from this day forth with our people."

Then, before the sun came up, the black crown dancers went over the horizon. Then the blue went over. Then the yellow and the white went over the horizon. And then the little dog. And that's the story of the origin of the sacred Crown Dance.

Edgar Perry

grandmother and the dog. The grandmother, it so happened, came upon the cave and heard the same "oooooohhhhh" sounds, as well as singing and the beating of a drum. She told the chief about the cave. Bringing everybody together, he told the grandmother, "Stay here at the mouth of the cave for four days and four nights. Don't go home. We'll bring you wood and food. Stay here and your grandson will come back." Knowing that her grandson was in the cave, she stayed. The first night, she heard the "oooooohhhhh" again and was scared. She heard the sound the second night. And the third night she heard the sound getting closer and ran back to the village. "I'm scared," she told the chief, "they're after me."

The chief led the people back to the cave. "We're going to stay here twelve nights," he said, "and we'll make our own crown dancers." You know, before then they had never seen crown dancers. But they made all four headdresses and the medicine man sang for twelve days. Then, on the last night, strange things began to happen. A group of four dancers came out of the cave. They were dressed in black with broad, black headgear. They stood on the east side and danced. Then a second group came out. Their headgear had three prongs and the headdresses were all blue. They

the ceremony. After they have been blessed and have gathered, or have been given, the materials necessary to make their headdresses, the medicine man has a sweat lodge built. As they are making their headdresses, the medicine man, dancers, and assistants bathe and purify themselves. Each time they enter the sweat lodge, they sing four sacred songs. Such participation of mind and body is required in order to invoke the spiritual presence of *gaan*, both during the preparation leading up to the dance and during the dance itself.

Perhaps at no time is the need for prayer and communal expression felt as intensely as in time of war. Among the White Mountain Apache, the 1991 Persian Gulf conflict brought about a revival of their War Dance. In the last century, if a war party was formed to avenge a death, a War Dance (again part of a larger ceremony) was held before the young men left their camps.[19] During the ceremony, warriors of each clan were called upon to dance with their weapons and demonstrate their bravery. During this ceremony, the warriors, their weapons, and the sacred objects that were made to protect them in war were prayed over and blessed.

While the White Mountain Apache War Dance may have been on the verge of becoming a lost tradition, the prayers and blessings that lay at the heart of the ceremony have always remained vital. Canyon Z. Quintero, a veteran of the Korean War, speaks about the power of White Mountain Apache prayer and its relevance to him during the Korean War:

> *And this medicine man, he's praying over here. It's strong. He looks at you every night, what you're doing over there. These people have strong power and their own prayer…. This old man, he's been in the scout, so many years, and he prayed for WWI, WWII, all these boys [to] come back [home]…. Boy, when you looked at that old man, boy, it was really something, real something. He know what to do with you. He got a cry in his voice, but he won't cry. Say he'll be there.*
>
> *[When I] came back over here with my mom, [I went to see that medicine man.] I said, "Remember me… remember you blessed me last year, when I was going across the sea, in the Apache way?" "Oh yeah, I remember you…. You was moving around all the time. I see you in the night and day time. I see you every day, and I was with you, beside you," he said. "Sometime I push you away," he said, "with my hands. You didn't feel me, you just go that way, and I follow you sometimes, you just run away from me," he said.*
>
> *"And you come back, and you're still a young man. Someday," he said, "look at me, look at me, someday you'll be like that someday. But don't worry about me, I've done my job already." So I look at him, patted him on the shoulder, and I started crying you know. Couldn't believe it, boy, my mama started crying, my god. I said, "You're a good man." So I'm thinking about him sometime, all the time. It's the way it goes. You feel his presence, his power. I did. I felt his presence, his power.*[20]

The White Mountain Apache War Dance is being revived at Holy Ground, a site on the reservation recently designated by the Tribal Council as "sacred and for exclusive use by persons practicing traditional Apache religion." Efforts are also being made to revive the dance by people whose grandfathers were Apache scouts. These people have personal memories of watching their grandfathers perform the dance.[21] It is their hope that the War Dance will become a meaningful tradition for the younger generation, who have no direct knowledge of the dance.

Another dance that is being revived at Holy Ground is the Hoop Dance. Like the Crown Dance, the Hoop Dance is performed as part of a healing ceremony.[22] The following description of a Hoop Dance is from a 1936 account.[23] A sick person is seated on a blanket in the middle of a dance ground facing east. One boy and one girl stand on the east, south, west, and north sides of him. All the boys are holding hoops and the girls are holding crosses. (This can be reversed.) When the medicine man starts to sing, the youngsters dance toward the patient, the boys placing their hoops over the patient's head and the girls holding their crosses just over his head. The hoops and crosses are raised and the youngsters dance back to their original positions. This dance is repeated as the medicine man sings four songs. Next, another man sings while the medicine man takes the hoop from the boy standing on the east and places it over the patient; the patient is then turned toward the south and the medicine man takes the south hoop and places it over the patient; the patient is then turned toward the west and the procedures are repeated until all the hoops are placed over the patient. The patient then stands up and steps out of the hoops. Similar procedures are repeated with the crosses. This entire ceremony can be repeated anywhere from one to four times that night.

Clearly, dance remains a profoundly important form of communal expression for the White Mountain Apache. Dancing helps White Mountain Apache people perceive the Creator's presence and healing power in their lives and to keep that perception alive. It is an affirmation of their cultural values. It is also a distinctive expression of their cultural identity. Dance represents tradition, pride in oneself, both as an individual and as part of a people. To this end, parents, community leaders, and elders are educating young people in school about dance. Three-, four-, and five-year-old children are taught dance in Head Start programs. Elementary schools have dance clubs, as do junior high and high schools. According to one sponsor, there are about twenty-five dance clubs in various schools on the reservation. And on 12 June 1992, the First Annual White Mountain Apache Traditional Song and Dance Competition was held. "I think that people should know about tradition," says Ramon Riley, sponsor of the competition. "[They] should know about where they came from, who they are, [and] that there are Apache songs and there are Apache dances. And they should be seen by young kids so that they will always know that they are Apache."[24]

This desire to foster and maintain tradition reflects the hope and trust that White Mountain Apache people have always had in dance, their belief that through dance the power of the Creator, the Giver of Life, extends through the community. "That we are one with this magnificent creation at the present time," says Ronnie Lupe, "that's what dancing is all about. It opens a door to you. You see things differently, a little more spiritually, with decency and humbleness, [and] with a lot of purity in your heart and body. That's what it means, dancing."[25]

I would like to thank Edgar Perry, director of the White Mountain Apache Cultural Center, not only for arranging several interviews, but for sharing with me his personal knowledge about White Mountain Apache dance. I would also like to thank George Arevalo, NMAI, for his research assistance and, in particular, for compiling the White Mountain Apache discography. Most of all, I would like to thank Chairman Ronnie Lupe, Marie Quintero Perry, Canyon Z. Quintero, and Ramon Riley for graciously sharing their time and talking to me about the meaning of White Mountain Apache dance.

1   Camp Ord was established in 1870. It was renamed Camp Mogollon, then Camp Thomas, then Camp Apache, and, finally, in 1879, Fort Apache. In 1881, U.S. Cavalry anxiety over the practice of a White Mountain Apache religious ceremony and dance, *na'ilde'* (the word, according to ethnographer Grenville Goodwin, has reference to "return from the dead") resulted in what soon became known as the Cibecue Massacre. An estimated eighteen Apache were killed, including the medicine man Noch-ay-del-kline, who had originated the ceremony (see William B. Kessel, "White Mountain Apache Religious Cult Movements: A Study in Ethnohistory" [Ph.D. diss., University of Arizona, Tucson, 1976], p. 73).

In the late-nineteenth and early-twentieth centuries, federal administrators involved in White Mountain Apache affairs made few attempts to acknowledge that the White Mountain Apache had a valued — or valuable — belief system. Albert B. Reagan, an administrative officer in the United States Indian Service on the White Mountain Apache reservation in 1901 and 1902, described the significance of several dances he witnessed as follows: "About two weeks before school each fall they inaugurated medicine dances and kept the children in constant turmoil to wear them out — they said it was done to make the child medicine-proof against white man's ways and medicines" (Reagan, "Notes on the Indians of the Fort Apache Region," *Anthropological Papers of the American Museum of Natural History* 31 [1930]: 313).

Throughout the twentieth century, Christian churches have labeled White Mountain Apache religion as "pagan" and have tried to suppress traditional practices. Fortunately, this attitude is changing and today at least one church is demonstrating both respect and support for traditional expressions of spirituality (see *Fort Apache Scout* [9 August 1991] and Anna Early Goseyun, "Carla's Sunrise," *Native Peoples* 4 [1991]: 8–16).

2   On the emphasis on healing in dance and religious ceremonies, Keith H. Basso writes that, in the past, the ceremonial system of the White Mountain Apache approached the Navajo in complexity and that, while there were a number of important rituals associated with hunting, warfare, and the onset of male and female puberty, the majority of their rituals were associated with curing or the bestowal of protection from illness. See Basso, "Western Apache," in *The Handbook of North American Indians*, vol. 10, ed. Alfonso Ortiz (Washington, DC: Smithsonian Institution, 1983), p. 479.

3   Also see Basso, *The Cibecue Apache: Case Studies in Culture and Anthropology* (Prospect Heights, Ill.: Waveland Press, 1986), pp. 45–47, for a discussion of White Mountain Apache concepts concerning sickness and taboos.

4   Ronnie Lupe, interview with author, Whiteriver, Ariz., 30 May 1992.

5   See Basso, *The Cibecue Apache*, pp. 42–44, for a discussion of the significance of sacred songs and supernatural power. Also see D. P. McAllester, "The Role of Music in Western Apache Culture," in *Selected Papers of the Fifth International Congress of Anthropological and Ethnological Sciences* (Philadelphia, 1956), pp. 468–72.

6   Women can also receive songs in dreams, but the singing of sacred songs in White Mountain Apache religious ceremonies is a male activity. Women, in addition to men, play an important role in ceremonies for the power they bring through massage. An important part of both the Sunrise and certain healing ceremonies, massaging is considered a sacred activity. During healing ceremonies that incorporate massage, women pull the pain out of a sick person through the rubbing, stroking, and kneading action of their fingers. See Basso, *The Cibecue Apache*, p. 66, for a discussion of the significance of massage during the Sunrise Ceremony.

7   Edgar Perry, interview with author, Fort Apache, Ariz., 27 May 1992.

8   The White Mountain Apache acknowledge three different ways of learning sacred songs. One is through dreaming, the second is by studying with a medicine man, and the third way is by "stealing" songs. If a man is studying with a medicine man, he will pay the medicine man, who will bless him and pray for him. Learning usually takes place in a sweat lodge. "They go to a sweat," says Edgar Perry, "and they sing in the sweat lodge four songs. And that's where they learn their songs. Four songs at a time. They go in and they go out. And they learn from the medicine man" (interview with author, 27 May 1992). If a man wants to "steal" songs, he follows a medicine man to different ceremonies and memorizes the medicine man's songs as he sings.

9   See Pliny Goddard, "The Masked Dancers of the Apache," in *Holmes Anniversary Volume: Anthropological Essays Presented to William Henry Holmes in Honor of His Seventieth Birthday, December 1, 1916 by His Friends and Colaborers*, ed. F.W. Hodge (Washington, D.C., 1916) p. 134.

10 See Basso, "The Gift of Changing Woman," *Anthropological Papers No. 76*, Bureau of American Ethnology Bulletin, no. 196 (Washington, D.C., 1966), pp. 113–73, and Basso, "The Cibecue Apache," pp. 53–72, for a comprehensive discussion and analysis of the Sunrise Ceremony. (Basso's work is based on fieldwork conducted in the 1960s and 1970s.)

Also see Goseyun, "Carla's Sunrise," 8–16, for a mother's account of the significance of the Sunrise Ceremony for her and her daughter, and Nita Quintero, "Coming of Age the Apache Way," *National Geographic* 157, no. 2 (1980): 262–71 for a girl's discussion of her own ceremony.

11 See Alan Ferg, *Western Apache Material Culture: The Goodwin and Guenther Collections* (Tucson, Ariz.: University of Arizona Press, 1987) for a more complete description and discussion of the ritual clothing worn by a young girl during the Sunrise Ceremony.

12 Marie Quintero Perry, interview with author, McNary, Ariz., 28 May 1992.

13 Edgar Perry, interview with author, 27 May 1992.

14 See Ferg, *Western Apache Material Culture*, pp. 117–25, for a more detailed description of crown dancers' ritual clothing and headdresses.

15 The forces of nature, such as thunder, lightning, and rain, are regarded as important sources of supernatural power.

16 Some men, who are frequently called upon to dance, are allowed to reuse their headdresses. Their headdresses are repainted for each ceremony in which they perform. Also, crown dancing is performed at social gatherings (inaugurations, parades, fairs, powwows, etc.) as well as for religious purposes. Headdresses used for social purposes are also blessed by a medicine man, but they may be used over and over again.

17 Edgar Perry, interview with author, 30 May 1992.

18 Ramon Riley, interview with author, Whiteriver, Ariz., 29 May 1992.

19 See Basso, ed., *Western Apache Raiding and Warfare: From the Notes of Grenville Goodwin* (Tucson: University of Arizona Press, 1973), pp. 246–52 and 279–83, for a discussion of the War Dance and Victory Dance. White Mountain Apache men served as voluntary scouts in the United States Army from 1872 until 1947. There were up to five scout companies at Fort Apache in the late 1800s.

20 Canyon Z. Quintero, interview with author, Fort Apache, Ariz., 29 May 1992.

21 See "Apache War Dance," in *Fort Apache Scout*, 24 January 1992, pp. 8–9, for a brief discussion of efforts to revive the War Dance.

22 In the past, the Hoop Dance was performed during lightning ceremonies — to cure people who had been struck by lightning or who had inadvertently used a piece of lightning-struck wood for some purpose.

23 This account was told to Grenville Goodwin by Joseph Newton. Goodwin was an ethnographer who worked among the White Mountain Apache in the 1930s. Newton was the medicine man with whom Goodwin worked. (According to Goodwin, Newton was an adopted member of the White Mountain Apache. He was originally Tonto Apache.) This account is taken from Grenville Goodwin's "Notes Concerning Religion, Curing and Ceremonials," pp. 57–58. Grenville Goodwin Collection, Arizona State Museum Archives.

24 Riley, interview with author, 29 May 1992.

25 Lupe, interview with author, 30 May 1992.

The Beauty, Humor, and Power of Tewa Pueblo Dance

JILL D. SWEET

From the moment the dancers and singers file out of the sacred ceremonial chamber, or kiva, a Tewa Pueblo village becomes a place of brilliant color, motion, sound, and excitement (fig. 90). The air is sweet with the aromas of freshly baked bread, simmering chili stews, and burning piñon. Family members who have moved to the urban centers for jobs come home, and the village is full of reunited kin. The people have gathered once again to celebrate what it is to be Tewa and what it is to be human. Seeking a sense of renewal, they dance and sing to "find new life."

Tewa ritual performances are communal public prayers that involve dancing, singing, percussive music, dramatic skits, and elaborate costumes. Sometimes the event includes scores of dancers and continues from sunrise to sunset. Typically the dance formation is composed of one or two long parallel lines (fig. 91). Dancers sing as they dance, or they may be accompanied by a chorus of men with one or more drummers. The movement style is contained and subtle. Repetitive, controlled, and relatively simple steps are executed in unison by dancers who hold their torsos erect and keep their gestures close to the center of the body (fig. 92).

Currently there are six Tewa villages, all located in the Rio Grande region north of Santa Fe, New Mexico (fig. 93). The names of these villages are Tesuque, Santa Clara, San Ildefonso, San Juan, Pojoaque, and Nambe. The people here are Pueblo Indians who speak the Tewa language. Other Pueblo groups are distinguished by the languages they speak — Towa, Tiwa, Keres, Hopi, or Zuñi. All these Pueblo groups are descendants of native peoples who have inhabited the American Southwest for at least two millennia. By the beginning of the fourteenth century, the ancestors of the Tewa migrated to the Rio Grande valley, where they established agricultural settlements. Ancient images left on nearby rocks suggest that the dance traditions of the Tewa are at least as old as their Rio Grande farming communities.

Tewa dance events can be discussed in terms of seasonal theme, degree of secrecy, and performance context. Such discussions help non-Tewa observers make sense of the great diversity of Tewa dance occasions.

90 DANCERS IN FRONT OF ONE OF THE KIVAS AT SAN ILDEFONSO PUEBLO, CHRISTMAS DAY, 1990

Tewa dances held in the villages throughout the year make up a series of public performances informed by a complex underlying cycle of private rituals. Each dance belongs to a particular season and reflects the concerns and traditional subsistence patterns associated with that season. For example, late winter and early spring dances mark the beginning of farming activities and signal the start of many agricultural dances that will be held throughout the summer. These agricultural dances are public prayers for fertility and feature corn, squash blossoms, butterflies, or basket motifs in costuming, gesture, and song. Clouds, rain, and lightning — all elements essential for agricultural success in the arid Southwest — are also prominent symbols (figs. 94–96). In contrast, during the winter months the traditional economy of the Tewa was hunting. Therefore, the winter dances, as public prayers for an abundance of game and successful hunts, feature deer, buffalo, elk, and other game animals as central dance figures and song subjects (figs. 97, 98).

91 A TYPICAL PARALLEL LINE
FORMATION DURING THE HOPI
CORN DANCE, AS PERFORMED
BY SANTA CLARA TEWA
DANCERS ON THEIR VILLAGE
FEAST DAY, 12 AUGUST 1974

92 TEWA DANCERS HOLD
THEIR TORSOS ERECT AND
KEEP THEIR GESTURES CLOSE
TO THE CENTER OF THEIR
BODIES. THE SOUND OF THE
GOURD RATTLE IS OFTEN
COMPARED WITH THE SOUND
OF SUMMER SHOWERS. 1974

94 THE BLUE CORN DANCE OUTFITS WORN BY SANTA CLARA TEWA DANCERS PROMINENTLY DISPLAY SYMBOLS FOR AGRICULTURAL SUCCESS. THE WOMAN'S TABLITA HEADDRESS IS PAINTED WITH IMAGES OF A RAINBOW, A SQUASH BLOOM, AND A CORN PLANT. SHE ALSO CARRIES AN EAR OF BLUE CORN IN EACH HAND. THE GEOMETRIC, EMBROIDERED BORDER ON HER WHITE MANTA REPRESENTS RAIN AND CLOUD FORMATIONS. THE YOUNG MAN WEARS A SQUASH BLOSSOM HEADDRESS. 1974

95 BUTTERFLY
DANCER AMY APPA
AT POJOAQUE
PUEBLO, 1990

A second way to distinguish Tewa dance events is based on secrecy. Secrecy has served the Tewa well as a device for protecting their ritual events from outside interference. Researchers and tourists quickly learn that most Tewa do not like to talk about their dances with outsiders and they consider direct questions to be rude. In fact, the most common complaint about the visitors who come to see dances is that they ask too many questions.

Some ritual events are closed to outsiders and held secretly in the kivas. The most secretive closed dances involve masked participants, embodying *Oxua* (or Cloud People). These masked dances have been hidden from outsiders ever since the early Spanish missionaries prohibited the people from publicly holding them. It was not uncommon for seventeenth-century missionaries — who considered this form of ritual performance "devil worship" — to burn the sacred masks and physically punish the dancers. Today, the only Pueblo villages where outsiders are permitted to witness these masked dances are Zuñi and Hopi, the two Pueblo village groups where the Spanish missionaries were less successful at suppressing native religious activities. And while this intolerance by the missionaries is primarily an attitude from the past, at all other Pueblo communities, including the Tewa villages, the masked dances remain private affairs, closed to non-Tewa spectators.

There are also open, but unpublicized, performances. When these dances are in progress, outsiders who arrive are permitted to stay, but they must keep their distance from the ritual action and usually they will not be permitted to take photographs or record the music. The dates for these dances are not predictable and often the Pueblo villagers themselves do not know when or if the event is going to take place until just a few days before it is held. Whether closed or open, unpublicized dances are scheduled by the native priests or requested by one of the internal village religious societies.

Finally, there are a group of dances that are open and publicized with predictable dance dates that may appear in local newspapers. The dates for these dances are predictable because most are tied to the calendar of Roman Catholic holy days. For these dances the Tewa expect many outside visitors. In fact, if the number of visitors is down from previous years, some Tewa people express disappointment. Most often these open and publicized events feature traditional native dances held on Christmas, Easter, or a specific saint's day. Because of the predictability of the dates and the publicity, these are the village dances that are most often seen by tourists who, at a few villages, may even be permitted to photograph the event.

Throughout the year each Tewa village celebrates its patron saint's day with mass, a procession to carry the *santo* (carved image of the saint) to an outside bower, and a full day of native dances in the village plazas. These open and publicized patron saint's day dances attract Pueblo people from other villages, as well as Navajo, Apache, Hispanic, and Anglo friends, and hundreds of tourists. On these "feast days" the homes are sites of sociability, with neighbors, relatives, and invited guests coming and going. Inside, the tables are typically laden with bowls of stew and platters of bread, tortillas, melon slices, cookies, and candy (fig. 99). In addition, there are usually native craftspeople selling jewelry and pottery during these dance events. When a saint's day falls in the later weeks of summer, Pueblo and Hispanic farmers also show up to sell their melons, chilies, and other

100 ON FEAST DAYS
EVEN DANCERS IN
CEREMONIAL ATTIRE
FIND A MOMENT TO STOP
AT ONE OF THE
CONCESSION STANDS
LOCATED BEYOND THE
DANCE PLAZAS. THESE
SANTA CLARA BOYS SEEK
REFRESHMENT DURING A
BRIEF BREAK BETWEEN
DANCE APPEARANCES.
1974

101 THE COLORFUL MATACHINES' DANCE,
OF SPANISH ORIGIN, IS PERFORMED ON DECEMBER
24TH AND 25TH AT THE SAN JUAN PUEBLO. A
VISITING GUITARIST PROVIDES MUSIC FOR THE
DANCE, WHICH FEATURES A CROWNED CENTRAL
FIGURE KNOWN AS MONARCA AND A LITTLE GIRL
CALLED MALINCHE. SOME TEWA PEOPLE BELIEVE
THE DANCE REPRESENTS A BATTLE BETWEEN THE
CHRISTIANS AND THE MOORS, WHILE OTHERS SAY
IT IS ABOUT MONTEZUMA AND CORTÉS. 1990

fresh produce. Often, at the outskirts of the village, there is a traveling carnival. All day long excited children can be seen running between the native dances held in the plaza and the homes of their relatives, the booths of visiting vendors, and the noisy carnival rides and concession stands (fig. 100).

The open and publicized Tewa dances performed in honor of Jesus or one of the saints reflect the coexistence of Catholicism and native religious tradition. Some Tewa people are more actively involved in church affairs than others. Regardless of personal commitment to Catholicism, however, most of the Tewa people are dedicated to the principles of their native religious system and remain quite cognizant of what is theirs and what is borrowed; what is native and what is Catholic; what is Pueblo and what is Spanish.

The Matachines' Dance, held near Christmas in some Tewa villages, exemplifies the Tewa people's awareness of origins. The Tewa enthusiastically present this dance but know it is of Spanish/Catholic origin, probably taught to their ancestors by Franciscan missionaries. The movements, costumes, and music of the Matachines' Dance are not typical of Tewa dances (fig. 101). Skips, hops, swing kicks, and polka steps dominate the choreography. The central dancers wear miters, reminiscent of a bishop's headdress, but with long, colorful ribbons attached at the back. Most often, visiting Hispanic musicians play sixteenth-century tunes on the violin and guitar.

Tewa dance events can be distinguished further in terms of the performance context. Some dances are held in the kivas, others in the village plazas, and some may be presented far from the villages in theatrical urban settings. Since the turn of the century, small Tewa dance troupes have performed short dance segments for non-Indian audiences. These theatrical, rather than ritual, productions contrast with the village events in several ways. First, they are held away from the kivas and village plazas that symbolize the heart of the Tewa world. Second, the dances, songs, and dance lines are abbreviated versions of the original forms. Third, dance segments are sometimes performed out-of-season (e.g., the presentation of an agricultural dance in the winter months). Fourth, participation in these outside performances is for fun and profit, while participation in village events is a communal ritual obligation or duty. In short, the performance context and purposes of these dances are significantly altered. Nonetheless, the Tewa dancers and singers who participate in these performances away from home believe that, if the dances are performed "from the heart," the sacred meanings and messages will still be present. Further, these performances for non-Indian audiences cultivate pride in Tewa expressive forms and in some cases have inspired revivals of particular dances that had fallen from the repertoire of a village.

Whether it is a dance reflecting agricultural or hunting concerns; one that is closed or open; or one performed within the village or at an urban center, all Tewa performances are elaborate events that bombard the senses. One sees, hears, smells, and feels the performance. And to the Tewa people these multisensual performances are vehicles for demonstrating, creating, and experiencing Tewa beauty, humor, and power.

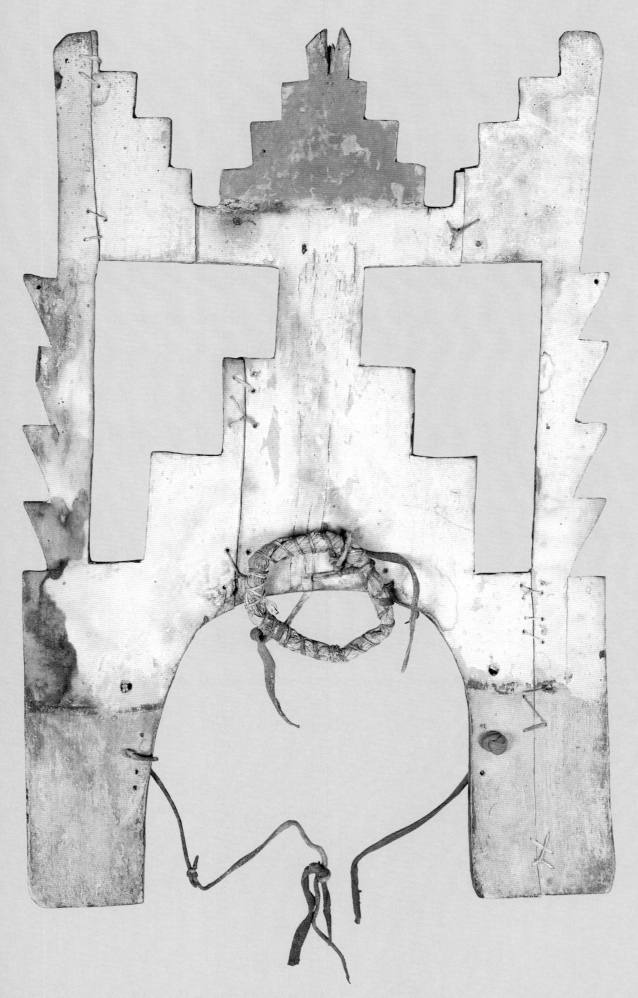

102 WOMAN'S WOODEN
DANCE HEADDRESS
ORNAMENT (TABLITA).
TESUQUE PUEBLO, NEW
MEXICO. NATIONAL MUSEUM
OF THE AMERICAN INDIAN,
SMITHSONIAN INSTITUTION,
NO. 6.436

S H A D E H

Shadeh is the Tewa word for dance. Translated literally, shadeh means "to be in the act of getting up, of waking up." By dancing, one awakens, arises in a heightened sense of awareness to the dance and participation in its meaning. To dance is to move with the song and sound of the drum and, hence, to participate in an ageless cosmic movement. The dance honors and recognizes the interactive role of human beings with the natural world. Songs entreat clouds and animals to come with their blessings into the human place, the village. The drumbeat is the heartbeat of the earth, which is thought about and made alive in dance. The heartbeat of the earth is physically felt when the Pueblo plazas vibrate with moccasined feet moving on the earth to the beat of the drum.

The moccasined feet are counterbalanced by the adornment of heads with feathers of birds and tablita headdresses graced with cloud and mountain symbols (fig. 102). Birds and clouds are of the sky, while mountains are of the earth, with summits that also touch the sky. Cloud, mountain, and bird symbols are sewn onto the women's mantas and men's kilts. Evergreen branches are placed within belts and headdresses and held in each dancer's hands. The boughs bring to the dance the everlasting life-strength of the encircling hills and four world-bounding mountains. Skins of animals — deer, antelope, buffalo, turtle, skunk, fox, coyote — carry the strength of the hills and mountains; the skins also symbolize the cyclic nature of life because they recall the animals who give themselves to the physical sustenance of human beings.

As they dance between female earth and male sky, connecting essential opposing elements of Pueblo philosophical thought and being, dancers evoke the human condition. Cycles of life — fertilization and the coming together of opposites in order to create life — are continual themes of Pueblo dance. Male dancers shake gourd rattles full of seeds. In certain dances, participants hold ears of mature corn, which represent the fullness of fertilization. In other dances, women hold baskets in front of them, as the male dancers move back and forth with lightning or zigzag wands.

On a larger scale, the shadeh connects the human place to the movement in the sky, to other simultaneous worlds below, and to the horizontal directions that embrace mountains, plants, and other animals. As such, the dance drama is of the middle place — between up and down, north, west, south, and east. The plaza, or *bupingeh*, is the "middle-heart-place." It is the central communal space where the community gathers to observe the ritual dance/drama of asking for, and receiving, life (fig. 103).

Seasons or cycles of time are honored in the dance calendar. Harvest, corn, and basket dances occur in the autumn, while animal dances happen in later winter to honor specific animals and to remind people of the interdependence of all animal life. Spring brings movement dances — such as the Geese Dance, which acknowledges and gives human energy to the birds in their flight to the north. In spring and summer, crucial agricultural seasons, rain and cloud dances assure another season of growth and continued sustenance of all life. Pueblo people thus honor the passing of time by dancing as a reminder to awaken, to participate in the connected flow of life around them.

Rina Swentzell and Dave Warren

103 RAIN DANCE, TESUQUE PUEBLO, CA. 1925. NATIONAL MUSEUM OF THE AMERICAN INDIAN, SMITHSONIAN INSTITUTION

Beauty, of course, is culturally defined and relative. For the Tewa, beauty is found in the illusion created by many dancers moving in perfect unison within a contained dance style. Beauty is also found in choreography and song composition that is repetitive and relatively simple, but punctuated with subtle variations. Most important, beauty is found in a respectful and sincere performance.

Dancing in unison is not only aesthetically desirable, but it underscores the Tewa notion that the needs of the individual are secondary to the needs of the whole community (fig. 104). The image of the entire group moving together should never be disturbed by someone who dances "too hard." In other words, a dancer who stands out from the others destroys the beauty of the group moving as one.

The illusion of one rhythmically moving mass is facilitated by the repetitive and relatively simple nature of the dance steps. Redundancy and simplicity allow a large group of non-specialists to learn the dance and to perform it in unison. This is important since almost everyone is expected to sing a few times each year and yet, there is no special training. Children simply start following their female relatives in the dance line, informally picking up the steps and style.

The Tewa people also see beauty in a controlled, understated dance style. Gestures do not extend far from the body's center and typically the steps are small progressions with little elevation. The women keep their gaze low and their manner demure (fig. 105). From the Tewa perspective this is how a beautiful woman should dance. The movements of the male dancers can be a little more exuberant and exaggerated, but a contained style is still essential.

Beauty is also found and expressed in the songs, which are closely tied to the meanings and the execution of a dance. The songs actually signal the dancers to make choreographic changes — such as a change in the directional orientation of the dance lines or a change in dance steps. Tewa song composers are admired for their creative skills in composing new songs, their ability to remember exactly old songs, and their skill at leading the singers to perform with clear strong voices that will "make the meaning straight." Like the dance movements, repetition and elegant simplicity are valued in song composition. These qualities can be found in the following translated traditional verse:

> *Oh, our Mother the Earth, oh our Father the Sky,*
> *Your children are we, and with tired backs*
> *We bring you the gifts that you love.*
> *Then weave for us a garment of brightness;*
> *May the warp be the white light of morning,*
> *May the weft be the red light of evening,*
> *May the fringes be the falling rain,*
> *May the border be the standing rainbow.*
> *Thus weave for us a garment of brightness*
> *That we may walk fittingly where the birds sing,*
> *That we may walk fittingly where the grass is green,*
> *Oh, our Mother the Earth, oh our Father the Sky!* [1]

97 A DEER DANCE AT
NAMBE PUEBLO,
CHRISTMAS EVE, 1990

98 BUFFALO
DANCERS AT SAN
ILDEFONSO
PUEBLO,
CHRISTMAS DAY,
1990

The beauty of the performance also results from the sincerity of the participants, who should approach the event "with respect." This includes the observers as well as the dancers and singers. Everyone present is responsible for contributing to the communal prayer through his or her dancing, singing, presence, and good thoughts. People are not watching to be entertained passively from a distance, but are there to be actively involved in a communal ritual obligation.

To say that participants enter the Tewa dance events with respect does not mean that these events are without humor. For the Tewa, as well as other Pueblo groups, ritual events often provide arenas for comic characters and clowns, who help bring together the serious and humorous. When the absurd plays a central role in a ritual performance, the Tewa sense of the ridiculous is made public and the paradoxical or perplexing aspects of life are explored and celebrated. The most common form of humor in Tewa events is mocking imitation. That is, Tewa comics and clowns parody foreign and local events, ideas, and people.

Tewa dancers perform two basic types of social parody to incorporate the foreign into their world — communal and individual. Both feature symbolic reversals and are most common during periods of seasonal transition. The communal parodies are ritual dance events in which all the dancers represent members of a non-Tewa group. The individual parodies feature one performer, or a small group of performers, who engage in an imitative drama while a larger village dance is in progress. These skits may occur between dance sets, during a lunch break for the larger group of dancers, at the conclusion of a dance, or simply off to the side of the main dance activity. The performers involved in the second type of social parody may be initiated members of a ceremonial clown society or simply individual volunteers with comic reputations.

The targets of Tewa social parodies have included Apache Indians, Comanche Indians, Navajo Indians, Catholic priests, tourists, and others. For the Comanche Dance all the male dancers dress as Plains Indian warriors, with feathered war bonnets, bone breast plates, or finely beaded vests (fig. 106). A chorus accompanies the dancers with songs that contain a few Comanche words. Some Tewa say that this dance commemorates a time when some Comanche warriors were "sent home crying" after a battle with the Tewa. For a Navajo Dance all the Tewa dancers will dress in Navajo ceremonial garb and may imitate Navajo dances or they may act out an aggressive trading situation since the Tewa regard their Navajo neighbors as shrewd traders. To imitate Catholic priests, Tewa ceremonial clowns might appear during a regular dance in their usual ceremonial attire, consisting of black-and-white striped body paint and loincloth to perform a mock Holy Communion or wedding. Tourists may be the target of a Tewa parody as well, sometimes with an emphasis on the visitor's passion for taking photographs of everyone and everything.

The importance of Tewa social parody is that the dancers, clowns, or comics — in poking fun at what they see as peculiar about others — reinforce the Tewa way of doing things as the correct way. The villagers laugh at the antics of their comics, and this laughter may occur in the middle of what otherwise seems to be strictly a serious ritual event. For the Tewa, laughter is a blessing and the sacred and the secular are often inseparable.

106 SAN JUAN
COMANCHE
DANCERS DRESS
FLAMBOYANTLY IN
EXAGGERATED
PLAINS INDIAN
ATTIRE. 1974

In addition to beauty and humor, Tewa dance events contain power. These ritual performances are life-affirming — they bring life to the culture as a whole and they bring life to the individual who may have temporarily forgotten the Tewa way to live. The gentle, subtle movements, colorful costumes, and strong voices singing poetically create a magical experience dedicated to the search for, and the renewal of, life. Some Tewa people talk about the ritual experience as one of seeking life, renewing life, or finding new life. One song composer stated it like this:

> Our ancestors used to tell us…Go there to the dance and ask the gods there to give good life — regain your life and make your life a longer life…. You go there like to go to church — to ask the spirits to give us better life.

Another Tewa consultant talked about the dances as experiences that could bring someone back to a good and beautiful path. He went on to explain that as people go through their daily life, they sometimes lose sight of the good way to live and through participating in a dance they can find their way again — find their place in the community and in the natural world. They are reminded that they are Tewa and that the Tewa way is their way.

The power of these life-affirming events can be experienced directly by participants in the form of psychological transformation. The repetitive rhythms of the songs, constant pounding of drums, shaking of rattles, and the effect of other small percussive instruments sewn to the costumes together create an environment of sound conducive to transformation (fig. 107). For some dances the participants must restrict their intake of food before or during the performance. Sometimes the dancers are up all night participating in private rituals before the full day of dancing, when they must push themselves to their physical limit (fig. 108). The percussion, dietary restrictions, and extreme fatigue all contribute to a state in which transformation is more easily brought about and communion with the gods is facilitated. Further, when the dancers take on the role of the buffalo, deer, Cloud People, or clowns, they take on the personality of the being they are impersonating. They become, in a very real sense, the animal or spirit. Hence, the experience is one of physical and psychological transformation to a heightened state of being (fig. 109).

Even those who simply watch the event all day can experience an intense transformation. The colorful costumes rhythmically moving in the bright sunlight create a strobelike effect and the drumbeat starts to feel as if it is coming up from the earth and entering one's body. The long line of dancers ceases to be made up of individuals and starts to look and feel like one large and powerful moving organism.

In such transformational states, cultural messages coming in several different forms — the music, song lyrics, costume designs, paraphernalia, movements, and dramatic action — all speak loudly to the individual. The powerful central messages about beauty, humor, life, what it is to be Tewa, and what it means to be part of a Tewa community are experienced fully.

A SAN ILDEFONSO EXAMPLE

A closer look at one Tewa dance event — an open and publicized occasion held each January twenty-third at the village of San Ildefonso — may help to bring together some of the various elements and performance qualities.

San Ildefonso or Po-oh-Ge-On-Wi (Pueblo Where the Water Drops) is located north of Santa Fe between US Routes 64-84-285 and Los Alamos on New Mexico Highway No. 4. It is a village with twenty-eight thousand acres of land. On January twenty-third, the village patron saint's day, each side of San Ildefonso presents a traditional dance repeatedly throughout the day. The first year this author witnessed the event was 1974. That year the south side of the village presented a dramatic Buffalo/Game Animal Dance, while the north side of the village held a colorful Comanche Dance. Public activities began the evening of January twenty-second as a prelude to the full day of dancing on January twenty-third. Fieldnote excerpts from this 1974 viewing are presented below:[2]

107 BELLS AT THE
KNEES AND TIN
TINKLERS ON
THE KILT OF A
DANCER FROM SAN
ILDEFONSO, 1989

108 A FATIGUED
AND PENSIVE SAN
JUAN DANCER
PAUSES BETWEEN
DANCE SETS, 1974

109 LIKE THE BUFFALO
HE IS IMPERSONATING, THE
EYES OF YOUNG SAN
ILDEFONSO DANCER
CECILIO MARTINEZ
REFLECT A WARINESS OF
HUMAN INTRUDERS. EIGHT
NORTHERN INDIAN ARTS
AND CRAFT FAIR, 1990

January 22, 1974 San Ildefonso

We arrived at the village around 6 pm and parked the car over by the church just north and west of the plazas. By 6:30 the first bells were rung calling the people to vespers, but only a few responded and entered this magnificent thick walled adobe church. After a second ring, more people arrived but by 7 pm when the service began, the church was still less than half full with about 125 people in attendance — 80% Native American, 15% Anglo, 5% Hispanic.

After the church service, the congregation formed a procession to carry the image of San Ildefonso through the village. We were directed into two lines with women on the left and men on the right. At the head of the line there was a San Ildefonso man carrying a cross, the priest and two acolytes, and the statue of San Ildefonso carried under a green canopy. This procession made one circuit around the plazas and then back to the church for a closing prayer. Everyone in the procession sang Dios Te Salve Maria as they walked. The plazas were lit by several stacked log bonfires and paper bag candle lanterns lined the roof tops of the houses and kivas.

It was getting very cold so after the procession we went to stand by one of the bonfires. At about 8 pm a man and woman could be seen near the stone shrine of the south side. Although I knew I must keep my distance and in the dark I could not see too clearly, it appeared that the man was in a breechcloth, body paint, moccasins, and had feathers in his hair. He was beating a small drum and chanting. The

woman had her head covered with a shawl that fell over her dress and she also wore moccasins. It looked like they both sprinkled sacred cornmeal on the stones and after about ten minutes disappeared into the south kiva.

We kept trying to keep warm by the heat of the fires. Once when the fire nearest us began to burn low some San Ildefonso teenage boys brought more wood. We were most grateful. At 9 pm about thirty men gathered just outside the north kiva and began singing and drumming. They moved to the north side stone shrine and stood around it in a semi-circle open to the east. After ten minutes they retreated to the north kiva.

At 9:15 a Game Priest, two Buffalo, one Buffalo Maiden, a Hunter and three assistants, eighteen Deer, and two Antelope emerged from the south kiva. These dancers were illuminated by the flames from the fires. It was very dramatic and dreamlike to catch shadowy glimpses of the animals. There now were about 300 people watching. The dancers came out for two fifteen minute appearances. By 10 pm they had gone back into the kiva and the observers began to leave.

112 SAN ILDEFONSO COMANCHE DANCERS CLIMB DOWN FROM THE NORTH KIVA, 1974

110 SAN ILDEFONSO DEER DANCERS PERFORM IN THE SOUTH PLAZA FOLLOWING THEIR DAWN ENTRANCE, 1974

January 23, 1974 San Ildefonso

Last night after vespers and the evening prelude performance we drove up to Los Alamos to stay with friends. It seemed like I just put my pen down and closed my eyes when it was time to get up and head back down to the village for the dawn ceremony.

We reached the village before the first morning light. After we parked the car we stood shivering in the dark by a small fire with about fifty other visitors. As we waited more observers arrived to see this dawn entrance. At 7:50 am six drummers and four singers gathered at the road intersection a few hundred yards from two eastern hills. Soon shouts could be heard coming from the saddle between these hills, and then we could see the silhouettes of the deer dancers with their large antlers etched against the dawn light. They were on top of the hills and slowly meandering down towards the village. They appeared so graceful, leaning on sticks and turning their heads. At the base of the hills they joined with the other dancers who appeared from between the hills. From there the Game Priest led the group towards the village by sprinkling a path of cornmeal from a decorated ceramic bowl. By now about

forty women wrapped in colorful blanket shawls had gathered so they could sprinkle cornmeal over the shoulders and arms of the passing animal dancers. Once they passed, all the observers followed these sacred creatures to the south plaza to see them dance for about fifteen minutes before entering the kiva (figs. 110, 111). During the day the animal dancers appeared four more times, one time in front of the church, but for that appearance the Game Priest did not accompany them . . . .

Each type of animal had a particular movement style. The music included a slow and a fast section and the animal dancers responded directly to these tempo changes. For example, during the slower sections the Deer meandered from side to side, periodically stopping as if frozen for a moment, and then taking a deep knee bend and rotating the upper body and head to change focus from one side to the other. It was like a deer feeding but alert to any sound that might signal danger. In the faster sections the Deer moved into two long parallel lines and leaning on their sticks danced briskly in place, kicking up their feet behind them. The white rain sash hanging down the back bounced and it made me think of white tailed deer bounding off and away into the woods. In contrast to the Deer, the Buffalo walked upright in a heavier gait. Each step was a shift in body weight from side to side and the knees were bent to create the lumbering walk of a heavy but very powerful animal. . . .

By noon dancers began to file out of the north side kiva dressed for a

Comanche Dance (fig. 112). There were sixty-one dancers and twelve singers with several drums. It amazed me how wild the men's Comanche Dance costumes were — a multitude of color combinations and variations on Plains Indian styles. There appeared to be no limit to the flamboyance and individual choice in dress. The women dressed less individualistically, all in brightly colored lace-edged shawls over their dresses.

The Comanche dancers performed their first dance sets in front of the church and all subsequent sets in the north plaza. The women stepped lightly in place with slight side-to-side pivots while the men repeatedly crossed in front of them with more exaggerated steps.

All during the day both sides danced in their respective plazas, taking twenty to thirty minute rest periods in the kivas between appearances. Once both the Buffalo/Game Animal dancers of the south side and the Comanche dancers of the north side were dancing at the same time because their appearances overlapped a little. Each side continued to dance, simply ignoring the drum beat of the other.

The village was full of people coming and going, watching, and visiting. At the busiest part of the afternoon there were no fewer than four hundred observers out in the plaza at any one time. Pueblo, Navajo, Hispanic, and Anglo visitors watched the dancing, listened to the songs, feasted, and most appeared to enjoy the festivities.

113 CANDICE ROSALIE
TES-PE, A YOUNG SAN
ILDEFONSO WOMAN,
DANCES THE ROLE
OF THE BUFFALO
MAIDEN,CONTRIBUTING
TO HER FAMILIES' AND
COMMUNITIES'
CELEBRATION OF WHAT
IT IS TO BE TEWA.
CHRISTMAS, 1990

104 TEWA DANCERS
MOVE IN UNISON AS THEY
PRESENT A SEGMENT OF A
BASKET DANCE OUTSIDE
THE VILLAGE AT THE
GALLUP CEREMONIAL,
1990.

105 THE CLOUD DANCE (ALSO
CALLED THE CORN MAIDEN
DANCE) AT THE SAN JUAN
PUEBLO, 1974. FOR THIS PRE-
PLANTING DANCE HELD IN
LATE WINTER, TWO FEMALE
DANCERS, WHO MODESTLY
KEEP THEIR EYES LOWERED,
ARE JOINED BY SCORES OF
MALE DANCERS.

Like other Tewa patron saint's days, January twenty-third at San Ildefonso is an event that simultaneously expresses native ritual meanings while honoring the village saint as an aspect of Catholicism that holds significance for the people. But unlike all the other Tewa patron saint's day celebrations, San Ildefonso's day falls in the middle of winter. As a result, at San Ildefonso the vendors are few and the carnival is nonexistent — in contrast to the warmer feast days at other villages. It can be, however, one of the most beautiful and dramatic open and publicized Tewa dance events.

The dance event is the most central Tewa expressive form — the key to their beliefs, values, and worldview. If something is important to the Tewa, most likely it will be explored or celebrated through dance and the accompanying songs. Further, this expressive complex — including costume design, music, drama, and unified rhythmic motion — is intimately tied to Tewa identity and cultural survival. Tewa consultants stated repeatedly that as long as the people continue to dance, they will remain Tewa. But if the dances are forgotten, the Tewa will cease to exist as a culturally distinct group.

Ever since colonization, outside observers have predicted that it was only a matter of time before the dances would be forgotten and the Tewa would become more like the newcomers of European descent. Nevertheless, in spite of the suppressive efforts through the years by Catholic and Protestant missionaries, politicians, and educators, the dances continue to be the vital lifeblood of the Tewa communities. Even in the smaller Tewa villages of Nambe and Pojoaque, where considerable cultural disruption occurred, the old dances are being revived with the help of song composers and elders from other Tewa villages.

At the turn of the century, when small dance groups began to perform short dance segments away from the villages, some observers assumed that this indicated secularization and a deterioration of the village rituals. This has not been the case, however. Rather, both types of performances — the village rituals and the outside theatrical productions — continue to thrive independently. And while the purposes and context may be different, the higher-order meanings will be present in either situation as long as the dancers approach the task "with a good heart." One Tewa man commented on presenting shortened dances in urban centers for non-Indian audiences: "You've still got to dance with your whole heart because the songs and dance still are sacred and bring beauty, no matter if you dance here [in the village] or out there."

Although many ancient traditions are regularly practiced by the Tewa, it would be a misconception to view them as isolationists "frozen in time." The Tewa people participate in contemporary society, adopting the technological innovations that they find useful. Many have blue-collar jobs, some hold college degrees, and some have professional careers. On important dance days, however, most will make every effort to return home and participate in the dance. This tendency to return home on dance days results from a desire to join with one's extended family and together celebrate what it is to be Tewa. The dance is where they will find beauty, humor, and power in the familiar songs and choreographic patterns. This is where key symbols of fertility and growth will be found in gesture, song, and costume design (fig. 113). In short, this is where they will find new life — regain their life and satisfy that periodic human need for spiritual renewal.

1   H.J. Spinden, *Songs of the Tewa* (New York: The Exposition of Indian Tribal Arts, 1933), p. 94.
2   The writing style of fieldnotes differs from standard professional prose. Fieldnotes are informal and personal
    documents that provide readers with a sense of the actual circumstances that ultimately influence the researcher's analysis.

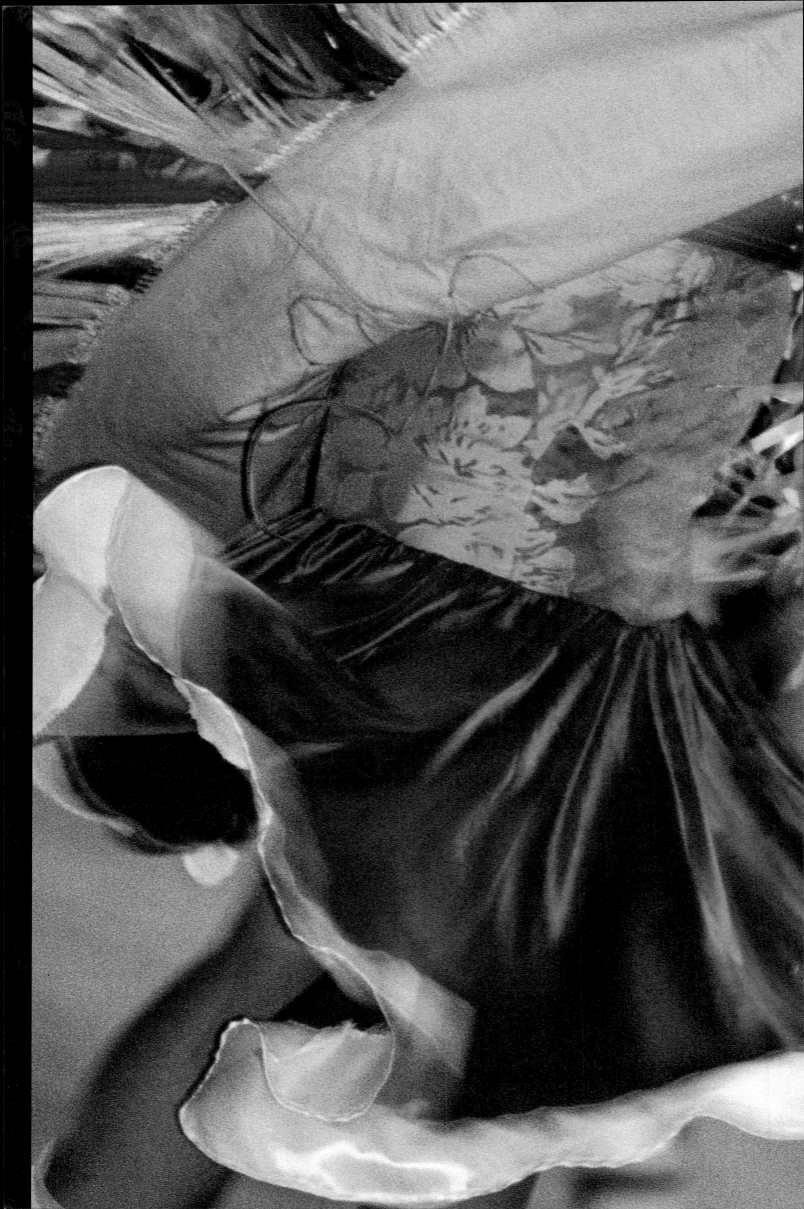

SOUTHERN PLAINS DANCE: TRADITION AND DYNAMISM

Thomas W. Kavanagh

Music and dance are integral parts of the social and cultural life of the native peoples of the Southern Plains (fig. 114). On practically every weekend throughout much of central and western Oklahoma and parts of nearby Kansas and Nebraska, Indian people gather for singing and dancing. These gatherings include everything from the most sacred rituals — the annual Sun Dance and Offerings Lodge of the Cheyenne and Arapaho — to the Black Legs Society of the Kiowa, women's victory dances in honor of great deeds worth remembering, and social dances for fun and friendship. Among the most popular and visible of these events are the powwows.

The term "powwow," derived from the Narragansett, an eastern Algonquian language, originally referred to curing ceremonies. The term soon passed into English as a word referring to any Indian gathering or as a verb meaning "to confer in council." In Indian Country, it came to mean a "secular event featuring group singing and social dancing by men, women, and children."[1] Although many of its elements are traditional, powwows are not unchanging continuations from the depths of time, but rather are the dynamic and creative expressions of Indian identity and pride, both for individuals and communities.

I n the course of a powwow, many different dances may be performed. One of them, the Round Dance, is a circle dance in which the dancers often hold hands with their neighbors while side-stepping to the left. Round dances often lead into the Snake-and-Buffalo Dance—called *aa nuhkana* (Horn Dance) in Comanche—in which the dancers unclasp their hands and imitate the motions of the buffalo. Comanche historian Joe Attocknie called the Buffalo Dance the favorite dance of his great-grandfather Ten Bears: "[His] Horn Dance reminded onlookers of the rocking, loping motion of a running buffalo; his fur bonnet's horns that he gently rolled in time to the music was a sight that was long remembered."[2] The Two-step — called the Owl Dance in the north — is the only couples dance; holding hands side-by-side, men and women follow the lead couples through a series of figures.

The Gourd Dance, which grew out of ceremonies associated with the men's societies, is still used by the revived men's societies, such as the Comanche Little Ponies and the Kiowa Gourd Clan, as well as by urban intertribal clubs.[3] Its name derives from the rattle carried by the dancers — formerly made from a gourd, the rattle is now commonly fashioned from aluminum salt shakers (fig. 115). In this two-part dance, an in-place bobbing step is followed by a forward-moving toe-heel step. During the course of a song, these parts may alternate five or more times. There are some variations in gourd dancing: Comanche gourd dances are almost line dances, with members of the men's societies dancing together side-by-side and moving forward as a line; Kiowa gourd dances are more individualized and active, with a "whip man" urging dancers to greater action.

In addition to these open-participation dances, powwows may also include what can be called performance dances — dramatic performances by solo or paired dancers. Among these are the Hoop Dance, in which an agile dancer weaves his way through a series of hoop figures; the Eagle Dance, in which the dancer imitates the soaring of an eagle (fig. 116); or the Spear-and-Shield Dance, which involves two dancers imitating warriors in hand-to-hand combat. These dramatic dances are staples of Indian performances for non-Indian audiences, but are rare at powwows in Indian Country.

115 GOURD DANCE RATTLE, MADE FROM AN ALUMINUM SALTSHAKER

116 STEPHEN MOPOPE (1898–1974), *EAGLE DANCER*, 1930, WATERCOLOR ON PAPER, 27.5 X 17.2 CM NATIONAL MUSEUM OF THE AMERICAN INDIAN, SMITHSONIAN INSTITUTION, NO. 22.8588

117 DWIGHT WHITE
BUFFALO DANCES A WAR
DANCE AT THE VIETNAM
VETERANS ANNUAL,
ANADARKO, OKLAHOMA,
MAY 1992.

Most of a powwow is given over to the War Dance (figs. 117, 118). This dance has its origins in the Inloshka and Hethuska societies of the Kansa (Kaw), Omaha, and Ponca, and in the Iruska of the Pawnee.[4] These were organizations of established warriors whose ceremonies were structured around a group of officials (including four officers chosen to wear the crow belts, feather bustles symbolizing crows flocking over a battlefield), a set of ceremonial and ritual acts invoking the heroism of war deeds, and an accompanying feast. The feast was often placed in the center of the dance arena and "stalked" by the dancers, who used either their bare hands to retrieve pieces of meat — thus the name "Hot Dance" — or the ritual forks carried by officers, who were comparable to the crow-belt wearers.

In the nineteenth century, the ceremony spread to many other tribes. When the Northern Plains tribes received it in the 1860s, they called it the Omaha Dance in recognition of its southern origins (fig. 119). It was also called the Grass Dance, after the braids of sweet-smelling grass worn in the bustles.

The tribes of western Oklahoma received the ceremony, which they called the Crow Dance, in the early 1890s, about the same time as they received the Ghost Dance, a round dance derived from the Paiute of Nevada. A religious movement, the Ghost Dance promised a return of the good life that had existed before the Europeans arrived. Participants were encouraged to trance, dream, and re-create the activities of the old days. These two dances were often combined in the same event, with the Crow Dance taking place during the after-

noon and the Ghost Dance at night (fig. 120). By 1893, people had stopped dancing the Ghost Dance; the Crow Dance continued, however, often in conjunction with other ceremonials, such as the Sun Dance.

In the late nineteenth and early twentieth centuries, these northern and southern versions of the Omaha/ Grass/Crow Dance and its ceremony developed in different directions. Among the prairie tribes of Oklahoma and Nebraska — the Osage, Omaha, Ponca, and Pawnee — the dance acquired elements of the *Midewiwin* (the "Dream" or "Drum Dance"), a ceremony centering on a large drum and offering revitalization features similar to the Ghost Dance.[5] Among those tribes, this version, called the Straight Dance, dispensed with the crow belt while retaining much of the ritual and many of the officers of the Inloshka societies. The dance, which has spread beyond the prairie tribes, attracts many straight dancers who do not belong to formal societies. The Straight Dance, however, remains relatively conservative both in choreography and in costume.[6] The dance's footwork is the basic toe-heel step and its motions are those of the feast-stalking aspect of the Grass Dance (fig. 121). The Straight Dance costume echoes its origins in the dress clothing of the prairie peoples: cloth shirt and leggings (both decorated with ribbon-work appliqué), crossed-beaded bandoliers, a headdress of deer-hair roach and an eagle-feather or an otter-fur turban, and otter-fur trailer (fig. 122).

Meanwhile, the tribes of western Oklahoma were developing an increasingly elaborate version of the ceremony, marked by individual embellishment. The exclusive right of the men's societies to participate was abandoned and the ceremony was opened to all, including women. The choreography, beginning with the basic toe-heel step, was enhanced to include acrobatic spins, turns, and splits. The result came to be called the Fancy Dance. In time, the Fancy Dance tradition developed in several directions, characterized not by choreography — they all involve intricate footwork — but by costume, with developments in bustles, headdresses, and other accoutrements.

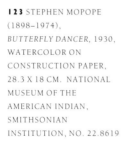

123 STEPHEN MOPOPE (1898–1974), *BUTTERFLY DANCER,* 1930, WATERCOLOR ON CONSTRUCTION PAPER, 28.3 X 18 CM. NATIONAL MUSEUM OF THE AMERICAN INDIAN, SMITHSONIAN INSTITUTION, NO. 22.8619

Instead of featuring crow belts worn only by society officers, the dance now allowed each participant to wear one or more bustles at the waist and at the shoulders and small bustles on the upper arms, all color-coordinated. In the 1930s and 1940s, these bustles were relatively small, often made out of pheasant feathers (fig. 123). A matching harness of beadwork was worn around the neck. From the 1930s through the 1950s, many fancy dancers wore a feather-crest headdress, an upright double row of feathers; others wore a deer-hair roach, though the short hair required that it be fastened to a headband.

By the 1960s, the feather crest had been replaced completely by the roach, which in turn was elaborated. Because one objective of the Fancy Dance was to show movement, the stationary feather was an obvious drawback. Thus, the "bobber" was invented, a pivoting see-saw platform holding sockets for two feathers, which bounce off rubber-band springs. At the same time, all of the bustles — at arms, back, and shoulders — had grown bigger and were made from larger feathers, such as turkey or eagle. This trend has continued, with the feather becoming the basis for further elaboration of color: the tips and bases of bustle feathers were often decorated with downy breast feathers ("fluffies"); in the 1970s, long rooster-hackle feathers, dyed in an assortment of colors, became available, and dancers quickly used them to make their bustles a blur of color. Recently, some dancers have added colored plastic streamers to the tips of their bustle feathers (fig. 124).

From the late 1980s to the present, some dancers have constructed their bustles in eagle feathers without fluffies. These feathers are sometimes so large that both the back and shoulder bustles are combined into a single bustle worn at the waist (fig. 125).

In the late 1970s, the so-called traditional dancers began embellishing their clothing in another direction. In addition to larger bustles, they often wear full face-paint, animal-skin headdresses, and whole bird-wing attachments at the shoulders. They carry various clubs or sticks in their hands (fig. 126). Many also dance counterclockwise around the arena, opposite to the standard clockwise movement. Although their presentations are not historically verifiable re-creations of old styles of dancing and costuming — which they claim are pre-photographic — in one sense, they continue the Ghost Dance/Crow Dance tradition of using the dance as a means of establishing an emotional connection with the values of "Indianness."

125 EAGLE-FEATHER BUSTLE. KEEPERS OF THE WESTERN DOOR POWWOW, ST. BONAVENTURE UNIVERSITY, NEW YORK, JULY 1992

124 FEATHER BUSTLES WITH STREAMERS. COMANCHE HOMECOMING, WALTERS, OKLAHOMA. JULY 1992

126 JOHN KEEL,
A MODERN
"TRADITIONAL"
DANCER AT THE
VIETNAM
VETERANS
ANNUAL,
ANADARKO,
OKLAHOMA.
MAY 1992

127 GRASS DANCERS
AT COMANCHE
HOMECOMING,
WALTERS,
OKLAHOMA.
JULY 1992

128 A SHAWL DANCER AT THE
KEEPERS OF THE WESTERN
DOOR POWWOW,
ST. BONAVENTURE UNIVERSITY,
NEW YORK. JULY 1992

129 NICHOLAS
WAUAHDOOAH, A YOUNG
MAN HONORED FOR HIS
FIRST DANCE, PRESENTS
A SHAWL TO THE COMANCHE
HOMECOMING PRINCESS,
LINDA BLACKSTAR.
MASTER OF CEREMONIES
WALLACE COFFEY
(WEARING HAT) IS
BEHIND HER. COMANCHE
HOMECOMING, WALTERS,
OKLAHOMA. JULY 1992

In recent years, a number of stylistic innovations from the Northern Plains tradition have found their way into Southern Plains powwows, including the style known as the Grass Dance (fig. 127). In this style, dancers elaborated their fringed capes to such an extent that their bustles — which included the sweet grass that gave the dance its name — have been eliminated altogether.

Women had always played a supportive role in the powwow — the traditional Woman's Dance, for example, is a modest toe-heel bobbing forward step that forms a rhythmic descant to the men's vigorous styles. In the late 1960s, however, young women began participating as feathered fancy dancers, even winning several contests. Recently, two women's fancy dances have been imported from the Northern Plains: the Shawl and Jingle-Dress dances (fig. 128), which combine the fancy-step and color of the men's Fancy Dance with traditional women's dress.

Powwows are as much community social events as dance performances; indeed, there is often only minimal separation of dancers from spectators. Powwows range in size from small local events of a single afternoon or evening, through three-day holiday weekend events, to large annual gatherings of a week's duration. At multiday powwows, many extended families will set up a camp. Each nuclear family sleeps in a separate tent or shelter — or, more recently, in a travel-trailer — while meals are communal within the camp group.

If the extended family is not camping, or if the powwow is a small one, each nuclear family may attend by itself, sometimes meeting other relatives for dinner. Young people will often attend powwows in groups of their peers. Camps are often composed of groups of four to eight young men who share a single tent, the cooking, and cleaning. Other peer groups might arrive in cars for the evening, which may be spent wandering the perimeter in search of friends.

Most powwows are not tribally exclusive, and members of many tribal groups, as well as non-Indians, can participate in a powwow's dances. This has often been interpreted as "pan-Indianism," a movement that focuses on a wider Indian identity, as opposed to one based on local, tribal affiliations. Powwows, however, are sponsored by, and associated with, members of particular tribal groups and the event's identification with that group is often made, albeit indirectly.

There is always an element of honor in a powwow, of prestige accrued through generosity. The small powwows are often sponsored by a family as public recognition of pride in the accomplishments of a family member. In such honoring powwows, the sponsors invite singers and dancers and provide a meal for all who attend. During the event, the sponsors will hold a "Special." During the Special, they will recount the honorable deeds being celebrated, dance the honoree around the arena to a special song, and then give away quantities of goods or cash (fig. 129). Comanche Homecoming was first organized in Walters, Oklahoma, in 1954 by a group of parents and other relatives of returning Korean War veterans and has continued as an event in honor of all Comanches.

The largest powwows are multitribal expositions where the focus is not so much on a community celebrating itself as on the demonstration of "Indian" dancing to a paying, non-Indian audience. The largest of these is the Red Earth Powwow in Oklahoma City; others include the annual Indian Exposition in Anadarko (Oklahoma), the Gathering of Nations in Albuquerque, and the Gallup Ceremonial (New Mexico).

TONKONGA: THE KIOWA BLACK LEGS MILITARY SOCIETY

The Tonkonga, or Black Legs Society, is one of at least eight Kiowa men's military societies or sodalities that existed in the nineteenth century (fig. 130). There are two versions of the story of how the society got its name: in one tale, the members return from a journey with their legs blackened by trail dust, while the second story relates how the Kiowas withstood attempts by an enemy to burn them out by setting fire to the prairie during a battle. The Black Legs are known to have existed at least as early as 1834, when H. L. Scott, in an unpublished ledger book, noted their role in policing a Kiowa buffalo hunt. During the nineteenth century, the Tonkonga also participated in the building of the Sun Dance lodge and in several of the many kinds of society meetings characteristic of the Kiowa.

The society was organized around two *pawtok'i* (leaders), one of whom was in command; two *adltok'i* (whipmen), who carried serrated whips as badges of office and served as sergeants-at-arms; two *awdok'i* or *ietek'i* (errand boys serving as helpers to the officers), who were *awdaytali* (favored boys); two *awdaymaton* (favored girls serving as princesses until they marry); and the regular members. While each member of a society considered every other as a brother, all members within a society were organized into designated pairs, with every member having a *kom* (friend or, more specifically, "society partner"). The two men forming a *kom* attended society meetings, danced

together, went on war and raiding ventures together, and cooperated with one another economically. These ritual relationships led to the formation of economic bonds and a sense of kinship between the two members, between their families, and throughout the entire tribe.

130 MEMBERS OF THE BLACK LEGS SOCIETY PARADING IN AT THEIR TWICE-YEARLY CEREMONY AT ANADARKO, OKLAHOMA, 1991

Kiowa military societies continued to hold social gatherings until around 1890, when they were forced by the U.S. military to give up their annual Sun Dance. From approximately 1912 to 1928, the Black Legs continued to hold annual dances on private Kiowa allotments (160-acre individual land holdings) near the community of Stecker, Oklahoma, until the deaths of older members, along with governmental economic sanctions, led to the group's cessation. The society was revived on 23 November 1958 by Gus Palmer, Sr., with the help of others. Palmer dedicated the revival to the memory of his brother Lyndreth Palmer, who was killed in World War II. Elderly Tonkonga members who were active in the 1920s taught the songs, dances, and traditions of the society to the younger veterans. As Palmer puts it, "The old people said, you younger men are entitled to carry it on. You men today are just like the men in the old days — warriors. You fought for your people."

Today, all of the society offices remain intact, with membership in the Black Legs requiring Kiowa descendancy as well as military service. The society also continues to hold mourning feasts, cedaring (religious prayer using incense), and the graveside singing of society songs for the families of recently deceased members. At each biannual ceremony, the society provides a meal to all attending. Using the men's lances and bonnets, female relatives and members of the Tonkonga Women's Auxiliary perform Scalp and Victory dances to open the afternoon events, while inside the society tepee the men prepare for the five types of society dances they will perform. One side of the tepee contains the designs from the famous Battle Tepee of Dohausen, the Kiowa tribal chief from 1833 to 1866, while the other side contains the divisional crests of modern-day Kiowa servicemen and the names of nine Kiowas who have made the supreme sacrifice for their tribe and country since World War I.

Once a year, the *Tsat'koigya* (or Reverse Dance) is held, during which a combat veteran must stop the drum and recite a personal victory or battle deed (fig. 131). Today the Tonkonga are frequently called the "Black Leggins" Society, as members wear black leggings (rather than following the earlier practice of painting their legs black) and red capes (in honor of a cape captured from a Mexican officer by Gool-Hay-Ee, an Anglo captive who was Palmer's great-grandfather). Members dance with individual lances, and a *pawbon* (a curved staff wrapped in otter fur) is still the society's emblem.

Since 1958, society membership has included Kiowa veterans of every war from World War I to Operation Desert Storm — including Pascal C. Poolaw, veteran of three wars and the most highly decorated American Indian soldier in history. The Black Legs, who frequently provide a color guard for various Native American cultural and educational events, continue to honor, recognize, and celebrate their Kiowa military heritage with biannual weekend ceremonies, commemorating their war dead on Armed Forces Day and Veterans Day. Palmer states, "As veterans, they fought for their land and their people, and therefore each dance is like a homecoming for veterans. Therefore, they should work together and stay together. Then they can feel good about coming out to celebrate and enjoy the songs and dances that were performed before this part of the country was opened up."

William C. Meadows and Gus Palmer, Sr.

131 THE TURN AROUND
OR REVERSE DANCE.
ANADARKO,
OKLAHOMA, 1991

There are four basic roles enacted by the participants at powwows: sponsor, principal, singer/dancer, and spectator. The sponsor is the group or individual that plans the event. The group may be a single family planning an honoring powwow or a formally organized powwow committee. The sponsors plan the event, provide for the facilities and rations for participants, and select the principals.

1 3 2 TRIBAL PRINCESSES AT THE VIETNAM VETERANS ANNUAL, ANADARKO, OKLAHOMA. MAY 1992

The major principals — the officials of the old Inloshka societies — are the Head Singer, Head Man Dancer and Head Lady Dancer, and the Announcer. Some of the larger powwows have a Princess, a young lady chosen to represent the sponsors at other powwows (fig. 132).

The Head Singer is one of the most important principals. He must know a great number of songs — including the special family and honoring songs — and be able to lead them, starting them "on key" and at the right tempo. Most singers belong to informal groups that practice together, and many powwows have an "open drum" — anyone who wishes may ask permission to sit at it and help sing. Until recently there were no named drums — formal singing groups — as on the Northern Plains. Since 1982, however, with the increased popularity of northern-style singing, named drums are becoming more prevalent.

For the Straight, Fancy War, and Gourd dances, the first song of a set is sung once through before the dance begins. The Head Man Dancer begins the dance; everyone follows his lead. The Head Man Dancer and the Head Lady Dancer often lead round dances and Two-steps as a couple.

The Announcer, in conjunction with the sponsors, keeps the whole affair running smoothly by alternating dances so that no one gets tired and the attention of the people is kept in focus. The Announcer is sometimes called upon to be the "talker," the person who recounts the honoree's accomplishments, at Specials.

At most powwows, the question of whether or not to dance is a purely individual matter. The primary restriction on dancing is the amount of time and money an individual is able to put into the preparation of dance clothing. For women, the choice is somewhat simplified: in all dances, the minimum costume is a fringed shawl. It matters not whether she is wearing the finest heirloom buckskin dress or the latest designer pantsuit, as long as she has a shawl she is considered to be properly dressed (fig. 133). The only comparable situations for men are the round dances, the Two-step (ladies' choice), and the special song performed during an honoring — for which street clothes are acceptable. In all other cases, some form of specific dance attire is necessary. In this regard, one reason for the popularity of the Gourd Dance is the inexpensive, minimal outfit: a rattle (see fig. 115).

The demands of the Fancy Dance make it an event for vigorous young men. Once the debilitating effects of age begin to set in, many fancy dancers switch to the slower Straight Dance. Fancy dancers regard the Gourd Dance as an "old man's dance" and complain that gourd dancers "want to hog the floor" (fig. 134).[7]

The majority of people at a powwow are spectators. This category includes everyone present, whether or not they are acting in any other capacity. Thus, outside the arena, even dancers are spectators. Because a powwow is a social event as well as a dance performance, the interaction among the spectators is as important as the dances themselves.

Except for events held to honor a specific person, most powwows feature dance contests, with prizes of up to several hundred dollars. Contests center around the various versions of the War Dance — the Fancy, Straight, and Traditional dances — and are divided into several age categories: tots, under six (fig. 135); junior, six to eighteen; senior, over eighteen. At some powwows, there is a "heavy-weight" division in both the Fancy and Straight dance classes for men weighing more than two hundred pounds. Judging is based on evaluation of

133 ROUND DANCERS,
SOME OF WHOM WEAR
SHAWLS OVER STREET
CLOTHES. VIETNAM
VETERANS ANNUAL,
ANADARKO, OKLAHOMA.
MAY 1992

135 TINY-TOT
WAR DANCER
AT COMANCHE
HOMECOMING,
WALTERS,
OKLAHOMA.
JULY 1992

134 GOURD DANCERS
AT COMANCHE
HOMECOMING,
WALTERS, OKLAHOMA.
JULY 1992

136 RIGHT AND BELOW, TRADITIONAL BUCKSKIN DRESSES. COMANCHE HOMECOMING, WALTERS,OKLAHOMA. JULY 1992

137 NIKKI OWINGS WEARS A JINGLE DRESS, WITH CONES MADE FROM SNUFF-CAN LIDS. VIETNAM VETERANS ANNUAL, ANADARKO, OKLAHOMA, MAY 1992

the dancers' style. In addition, since a contest dancer must stop on the last beat of the song, he must know the songs as well as a singer does. "Trick" songs that do not follow the normal structure are used to test a dancer's knowledge. A point system, with credit given for participation in the whole event, is used at some powwows to ensure that dancers stay for the duration of the powwow, not just for the night of their contest class.

The women's contests are categorized more according to dress than choreography: the "traditional" style (a term constantly modified) buckskin dress and the reservation-period cloth dress, often of blue and red (fig. 136). As mentioned, shawls and jingle dresses are also recent contest styles (fig. 137).

Dance on the Southern Plains is at once traditional and dynamic, recalling and reinforcing the old values of community pride and participation, war honors, and generosity, while at the same time being subject to constant innovation and regeneration.

Sultan Park, near Walters, Oklahoma, is usually a quiet spot on the banks of Cache Creek. In midsummer, Mayflies circle lazily over the water. In the distance, a farmer may be working his field after the winter wheat harvest, while the engines pumping the oil wells drone on. But for several weeks in July, Sultan Park is astir with activity, for it is the site of the Comanche Homecoming Powwow. Held about the third weekend of July, Homecoming is the high point of the social year for Comanche powwow people. While its immediate origins date to an event held in honor of Korean War veterans, it has antecedents in events held after both World Wars in tribute to returning soldiers. In its present form, the powwow honors all Comanches.

Soon after the conclusion of one year's event, preparation begins for the next. In the subsequent months, the Homecoming Committee will meet several times to discuss the selection of the principals, the Head Man and Head Lady dancers and the Head Singer.

During the winter and spring, the committee and newly selected principals hold a series of benefit dances to raise funds for the upcoming powwow. Soliciting donations from the community, the committee also purchases Pendleton blankets, handmade shawls, and other items to be auctioned or raffled off. These funds provide prize money for the contests and cover rations to feed the campers.

About the first of July, families begin to visit Sultan Park to claim or reclaim their camping spots. Many use the same spots year after year. Over the next few weeks, in evenings and on weekends, they gradually establish camps. Each campsite usually includes one or more canvas tents with attached awnings and possibly a tepee; bedsteads, small wood camp stoves, even refrigerators will be moved to the site. With the abundant willow brush that grows along the creek, some families build domed or flat-roofed arbors. The committee also begins preparing the circular dance ground, which will be the focus of the powwow's activities.

The dance program begins on Friday afternoon with a Brush Dance, derived from the old Sun Dance, in which dancers approach the arena with tree limbs and branches to finish the dance lodge. The Flag Song, an Honoring Song functioning as the national anthem, accompanies the raising of the American flag. The afternoon is spent in gourd dancing.

Following a break for dinner and more gourd dancing, the evening begins with a Grand Entry parade featuring all the dancers (fig. 138). During the next several hours, the program alternates between non-contest,

1 3 8 GRAND ENTRY
PARADE AT COMANCHE
HOMECOMING, WALTERS,
OKLAHOMA. JULY 1992

intertribal war dances, the social dances, round dances and Two-steps, and the beginning of the contest series, with the event often ending after midnight.

The end of the formal program does not, however, signify the end of dancing: the "49 Dance," a much looser Round Dance, may last until dawn. Probably derived from the *Nuhohtsahe*, the Swaying Dance held the night before a war party departs, 49s include a good deal of bawdy humor and trysting. Many 49 sings have English words, such as the classic "One-eyed Ford":

> *When the dance is over sweetheart,*
> *I will take you home in my One-eyed Ford.*
>
> Or
>
> *You know that I love you sweetheart*
> *But every time I come around*
> *You always say you gotta go*
> *You know goddammed good and well that I love you.*

Because these activities were frowned upon by government officials and church leaders, 49s were formerly held some distance from camp. In recent years, however, Homecoming 49s have been held in the arena itself, in an effort both to recognize their basis in Comanche culture and to minimize the dangers from late-night drinking and driving.

Saturday begins late in the morning and is a day of socializing with family in camp and with friends in other camps. Many Comanches use Homecoming as the catalyst for family reunions, with relatives coming in from across the country. At the 1988 Homecoming, one set of cousins numbered almost 250 individuals. Rations — meat, flour, bread, and other commodities — are distributed to all camps on Saturday, and the afternoon is spent preparing the evening meal. Many camps take pride in feeding all comers, announcing that any visitors who might not have a place are welcome at their table. Dancing begins again in the late afternoon and follows the same program as before: gourd dancing, followed by the Grand Entry, intertribal and contest dances, social dances, and a 49 until dawn.

On Sunday, at a brief meeting in the arena, the committee for the next year is selected. There is dancing in the afternoon and evening, with the senior-division contests often lasting until after midnight. On Monday, the work of breaking camp begins. By the next weekend, Sultan Park is back to its usual quiet, broken only by the sounds of summer.

1   William K. Powers, "Contemporary Oglala Music and Dance: Pan-Indianism vs. Pan-Tetonism," in *The Modern Sioux*, ed. Ethel Nurge (Lincoln, Nebr.: University of Nebraska Press, 1970), p. 271.

2   Francis Joseph Attocknie, "The Life of Ten Bears and Other Stories of Our People" (unpublished manuscript).

3   See Thomas W. Kavanagh, "Recent Socio-Cultural Evolution of the Comanche Indians" (Master's thesis, George Washington University, 1980). Also see James Howard, "The Plains Gourd Dance as a Revitalization Movement," *American Ethnologist* 3 (1976): 243–59.

4   Although these three society names are clearly derived from the same word, the meaning of the word is unknown, as is its original language. Some Osages give its meaning as "playground of the eldest son" [see Alice A. Callahan, *The Osage Ceremonial Dance I'n-Lon-Schka* (Norman, Okla.: University of Oklahoma Press, 1990)], while Clark Wissler gives *Iruska* as "the fire is in me," as well as referring to the roached headdress ["General Discussion of Shamanistic and Dancing Societies," Anthropological Papers of the American Museum of Natural History, 11 (1916): 859–60].

5   Thomas Vennum, "The Ojibwa Dance Drum: Its History and Construction," *Smithsonian Institution Folklife Studies* no. 2 (1982).

6   Callahan, *The Osage Ceremonial Dance*, p. 2.

7   See James Howard, "The Plains Gourd Dance as a Revitalization Movement," *American Ethnologist* 3 (1976): 253.

Northern Plains Dance

Lynn F. Huenemann

I n 1884, as part of its efforts to prohibit certain Indian ritual practices, the United States Government banned participation in a number of Indian ceremonies. For the tribes of the Northern Plains, this prohibition applied directly to the Sun Dance, a central religious rite, but it also impinged upon dances of the warrior and dream societies. Although some of these activities continued away from government scrutiny, it was not until 1933 that the government lifted its ban and dance activities resumed in the changing contexts of reservation and "Americanized" life.[1]

Today, dance and dance events — including the songs, dance dress, and gatherings of the people — are among the strongest overt expressions and measures of the perpetuation of Indian life and culture among the people of the Northern Plains tribes. Although the powwow is the most visible public dance complex shared by Northern Plains peoples, participation in the ceremonial Sun Dance has increased in some areas and winter social dances are still held in community halls and some homes (fig. 139).[2]

In earlier times, male warrior society members were the primary participants in the warrior-related dance complex. Today, however, powwows are more open — men, women, and even young boys and girls dance to express, explore, and celebrate their "Indianness" (fig. 140).[3] This participation by young and old dancers, along with the large cash prizes at contest powwows, indicates that Indian dance and music are alive and well and that they will remain a significant element of Indian culture and group life in coming years and generations.

140 A YOUNG
SHAWL DANCER
AT THE GALLUP
CEREMONIAL,
NEW MEXICO,
1990

139 WAR DANCERS AT THE GALLUP
CEREMONIAL, NEW MEXICO, 1990.
THE PHOTOGRAPHS ACCOMPANYING
THIS ESSAY INCLUDE PICTURES OF
POWWOWS AND DANCERS OUTSIDE
THE NORTHERN PLAINS AREA AND
STYLE PROPER, ILLUSTRATING HOW
NORTHERN PLAINS POWWOW
PRACTICES HAVE DIFFUSED
THROUGHOUT OTHER TRIBAL
AREAS OF THE UNITED STATES.

141 THE STRUTTING
POSTURE IS SEEN IN
THIS DAKOTA WAR
DANCE OF 1929.
NATIONAL
ANTHROPOLOGICAL
ARCHIVES, NEG. NO.
3675-C1

The Northern Plains culture and dance area is generally considered to be between the Rocky Mountains and the wooded lakes country of Minnesota and Ontario, covering the Dakotas, Wyoming, Montana, Alberta, and Saskatchewan. The corresponding tribes are: the Lakota/Dakota, Northern Cheyenne, Shoshone, Arapaho, Crow, Flathead, Gros Ventre, Assiniboine, Blood, Blackfeet, Plains Cree, and Plains Ojibwa, among others. Certain other tribes to the west —including the Ute, Taos, and various tribes in Washington, Oregon, and British Columbia —also share certain dance elements of the Plains tribes. These tribes speak languages primarily from the Siouan and Algonquian linguistic families, which are unrelated. While each has its own traditions and styles of dress and dance, these tribes also share many related and analogous practices in terms of dance and dress styles, types of dances, and types of dance complexes and events.

Northern Plains dance, dress, and song styles have been distinguished from Southern Plains styles by secondary details such as feather bustle construction, song tessitura (northern songs are usually higher than southern), drumming patterns, and etiquette. The overall aesthetic of northern styles tends to be looser or freer, while southern styles tend, comparatively speaking, to be more controlled or more formal and reserved.

The dance practices of the Lakota or Dakota Sioux people are representative of the Northern Plains area. These people, popularly referred to in English as the Sioux, comprise seven major divisions and refer to themselves variously in the three respective dialects of their language as the Lakota, Dakota, or Nakota people. The Lakota people have home reservations west of the Missouri River in North and South Dakota. Dakota groups live in the Dakotas and Minnesota and in Canada, while Nakota speakers live in Montana, near the Dakota speakers. Eastern and northern groups also share some cultural characteristics with Algonquian and other Siouan tribes, including the Ojibwa and Winnebago.

The earliest origins of Plains Indian dances remain obscure, but origin stories and explanations exist for the Sun Dance, for some warrior societies, and for some social dances and modern dance styles. It is clear that earlier male grass dancers imitated animals as well as hunting or warrior actions.[4] Such imitative, pantomimic actions are seen today in the Sneak-up Dance, in which dancers crouch to sneak-up and scout the enemy, and in some versions of the Pick-up Dance, in which a dancer (or set of four dancers) dances to pick up an eagle feather that has dropped from a dancer's outfit. They circle and approach the fallen feather as they would surround and attack an enemy. Each then extends his hand or fan over the feather as if counting coup on it — i.e., each imitates touching an enemy to gain war honors. Veterans are normally chosen to perform the Pick-up Dance because only a veteran has the right to wear, or pass on the right to wear, eagle feathers as part of dance dress.

Lakota and Dakota people have also attributed the traditional male grass dancer style to the imitation of the strutting of the male prairie chicken, and at least one commentator has indicated a courting as well as warrior function for the dance (fig. 141).[5]

During the eighteenth and nineteenth centuries, the Lakota/Dakota tribes had numerous soldier organizations or warrior societies. Each society, such as the Cante Tinza (Strong Hearts) and the Tokala (Foxes), had its own songs, dances, and dance regulations, as well as specific dress items and paraphernalia worn or carried only by particular officers and members.[6] These warrior society dances, dance styles, dress items, and paraphernalia are the origin of, and basis for, many of today's powwow outfits and for particular dances and dance procedures.

One society, the Omaha — and the Omaha Dance, which came to the Lakota from the Omaha tribe — became the basis of traditional powwow practices, including use of the eagle-feather bustle and the porcupine-hair "roach" headdress (fig. 142).[7]

During the latter nineteenth century, the warrior societies declined. At the same time, intertribal contact was spreading the Omaha Dance. A general powwow type of dance became common. It also became more social in nature, and even women and children, who had had only limited participation in the warrior dances and societies, now took a more active part.

The reasons for performing the Sun Dance, the Ghost Dance of the 1880s, and even the warrior society dances obviously go beyond performance. Dances portraying a warrior's exploits served directly to recount and reward such deeds. The early Sun Dance also contained warrior-related elements, and dancers frequently were warriors dancing their fulfillment of vows.[8] Further, all dances involved the individual's and the people's relationship with mystic power or powers in the universe, both spiritual and material. Dancers dance to fulfill religious vows, to acquire or celebrate power or protection, or to bring blessings upon themselves or relatives or the people. Dance dress outfits use sacred eagle feathers (fig. 143), cosmic designs, and elements such as red paint in the hair part that come from other ceremonies. Even a drum may be named and blessed.

Thus, there were and are many specific prescriptions and proscriptions about proper procedure and participation. Even in today's more secularized and social powwow settings, specific etiquette governs dancers' and others' behavior or movements around the dance arena or at the drums, or when handling certain dress items and paraphernalia. At the same time, as indicated below, there are also social dances today that are done purely for the enjoyment of dancers and spectators.

In his book, respected traditional Lakota singer and dancer Ben Black Bear, Sr., provided this marvelous explanation of the Omaha Dance — i.e., general contemporary powwow dance and dancing:

> *I will now tell of dancing and how many men and women among you have no interest in it. Many of you*
> *who dance (and will dance) know the beauty of it … and know that it is the highest form of enjoyment.*
> *What evil things you had planned to do, you will not do. You will keep your mind on only the dancing*
> *and your body will be well; it will not be fat. Your body will be very well. And your arms and body will be*
> *well. Whoever dances is never sick as long as he dances. Going to dances is good fun, and also, dancing*
> *can make your disposition good. If someone does not do this, I do not know why he is on this earth.*
> *People use the dance to lecture those who like to strike their families. While you are alive, you give*
> *homage to the Great Spirit, and you will do favors for others, and then you will enjoy yourself. If one*
> *does not do those things, he will explode within himself. These three things are the highest in law. . . .*
> *Realize this. These are truths. So be it.*[9]

144 DANCERS,
FAMILIES, AND
OUTSIDE VISITORS
ENJOY THE
ACTIVITIES AND
SOCIALIZING AT THE
MICHIGAN STATE
UNIVERSITY
POWWOW, AUGUST
1992

146 A FANCY
DANCER AT THE
GALLUP
CEREMONIAL,
NEW MEXICO,
1990

Today a powwow is a get-together by the people to dance, look on, and visit (figs. 144, 145). The main purpose may be social, but civil and even religious ceremonial elements remain important, such as honoring a veteran or other person with honor songs, or receiving a family back into public life after a period of mourning. Through these practices, powwows help to sustain traditional values and tribal and kinship ties.

Dance is by nature visual movement (fig. 146). And full-dress Northern Plains powwow dancing is self-consciously visual in movement and dress. Newcomers visiting and watching a major powwow are invariably struck by the bright colors and elaborate detail of the feathered, quilled, beaded, appliquéd, fringed, and otherwise decorated dance outfits and the varied individual movements and styles of the dancers (fig. 147). In recent years, there has been a renaissance in both traditional and modern-style dance clothing. Indian people enjoy and appreciate the effects of this creativity; many do so with the practiced eye of the connoisseur, noting smaller details of style and correctness. And even in non-costume social dances, such as the Rabbit Dance, subtleties of movement and style are noted by discriminating viewers as well as dancers.

Nevertheless, traditional Lakota and Northern Plains Indian dancing are never conducted in a Western "art for art's sake" fashion. Lakota dances, while complete, legitimate artistic performances, are also always social and cultural events. The dancers and singers, even while enjoying and displaying dancing and singing as such, do not dance as separate from the people (as audience) or the social setting. Rather, the dances and songs are vital parts of the gathering of the people. Singers are absolutely necessary, and dancers essential, to powwows and related events.

Although the Lakota people call a local dance or larger intertribal powwow a *wacipi* (dance), dancers are most often thanked by those putting on the event, not for their fine performance, but for "helping out." The dancers dance neither for themselves nor just to present a performance to the audience, but to help make the gathering of the people and the continuation of tribal culture possible and effective. One dances with, for, on behalf of, and in relationship to the people and the social, cultural purposes of the event. Active, prominent dancers are recognized and appreciated not only for dance prowess, but for their leadership and consistent contribution to the life of the people by making events possible and successful. Similarly, good singers are those not merely with good voices, but with the knowledge and memory of the various specific songs needed or requested. Such memory is important to the people.

The social importance does not exclude personal enjoyment. Again, Black Bear says:

> In the dances the reason why the men, young men, boys, women, young women and girls dance the
> Omaha is that they are enjoying themselves. The fine looking outfits they are wearing, they are showing
> off and whatever the dancers want you people to see is how they use their arms, their legs, their neck and
> their whole body. How good they look is something to enjoy. When you dance, you will like it. You will
> like only it. After you finish praying and helping others, you will always remember the dance next. You
> will enjoy yourself and you will think of nothing bad. If you would notice, those dancers treat each other
> well. So be it.[10]

147 THIS ROUND DANCE SHOWS THE
VARIETY, COLOR, AND ELABORATE
DETAIL OF POWWOW CLOTHING.
NAVAJO NATION FAIR, WINDOW ROCK,
ARIZONA, 1989

149 GRAND ENTRY PARADE,
SHOWING NAVAJO TRIBAL MEMBERS
IN TRADITIONAL NAVAJO DRESS
PRECEDING THE POWWOW
DANCERS IN THE ENTRANCE, AT THE
NAVAJO NATION FAIR, WINDOW
ROCK, ARIZONA, 1990

148 AROUND A SOUTHERN
DRUM, A MOMENT OF
SOLEMN REMEMBRANCE
OF A DECEASED LEADER.
THE GALLUP CEREMONIAL,
NEW MEXICO, 1990

Powwows are thus a major performing arts form in contemporary Indian culture that offers an important performing experience for participants. But, more than this, they bring the people together specifically as members of a tribe or as Indian people. Powwows help sustain particular social or kinship positions, relationships, and values — through the honoring songs; the giving of gifts to selected people; through the choices of head singers and dancers and other positions; and through the procedures, etiquette, and explanatory speeches incorporated as part of the proceedings (fig. 148).

These events provide one arena, one setting in which traditional and neotraditional ways can be acted out and verbalized, and in which Indian identity can be openly and directly expressed, practiced, and promoted — in contrast to many other settings, in which Indian people must survive in the dominant society.

A powwow consists of many different program items and elements. The event or program normally begins with the Grand Entry, a flag song, and an invocation. The Grand Entry is the parade entrance of all costumed dancers (fig. 149). Spectators generally stand in honor of the dancers, and of the flag — traditional staff and/or U.S. flags — carried by the lead dancers. The song used may be a general intertribal Omaha or specific parade or grass-flattening song.

The flag song or national anthem is a specially composed song with a text honoring flag and country. Many tribes have their own flag song. The text of the Lakota National Anthem states the words of a soldier:

> *Tunkasilayapi tawapaha kin oihanke sni najin ktelo*
> *Iyohlate oyate kin wicicagin;*
> *ktaca, lecamon.*
> *(The flag of the United States will fly forever.*
> *Under it the people will grow and prosper;*
> *Therefore have I done this [fought for my country]).*[11]

Everyone stands without dancing for this. This song, like "The Star Spangled Banner," is also used on other formal occasions. In Indian schools serving Lakota and Dakota students and communities, for example, it is sometimes sung at the start of school graduation ceremonies and before basketball games.

Following the flag song, the person who is asked to pray the invocation then offers a prayer, either in a traditional Indian or Christian manner, depending on his personal belief and practice. This may be followed by a welcome from the head of the committee or organization sponsoring the powwow.

Various kinds of dances are usually performed during the course of a powwow. The Sneak-up Dance, also called the Scouting or Wounded Warrior Dance, is often done first. The dance is traditionally performed by male dancers who imitate the sneaking up on, and battle with, the enemy; today children and women often join in.

One version of the song tells of a brave warrior who has been wounded in battle and is being carried back by his comrades:

> *Le yuha manipe;*
> *eca blotahunka ca wisoseyape.*
> *(They are carrying him;*
> *he was a very brave man, so they wounded him).*[12]

The main kind of general dancing that makes up the core of the Dakota and Lakota people's powwows is called the Grass Dance — referring to the earlier Grass Dance society dance style and the braided sweet-grass worn in dancers' belts — or Omaha Dance (so-called because they received this dance from the Omaha people). At today's powwows around the country this general dancing is also termed intertribal dancing, since members of various tribes are often present. The songs may have words, but often use only vocables (singing syllables). Among the Winnebago, Omaha, Eastern Dakota, and several other Siouian-speaking people, the traditional songs, forms of dancing, and dance event are called *Helushka* (War Dance), referring to the respected male warrior dancers.

Several additional dances are often included in the powwow event. The Round Dance is a circle dance that derives in different tribal areas from earlier victory or friendship dance forms. Today it is done as an open dance in which everyone, including visitors, may participate, whether in powwow dance dress or not.

The Rabbit Dance and Two-step are social partner dances done for fun; the texts to the dances are often love songs. They are "ladies' choice" dances and participants need not wear any special dance or traditional dress. A typical Rabbit Dance song (with English words) says, "Dearie, why don't you look at me? I know you will come back to me, so I don't worry."[13]

Several other special kinds of dances may be inserted into the powwow sequence between inter-tribal dances. These can be older dances from a particular tribe's traditional practices that are not part of the powwow customs directly, such as the Winnebago Snake or Bean dances. They can be social dances, such as the Northern Plains Owl Dance (Oklahoma Two-step; fig. 150). Or they can be newer fun dances, such as the Dollar Pick-up Dance or Men's Fancy-Shawl Dance.

During intertribal dancing, a number of specific dance and dress styles can be clearly distinguished for both men and women. During contest powwows, these styles are used as dance contest divisions or categories. Specific details of costume style, such as the type of beadwork design or feather-bustle construction, may identify and distinguish the specific tribal identity of individual dancers, but the following styles and categories are generally recognized and used in the Northern Plains region today.[14]

150 A TWO-STEP (ALSO KNOWN AS THE OWL DANCE) AT THE MICHIGAN STATE UNIVERSITY POWWOW, AUGUST, 1992

From the latter years of the eighteenth century, until it reached its apex in the 1880s, one ceremony loomed above all the rest as typical of the transformative process and worldview of those who had left behind their woodland traditions and re-created themselves into the peoples we know today as the Plains tribes. That ceremony is known by many names by different tribes—the Sun Dance, They Dance Staring at the Sun, the Thirst Dance, the Medicine Lodge, and the Dance for the World (fig. 151).

The whole ceremony is not technically a dance. While dancing in place or bobbing to the sound of the drum and sacred songs over an extended period of time does take place, this aspect is only part of a series of other complex and profound rituals that make up the Sun Dance.

At the appointed time of year, in the summer, sometimes near the summer solstice, the tribe (or, in some cases, several allied tribes) would gather in great camps on the Plains. After selecting sacred leaders and associates, the participants would enter into a four- or eight-day period of fasting from food and water. Practicing ritualized behavior and restraint, the people would demonstrate awesome respect for the sacred drama of re-creating the world and all that is in it in a miniature version of the cosmos. This miniature version took the form of a sacred lodge, circular in shape, walled in and roofed over by some tribes, but always made of natural materials (posts and beams of newly cut trees, foliage, vines, and reeds).

A sacred tree, or *axis mundi*, is placed at the center and the lodge is demarcated into the four quarters of the universe, which are marked by smaller decorated trees or sacred altars. Offerings of precious animal skins— and, in modern times, brightly colored yard goods, a once-precious trade item — adorn the sacred tree and those of the four quarters. Other esoteric offerings (almost always including tobacco) are placed on the crotch at the top of the sacred tree.

In solemn procession, the accoutered participants, sacred leaders, singers and drummers, and audience enter these sacred worlds and proceed to offer themselves up as sacrifice to the ancient gods, in thanksgiving for life itself and all that sustains life. In due time, each individual's vow to undergo this sacrifice becomes part of a great collective prayer for the life of all things and all peoples of this world.

The elements of the Sun Dance are simple—dancing in place, the sound of an eagle-wing bone-whistle blowing in rhythm to the great drum (or drums), and the ancient voice-prayer-music of the singers as they address the Sun and other powers of the universe: *"Oh, holy powers, we honor you this day that we may live. Have pity on me. Accept my suffering this day in reciprocation for all you have given us."*

The essence of the prayer rises out of the teachings of the shamanic tradition of communion with the gods via sacred acts: music, dance, visual-arts compositions, and projection of one's will into the heart of the experience of relationship. First and foremost in this relationship is the recognition that humans are but one of many beings among all the plants, insects, reptiles, birds, other animals, minerals, and hidden mysteries of the earth itself. Tribal teachings emphasize that all are children of an infinite and ongoing process that transcends our most basic understanding of time itself.

At the heart of the Sun Dance prayer is a cyclical view of time and process, this great circle of life that various tribes call "That Which Moves," "The Great Holy," "The Great Spirit," or "The Great Mystery."

It is this concept, or its perceived parts, that the tribes in their sacred lodges have demarcated and manifested as symbol in their visual arts, music, oratory, poetry, dance, drama, and vernacular architecture.

Through the use of these forms in ritual, tribal people interact; they express, celebrate, and reaffirm their relationship to the originating powers of their very being and their particular roles in the great cyclical potency that governs all dimensions of the environment that sustains them — as long as they behave as stewards and respect it and reciprocate in a benevolent manner.

Arthur Amiotte

Editor's note: Some of this material has also appeared in Arthur R. Huseboe and Arthur Amiotte, *An Illustrated History of the Arts in South Dakota* (Sioux Falls, So. Dak.: Center for Western Studies, Augustana College, 1989), pp. 123–24.

151 PROBABLY LITTLE CHIEF (1854–1923), *SUN DANCE ENCAMPMENT* (SOUTHERN CHEYENNE), INK, GRAPHITE, AND WATERCOLOR ON PAPER, 59.5 X 65.8 CM. NATIONAL MUSEUM OF THE AMERICAN INDIAN, SMITHSONIAN INSTITUTION, NO. 11.1706

LITTLE CHIEF (KOWEONARRE), A SOUTHERN CHEYENNE PRISONER OF WAR INCARCERATED AT FORT MARION, FLORIDA, WAS LISTED AS A "RINGLEADER" AT THE TIME OF HIS 1875 ARREST ON UNSPECIFIED CHARGES. EAGLE HEAD (MINIMIC) AND GREY BEARD, ARRESTED AT THE SAME TIME, ARE REMEMBERED IN THIS WORK THROUGH THE DEPICTION OF THEIR PAINTED LODGES. THE DRAWING CAPTURES THE GREAT SOCIAL AND SACRED ACTIVITY ASSOCIATED WITH THE SUN DANCE. TWO BOYS ENGAGE IN A HORSE RACE IN THE LOWER RIGHT CORNER. SOLDIER SOCIETIES STAGE THEIR DANCES AT EACH CORNER WITHIN THE CAMP CIRCLE. THE FAMED CHEYENNE DOG SOLDIERS, CLEARLY IDENTIFIABLE BY THEIR DISTINCTIVE HEADDRESSES, ARE SEEN IN FRONT OF THE MEDICINE LODGES IN THE LOWER LEFT QUADRANT OF THE CIRCLE. THE MEN IN THE HILLS ARE SEEN ENGAGED IN SACRIFICE, PURIFYING THEMSELVES THROUGH THE SWEAT LODGE, OR MAKING THEIR WAY TO THE SUN DANCE LODGE, WHICH IS FESTOONED WITH NUMEROUS OFFERING CLOTHS.

Men's Traditional. The traditional men's dance style and dress come from earlier, nineteenth-century warrior society dance styles and dress items. Men usually wear one eagle-feather bustle at their waists, and a porcupine-hair roach headdress with one or two eagle-tail feathers standing upright in the roach. The dance style is flat-footed and earth-bound, but may include active head and upper body movements portraying hunting, tracking, or fighting actions.[15] In traditional men's and women's dances, specific tribal dance styles and dress — including specific kinds of feather bustles, beadwork designs, and bandoliers — are generally observed in some detail; there is less pantribal blending than in the modern Fancy and Shawl dance styles. Young people and children also may dance in any of the styles being described here.

Women's Traditional. Women's traditional dance dresses are usually full-length and made of either buckskin or tradecloth (fig. 152). The dance style is modest, consisting of either a single or double step going forward around the dance circle, or a vertical movement sometimes called a "washboard" motion done in place with only very subtle foot movements.

Men's Northern-Style Grass. This dance and costume style originated in North Dakota in the early 1900s and has again become popular. These costumes commonly use fringed V-shaped shirt yokes and fringed shirt and pants seams.[16] Dancers do not wear a bustle and may use a side-to-side swaying motion (fig. 153).

Men's Fancy. After World War II, the men's traditional dance and dress styles saw increasingly fancy and colorful innovations, especially in the beadwork and larger bustles worn. Today's fancy dancers usually wear two bustles, one at the back waist and one at the back of the neck; they dance with more elevated foot and leg movements, and use many visual elements in both costume, face paint, and movements to attract the judges' attention during dance contests (see fig. 146).

Women's Fancy-Shawl. Women traditionally wear a shawl as a sign of proper etiquette when dancing or otherwise called into a dance arena. For younger women, however, the traditionally restricted dance style has been replaced with a more vigorous style not unlike the men's Fancy Dance. Younger shawl dancers may wear only a shawl over day-to-day street clothes, but fully outfitted fancy-shawl dancers wear beautiful cloth dresses, beaded moccasins and leggings, and a shawl, or beaded or decorated cape (fig. 154).

152 A HEAVILY BEADED TRADITIONAL BUCKSKIN DRESS WITH MATCHING LEGGINGS. NAVAJO NATION FAIR, WINDOW ROCK, ARIZONA, 1989

155 JINGLE-DRESS
DANCER, NAVAJO
NATION FAIR,
WINDOW ROCK,
ARIZONA, 1989

Women's Jingle-Dress. This dance and dress style is named from the tin, cone-shaped jingles that are sewn in rows around the dress to move and jingle against one another (fig. 155). The dress style, which has some parallels with that of the northern style grass dancers, also began in the early 1900s. One story attributes its origin to a dream by an Ojibwa holy man in Minnesota, in which four women appeared in jingle dresses. From there the dance spread to North Dakota and Montana. Today it has regained popularity among women of all ages.[17]

Two important ingredients of most powwows — honor songs and give-aways — are more significant as social activities than as dance performance. An honor song is sung in honor or in memory of a specific person or group, usually with the person or group's Indian name inserted into a text recognizing their bravery or generosity. When the song is sung, the person being honored is accompanied around the dance floor by those requesting the song or by other relatives and friends who dance to honor the person.

A person may request an honor song for another person (or themselves) and may request also a "Special"—that is, an opportunity to "give away." Give-aways are used to honor a person, or to express appreciation for an honor given to a person. When a person has been honored in some fashion, or there is a special event that someone wishes to commemorate, the person (and/or the person's relatives) will give goods or money to the singers and other people in a spirit of acknowledgment and appreciation. This sharing is a traditional way of maintaining ties and bonds among the people.

Powwows sometimes end with a closing song during which the drum retires and the dancers dance and exit following the drum.

The organization of powwow events today often includes the selection and use of a Head Man Dancer. This stems from early warrior society dance organization and practices. One of these roles is the position of Whip Man. This person was a dancer who carried a whip to make sure that dancers participated when expected or required. Today both Head Man and Head Lady dancers are chosen to lead the dancers.

A selected drum (singing group) may also be invited to serve as the Head Drum or Host Drum to provide selected songs when needed. Other drums are also welcome. A small powwow may have only one or a few drums; some very large intertribal powwows will have twenty or more (fig. 156).

156 TWO DRUMS AT THE KEEPERS OF THE WESTERN DOOR POWWOW, ST. BONAVENTURE UNIVERSITY, NEW YORK, JULY 1992: YOUNG NATION DRUM (ABOVE) FROM THE TONAWANDA INDIAN RESERVATION, AND WHITE FISH BAY, MICHIGAN

The Stoney Reserve is located sixty miles west of Calgary, Alberta, in Canada. Lying at the foothills of the Canadian Rockies, the reserve (as tribal lands are referred to in Canada) encompasses an area marked by the majesty and surrealism of the mountains as they rise out of the buffalo-grass plains (fig. 157). The prairies are peppered with family farms and cattle ranches. Even in the midst of summer you can sense the chill northern winds to come when you see the stacks of baled hay and board windbreaks in the cattle pastures awaiting their calling for the winter months.

The Stoney people are hunters. It is common for tribal members to set up a hunting camp for two or more weeks at a time to hunt, gather, fish, and cook in preparation for winter. Hunting camp for modern-day Stoneys is a time of respite and family togetherness—less a necessity than a matter of maintaining a lifeway.

Chief John Snow says that the Stoney people "are members of the Great Sioux Nation who spoke a dialect of the Nakota branch of the Siouan language family." A very large percentage of the Stoney population speaks the language today— from the oldest to the youngest, the people tend to carry on casual conversation in Stoney.

The importance of dance and its place in Stoney society can be seen in a variety of settings on the reserve. From the Trans Canada Highway you can see two Sun Dance lodges that are going back to the earth. Identifiable by the colored cloth that has been hung and tied to the central pole of the structures, the lodges represent one of the most sacred ceremonies of the Stoneys. Reflective of self-sacrifice through fasting for the good of all people, and indicative of the fulfillment of an individual commitment by the Sun Dance maker (the person who actually sponsors the ceremony), the ceremonies occur during the summer months and are

integral to the cultural continuity of the Stoney people. Each Sun Dance lasts four days. During the summer of 1992, there were four different ceremonies on the reserve.

The Stoneys, not unlike other groups of Native Americans, have a history wrought by misfortune — their land diminished and resources depleted at the hands of non-native governments and unscrupulous individuals. The Stoneys' adaptation to their changing circumstances, while maintaining cultural continuity in the face of these pressures, is testimony to their vitality.

During the summer of 1992, the Stoney people hosted the Indian Ecumenical Conference, a gathering of native religious leaders and elders, which included a community powwow. The Nakoda Nation Singers kicked off this small and

157 THE SACRED MOUNTAINS OF THE STONEY PEOPLE ARE THE BACKDROP FOR THE INDIAN ECUMENICAL CONFERENCE CAMPSITE. STONEY RESERVE, ALBERTA, CANADA, 1992

intimate event, held primarily for the conference attendees, with the Grand Entry song. Following the Grand Entry were a good range of dances that included intertribal war dances, round dances, the Sneak-up Dance (a men's dance that recalls the courting ritual of the prairie chicken), a Women's Traditional Dance, the Grass Dance, and the Owl Dance (similar to the Two-step among Southern Plains tribes). Although the powwow was brief, it was a further demonstration of the people's commitment to their traditions (figs. 158, 159).

As in any encounter of this nature, non-group members can never really experience the security and identity of the group. Being among the Stoneys, however, gives an observer the sense that these people are fully involved in the social structure and maintenance of their nation. With the kind of group integrity and cultural activities that the Stoneys and other native peoples continue to protect and practice, native self-expression through dance and music will survive and prosper into the unknown future.

Fred Nahwooksy

159 VERN HOULE DOING THE SNEAK-UP OR CHICKEN DANCE, STONEY RESERVE, 1992

**M**any intertribal powwow songs have no words and use only vocables. Songs for more specific dances or uses, such as flag songs and honoring songs, have texts that relate brave deeds or that encourage the people.[18] Most songs sung for the types of dances done at powwows follow a common song structure. This form is used for intertribal, Round, Rabbit, Two-step, and Omaha or War Dance songs:

> *the lead singer starts the song (melodies start high);*
> *the lead phrase is "seconded" (repeated) by the group;*
> *the main body of the song (the chorus) is sung through and repeated;*
> *the lead singer then "picks up" (starts) the song over again.*

If the song has words, it is usually sung through first, using only vocables, with the words sung the second time through the chorus.[19]

In contrast with the ascending contour of many European melodies, Plains Indian songs start high and generally descend phrase by phrase to the end of the song or chorus. Each type of song has a stock vocable and rhythmic ending formula, such as *weyaheyeyeyeyo* for War Dance songs. Powwow songs are generally short; certain songs are traditionally sung four times through, with the chorus or song repeated as a "tail" during soldier-related songs, while intertribal dance songs may be sung any number of times through.

Thelonius Monk is credited with observing that "talking about music is like dancing about architecture." An attempt to convey or experience dance through writing is no doubt equally elliptic. Nevertheless, four characteristics of Northern Plains dance that indicate both performance and social aspects of the dancing and dances, and of the tribal societies, should be noted. First, the dance is historically male dominated. Male participants have a more prominent role and use more vigorous leg and body movements. In warrior society dances and in earlier traditional powwow forms, women were restricted to dancing in a reserved manner around the edge of the dance area. This reflects the male leadership found traditionally among the Northern Plains tribes in matters of government and religion.

Exceptions, such as the virgins' roles in the Sun Dance or women's performance of the Victory Scalp Dance have their explanation in the stories and in the high respect accorded women, particularly sisters, in Lakota values and ideals.[20] Today, the active style of women shawl dancers and jingle-dress dancers in the center of the arena must also reflect the changing roles and relationships of men and women in non-dance settings (fig. 160).

Second, the central male dance forms are quite individualistic. Although this is often sublimated in the Sun Dance, powwow dancers dress and dance, within the parameters of each identified genre, in individual and individually decided and designed styles. This is an expression of the free mobility of the individual and of the extended family and larger combined family groups or bands in Plains life. Dances such as the Round (circle) Dance are prescriptive only for the basic formation and step; this flexibility can be thought of as reflecting the unity and egalitarianism of the camp circle and social unit.

A third characteristic is that the dance posture and steps are essentially earth-bound and earth-oriented. Traditional steps are flat-footed, and accented movements are generally in an earthward or downward direction. This contrasts directly with the vertical, upward orientation of the epitome of classical European dance, the ballet, and expresses the mother-earth aspect of Lakota and Indian belief.[21]

Finally, the level of difficulty or complexity of the dances allows and provides for general participation. The dance is not professionalized to the exclusion of the people. The best elaborate and subtle details of dress and dance style are recog-

nized and appreciated, but people dance not as dance specialists, but as members of the family and tribe. The few specialized dances, such as the Hoop Dance, that require years of practice remain the exceptions and are usually used as special program entertainment dances (fig. 161).

Music and dance are central in and to the cultural life of Indian peoples. More than options or accessories, they remain at the heart of cultural matrices and provide an understanding of Indian beliefs and social life. Further, they are among the elements and domains that remain most overtly Indian in Indian peoples' individual and collective lives. Northern Plains song and dance activity continues within both rural reservation and urban Indian communities with visible and vigorous strength.

Moreover, in recent years intertribal powwows of the Plains type have become a vehicle for pantribal expression of Indian identity in all reaches of the United States, from New York State to Los Angeles to the Southwest, even among many members of tribes such as the Navajo and Hopi, for whom the powwow is a totally imported form. The predominant influence in much of this current practice, both in dance and singing styles, is that of the Northern Plains (Southern Plains practices, including the Gourd Dance, war dances, and drumming and singing styles are also spreading, but northern styles seem to be dominant, especially among the young).

Among a widening circle of Indian people, performing and understanding Northern Plains Indian dance and song continue to be a means of guarding and sustaining either specific Northern Plains cultural ways or a more generalized Indian identity within a Western society that usually has little appreciation or understanding of the content and richness of these dance and song traditions. Nevertheless, the creativity and cultural continuity that mark these activities today give clear evidence that Northern Plains dance and song will continue to provide a strong center and outlet for cultural energy in Indian life for generations to come.

1   John Collier, *Indians of the Americas* (New York: Mentor Books, 1947; slightly abridged, 1964), p. 137.

2   Dance complex refers to the interrelated elements of dance performance, the dance event, and related activities and beliefs associated with sponsoring, performing, and conducting the total event.

3   Elizabeth S. Grobsmith, *Lakota of Rosebud: A Contemporary Ethnography* (New York: Holt, Rinehart and Winston, 1981), p. 52.

4   See William Powers, "Comment," *The Singing Wire* 5, no. 3 (1969): 9–10. Also see Lynn F. Huenemann, *Songs and Dances of Native America: A Resource Text for Teachers and Students* (book and tapes), (Tsaile, Ariz.: Education House, 1978), p. 94.

5   William Powers, in a paper given at the Society for Ethnomusicology Annual Conference, discusses the courtship function of grass dancing. Strutting prairie chicken was described by Asa Primeaux (Yankton Dakota) in a lecture to one of my classes at Navajo Community College, ca. 1979.

6   Frances Densmore, *Teton Sioux Music*, Bureau of American Ethnology Bulletin 61 (Washington D.C.: Smithsonian Institution, 1918; reprint, 1972), pp. 101–109.

7   James H. Howard, "Notes on the Dakota Grass Dance," *Southwestern Journal of Anthropology* 7, no. 1 (1951): 82–85.

8   See Densmore, *Teton Sioux Music*; also see a series of articles on American Indian music by William K. Powers, in *American Indian Tradition* 7–8, nos. 3–4 (1961–62).

9   Ben Black Bear, Sr., and R.D. Theisz, *Songs and Dances of the Lakota* (Rosebud, So. Dak.: Sinte Gleska College, 1976), p. 27.

10 Ibid., p. 37.

11 Huenemann, *Songs and Dances*, p. 97.

12 Ibid., p. 94.

13 Ibid., p. 128.

14 Parts of these descriptions are based on the author's previous writings. For other similar descriptions of dance styles and categories, see George P. Horse Capture, *Powwow* (Cody: Buffalo Bill Historical Center, 1989); and Black Bear and Theisz, *Songs and Dances*, pp. 15–20.

15 See Powers, "Comment," p. 10, and Huenemann, *Songs and Dances*, p. 94.

16 See James H. Howard, "Northern Style Grass Dance Costume," *American Indian Hobbyist* 7, no. 1 (1960): 20. The outfits using the V-shaped fringed shirts have been attributed to the influence and use of cowboy shirts and styles, but they may have also come directly from earlier Indian shirt and leggings styles. Men's nineteenth-century Ghost Dance shirts often used a fringed V-shaped yoke, similar to that of the Grass Dance shirts.

17 See Horse Capture, *Powwow*, p. 27.

18 The best source for ordering recordings of Indian songs of the Northern Plains and other tribal areas is Canyon Records in Phoenix, Arizona, since they sell both their own excellent recordings and those of several of the other significant recent and current recording companies that have produced good Indian recordings (including Indian House Records, Library of Congress, Folkways, Soundchief, and others).

19 See Huenemann, *Songs and Dances*, p. 82, and Powers, *American Indian Music* 7: 28–29.

20 For an excellent description of, and for insight into, these and other traditional Lakota and Dakota values and ideals, see Ella C. Deloria, *Speaking of Indians* (New York: Friendship Press, 1944; reprint, 1983).

21 See Huenemann, *Songs and Dances*, p. 202.

CONTEMPORARY ALASKA NATIVE DANCE: THE SPIRIT OF TRADITION

MARIA WILLIAMS

During the period of Alaska's colonization, which began in the late eighteenth century, all traditional practices (including the performance of music and dance) were suppressed by Christian missionaries and the Western ethnocentric educational system. Since the mid 1970s, however, music and dance performance has been on the rise and is now openly embraced and publicly celebrated. It is a testament to human survival and the gift of adaptability that some of the indigenous cultures of Alaska have been able to retain their music and dance practices.[1]

Native Alaskans have coped admirably with these pressures. In the tide of change brought by Westernization, Americanization, and technological innovations, the indigenous people of Alaska persevere and continue to express themselves and their cultures through their own languages and traditional value systems, which include music and dance performance (fig. 162).[2] In fact, many visible aspects of traditional (or pre-contact) culture exist and form a viable part of present-day life in Alaska.

162 LEAD DRUMMERS
DRUM IN DANCERS
DURING THE GRAND
ENTRANCE OF THE 1990
"CELEBRATION," A
BI-ANNUAL GATHERING OF
CLAN GROUPS, FAMILIES,
AND INDIVIDUALS TO
CELEBRATE THE TLINGIT,
HAIDA, AND TSIMSHIAN
CULTURES.

Today, traditional music and dance practice reflects many realities — adaptations in performance context, group membership, length of performances, purpose/intent of performance, and so forth. These changes are made both consciously and subconsciously by performing groups or organizations that sponsor traditional performance. They are really extensions of a normal process of growth and adaptation (although greatly intensified since the mid eighteenth century because of colonization).

The idea of change in Native Alaskan cultures is often compartmentalized by Western scholars into two areas: the "idyllic" pre-contact period and the post-contact period. Change in relation to post-Western contact is often measured by response or reaction to

163 THE LAST TRADITIONAL CEREMONIAL HELD AT KLINQUAN BEFORE EVACUATION OF THE VILLAGE TO HYDABURG, ALASKA, CA. 1900. THE RESETTLEMENT QUALIFIED THE HAIDAS FOR PROGRAMS UNDER THE TERRITORIAL BUREAU OF EDUCATION — THUS HELPING THEM SURVIVE IN AN INCREASINGLY COMPLEX AND CHANGING SOCIETY. NATIONAL ANTHROPOLOGICAL ARCHIVES, SMITHSONIAN INSTITUTION, NEG. NO. 72.508

colonialism and imperialist forces. The concept of change, and even tradition, must be viewed as a continuum. Native Alaskans have experienced change, adaptations, and development throughout time, not just since 1800. Although accelerated change has occurred because of the tremendous imposition of Westernization (with the resulting cultural losses in such areas as religious practice and language), one must allow for the fact that change—going back thousands of years before any outside contact—has always been an important aspect of survival for Native Alaskans. Indigenous societies have also made their own choices and created their own strategies in attempting to survive in a hostile geopolitical environment (fig. 163).[3]

The concept of tradition must also incorporate the historic continuum of what has been the cultural practice or norm. Native

164 THE KODIAK ALUTIIQ DANCERS WAS FORMED IN 1989 TO PRESERVE THE ALUTIIQ CULTURAL HERITAGE. THE DANCERS' TRADITIONAL DRESS, LIKE THIS "SNOW-FALLING" PARKA, WAS BASED IN PART ON RESEARCH DONE BY THE SMITHSONIAN'S NATIONAL MUSEUM OF NATURAL HISTORY FOR ITS EXHIBITION *CROSSROADS OF CONTINENTS: CULTURES OF SIBERIA AND ALASKA.*

Alaskan dancers are the contemporary custodians of their customs and cultural sense of being (figs. 164, 165). The use of the word "traditional" here refers to recognized practices that have come from previous generations, that fit in the cultural framework, and that are not regarded as "modern" or "contemporary"— terms that indicate a large degree of change or a significantly different approach from the cultural expressions of previous generations.

E arly Western contact in the eighteenth and nineteenth centuries was documented by the crews of whaling vessels, Russian explorers, and Canadian fur trappers through ships' logs and correspondence. By the nineteenth century, Western exchange, missionization, and exploitation of natural resources increased — prompted in part by the constant presence of Christian missionaries and various governmental and military officials. In 1741 Vitus Bering, a Danish explorer, "claimed" Alaska for Russia, which in 1867 "sold" it to the United States. In 1959, Alaska became the forty-ninth state of the United States. Today, although English is commonly spoken and people live in Western-style homes, many of the traditional languages are still used and subsistence hunting is more the rule than the exception in most native villages.

On the superficial level, music and dance seem unaffected by many of these forces; on closer examination, however, traditional music and dance performance (which had been suppressed by the U.S. Government in all areas of Alaska) has been on the increase for the last fifteen years. Many young people often perform with their village dance groups, and there are increasing numbers of events, such as regional dance festivals and gatherings, that feature traditional music and dance (fig. 166).

165 A KODIAK ALUTIIQ
DANCER, WEARING A
KONIAG SPRUCE-ROOT
HAT, PERFORMS THE
SHOO-NAH-ME SONG:
"WE THE PEOPLE OF
KODIAK ARE SINGING/
DANCING JUST LIKE
OUR ANCESTORS
HUNDREDS
OF YEARS AGO." 1991

166 AT THE ALASKA STATE
FAIR IN PALMER, THE
KODIAK ALUTIIQ DANCERS
RE-CREATE TRADITIONAL
SONGS AND DANCES.
SINGING *AH-LAH-HAY*, THE
DANCER AT THE RIGHT
"SWEEPS THE CLOUDS
AWAY." ABOVE, A DANCER
USES A "WHISTLING MASK"
FOR HIS COURTING SONG
OO-NU-GU: "TONIGHT,
TONIGHT, I WILL COME,
BRING A LITTLE TEA WITH
ME. WHEN DOGGIE, DOGGIE
BARKS AT ME, DON'T THINK
I'M A BOOGIE MAN."

DANCE RATTLES OF THE NORTHWEST COAST

On the Northwest Coast of North America, dances, songs, and ceremonies are accompanied by an extra-ordinary array of regalia, including a wide variety of dance rattles. Made of indigenous materials such as wood, horn, and shell, rattles display sublime artistic creativity as well as great variation in form. Rattles are generally of two kinds, strung and vessel. The first, made from clusters of small objects arranged loosely on a circular frame or in rows on a staff, clatters softly when shaken. The second, made from a hollow container (often fashioned in two halves) and fitted or carved with a handle, is partially filled with pebbles, shells, seeds, or other small objects. The dancer holds the rattle in his or her extended hand, shaking it at appropriate times.

Some rattles were used by native doctors (fig. 167). These included rattles made in a round or globular shape and those in the form of a crane or an oystercatcher, a long-beaked shore bird. Other bird rattles depicting grouse, kingfisher, hawk, and, most commonly, the raven were, and are, used in dances on social and ceremonial occasions, particularly the important gift-giving feast known in English as the potlatch.

Raven rattles, a distinctive Northwest Coast art form, were found throughout the coast at the time of European contact (fig. 168). They are said to have been created originally by Nishga carvers of the Nass River area and traded from Alaska to as far south as Vancouver Island. Known everywhere as "Chiefs' rattles," they were part of the ceremonial regalia used by people of high rank at potlatches and other important occasions. Tlingit doctors sometimes used Raven rattles in addition to other kinds.

Although no two Raven rattles are exactly alike, the general style makes them instantly recognizable. Raven carries on his back a human figure, often joined at the tongue with a frog or kingfisher (a bird that makes a rattling noise as it dives for fish). In Raven's beak is a small, red block, which is sometimes interpreted as a box containing daylight. On his belly is carved a face, which is sometimes described as that of a hawk, but is also seen as an ancient, powerful sea monster — a reference to the sea as a source of wealth and life.

Raven, or Yehl, is the great culture hero of the Northwest Coast, a Creator/Trickster who brought gifts to the people through his cleverness and ability to transform himself into many disguises. One tale tells how Raven changed himself into the baby grandchild of a great chief, who kept the world in darkness by hiding the sun and moon in wooden boxes. When the indulgent grandfather gave the boxes to the baby as toys, Raven seized the sun in his beak, flew out the smokehole of the house and let daylight burst upon the world. Raven dance rattles may depict this Light-bringer.

The figures on Raven's back remain an enigma, but they suggest themes and values still important today — the oneness of life, the possibility of transformation, the power of the spirit. Because of their beauty, and their mysterious complexity of form, Raven rattles are often exhibited in museums as art objects. But for the people who made and use them, they are something more — a view of a universe rich in poetry and hidden meaning; a symbol of tribal and clan history; a visible image of stories told by grandparents to the children down through the generations.

Mary Jane Lenz

There are five main cultural or ethnic groups in Alaska (fig. 169): Inupiat (formerly northern Eskimo), Yupik (formerly southern Eskimo), Alutiiq/Aleut (of Kodiak Island and the Aleutian chain), Athabascan Indians (of the interior and south-central areas of Alaska), and the Tlingit, Haida, and Tsimshian Indians of southeastern Alaska (the northernmost part of the Pacific Northwest Coast culture area).

There are vast differences, yet many similarities, among the Native Alaskan groups. It is important to understand that Alaska is an immense area, covering more than 440 million acres — one-fifth the size of the continental United States. The native people of Alaska have formed social, economic, and cultural systems that correspond to their particular areas of residence, creating a rainbow of societies, each uniquely adapted to its physical environment.

hange has been rapid for Native Alaskans and traditional cultures have had to adjust quickly. Many different policies and events have affected the state, including changes in international claims of ownership, religious influence, technological innovations, educational practices, and epidemics brought by non-natives (the latest being tuberculosis, which reached its peak in the 1950s). These have been imposed on Alaska's indigenous people and illustrate larger geopolitical pressures that have affected present-day Native Alaskans.[4]

In 1971, native leaders began working with the U.S. Government to attempt to settle aboriginal claims. During the late 1960s, because of the discovery of vast oil fields in the north slope region, the federal government pressured the state of Alaska over issues of land ownership and aboriginal claim. The Alaska Native Claims Settlement Act (ANCSA), passed by Congress in response to these pressures, stipulated that a certain amount of money and land was to be paid or deeded to the aboriginal peoples of Alaska.[5] Twelve corporations were formed and organized around geographic and ethnic regions to distribute the land and money. These regional corporations have had major impact on the overall political climate of Alaska and continue to fill vital roles in the lives of all Native Alaskans. The corporations are charged with survival, showing a profit, and developing and protecting the cultural, social, and economic integrity of their shareholders.

Interestingly enough, ANCSA, basically an experiment in social engineering, has had a far-reaching impact on cultural practices. The birth of the regional corporations and their sister non-profit organizations has spawned a strong network of support for many traditional music and dance events. ANCSA created a new political climate for Native Alaskans, now endowed with political independence and recognition of their rights, which has contributed to a greater cultural vitality. Many of the corporations have offered financial support and encouragement for traditional performing groups, resulting in changes in performance context, sponsorship, and support. The non-profit arms of many of the corporations are actively involved in cultural projects or programs. By the late 1970s and early 1980s, ANCSA was a new source of sponsorship for many performing groups.

The following examples show how traditional music and dance performance has been remodeled in order to survive and remain a viable part of contemporary life. Each illustrates activity occurring in public performance.[6]

T he Tlingit, Haida, and Tsimshian people of southeastern Alaska gather every two years to celebrate their cultures and traditions through dance performance. In "Celebration 1992," forty different dance groups, with more than one thousand dancers, performed (figs. 170, 171). The four-day event is sponsored by Sealaska Heritage Foundation, the non-profit arm of Sealaska Corporation, one of the native corporations formed in 1971 as a result of the ANCSA. Sealaska Heritage Foundation hosted the first celebration in 1982. In the early 1980s, David Katzeek, president and CEO of Sealaska Heritage Foundation and one of the traditional leaders of the Thunderbird-Eagle clan, listened to his elders' admonitions on the importance of preserving traditional cultural expressions. The goal, thereupon, of the first Celebration was to perpetuate the culture and language of the Tlingit, Haida, and Tsimshian people by sharing the knowledge and

meaning of clan songs, ceremonial regalia, and dances (fig. 172). In 1992, at the fifth Celebration, Katzeek stated, "Our elders have again provided leadership to our people as we face new challenges. They have led us in the struggle to preserve and renew those cultural values which have been, and are still used today, the real treasures of our people."[7] David Katzeek is also a dancer and singer who actively performs with his Thunderbird family, a clan of the Eagle tribe, originally from the community of Klukwan.

171 TLINGIT DRUMMERS DURING THE GRAND FINALE OF CELEBRATION 92, JUNEAU, ALASKA

170 TLINGIT DANCERS IN REGALIA AT CELEBRATION 92, JUNEAU, ALASKA

172 IN THE PAST, BOX DRUMS WERE USED PRIMARILY IN RELIGIOUS OR SPIRITUALLY ORIENTED ACTIVITIES. DUE TO CHRISTIAN PRESSURES, THESE TYPES OF EVENTS HAVE BEEN SUPPRESSED AND THE DRUM IS RARELY USED TODAY. THIS LATE 19TH-CENTURY WOODEN DRUM IS PAINTED WITH AN OWL CREST DESIGN; THE EYES ARE INLAID WITH HALIOTIS SHELLS. TLINGIT. ALASKA. NATIONAL MUSEUM OF THE AMERICAN INDIAN, SMITHSONIAN INSTITUTION, NO. 19.9099

It is important to note the context of the Celebration series, which does not have a connection to historic practices. As a modern event that enables clans to gather and sing traditional songs, wear regalia, and perform time-honored dances, it is a new vehicle for preservation. Some of the groups are traditional clans, others are combined clans from specific villages, and still others are related family members (fig. 173). The event reflects innovations that incorporate and reflect the modern world, while retaining traditional practices. The dance and musical styles emphasize the regalia worn by the performers (fig. 174). These are emblazoned with the clan crest of the performing group (fig. 175). When the performers complete a dance, they turn their backs to the audience so that they can properly display their crest emblem, which appears on the backs of their woven or button robes (figs. 176, 177). Some songs/dances are enactments of clan histories or events and some are theatrical.

The event does not take the place of traditional activities, but rather adds a new dimension to them. This is a region-wide gathering that reaches out to many individuals, especially those of younger generations, and involves them, thus providing support for a continuity of cultural knowledge and pride. Sealaska Heritage Foundation represents the latest development in a patronage system — a modern post-ANCSA organization taking responsibility for encouraging cultural activities.

173 GEORGE RAMOS, LEADER OF THE MT. ST. ELIAS DANCERS, A MULTIGENERATIONAL DANCE GROUP FROM THE TLINGIT VILLAGE OF YAKUTAT, PERFORMS AT CELEBRATION 90, JUNEAU, ALASKA.

175 THERE ARE TWO
MAIN MOIETIES IN
TLINGIT SOCIETY, THE
RAVEN AND THE EAGLE,
WITH NUMEROUS CLANS
UNDER EACH. DANCER
PAUL MARK'S MOOSE-
HIDE TUNIC IS BEADED
WITH A RAVEN AND A
SOCKEYE SALMON
CREST. CELEBRATION 90,
JUNEAU, ALASKA

174 A TLINGIT DANCER
AT CELEBRATION 90
IN JUNEAU, ALASKA. THE
CEREMONIAL HEADPIECE
IS A *SHAKEEUT*, MADE
OF A CARVED FRONTLET
WITH SEA-LION
WHISKERS AND ERMINE.

176 WEARING A
BUTTON ROBE, A
TLINGIT WOMAN,
RACHEL JACKSON,
FROM HAINES
PERFORMS WITH THE
GEISAN DANCERS AT
CELEBRATION 90.

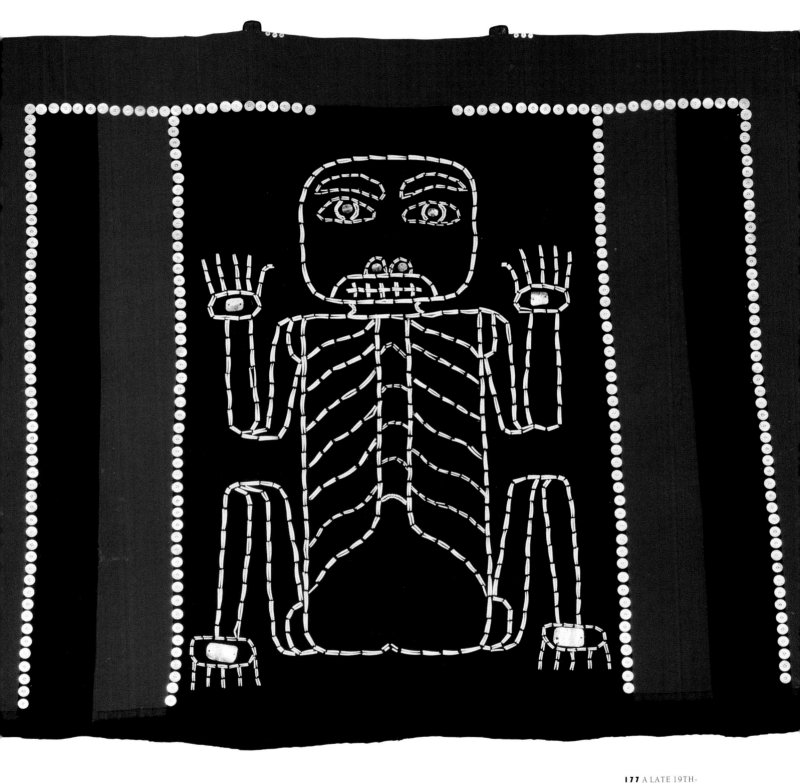

177 A LATE 19TH-
CENTURY BUTTON
BLANKET, WITH
BROWN BEAR CREST.
HAIDA. PRINCE OF
WALES ISLAND,
ALASKA. NATIONAL
MUSEUM OF THE
AMERICAN INDIAN,
SMITHSONIAN
INSTITUTION,
NO. 16.2769

178 CHARLES TIULANA OF THE KING ISLAND INUPIAT GROUP PERFORMING THE MEDICINE MAN DANCE, 1991

179 THE KING ISLAND INUPIAT DANCERS PERFORMING THE WOLF DANCE AT ALASKA FEDERATION OF NATIVES/QUYANA NIGHT, ANCHORAGE, 1991. THE YOUNGER GENERATION DANCES, WHILE THE ELDERS FACE THEM DRUMMING.

180 LEAD DRUMMER EARL MAYAC OF THE KING ISLAND INUPIAT DANCERS PLAYS A SUSPENDED BOX DRUM FOR THE WOLF DANCE. ALASKA FEDERATION OF NATIVES/ QUYANA NIGHT, ANCHORAGE, 1991

The Inupiat people of King Island, Alaska, no longer live on their home island. They were forced off their small island home in the late 1960s by governmental mandate. The almost five hundred residents moved to other cities in Alaska — mainly Nome, Fairbanks, and Anchorage. Paul Tiulana, recognized elder and leader of the Anchorage King Island people, has kept his community together by highlighting the importance of cultural knowledge. The King Island Inupiat group has performed the traditional songs and dances of their home for many years (fig. 178). They have performed at the Smithsonian in Washington, D.C., at the 1990 Los Angeles Festival, throughout the United States, and all over Alaska. In doing so, they have stayed together. It is a profound expression of identity that these people have retained their cultural integrity, despite the loss of homeland.

One of the more complex performance pieces in the King Island repertoire is the Wolf Dance (figs. 179, 180). Because of production size, sets, complex choreography, and elaborate regalia, it is rarely performed. In its entirety, this beautiful and intricate piece can last days. The Wolf Dance deserves to be regarded as the cross-cultural equal of Wagner's *Ring* cycle or the *Mahabharata*.

The Wolf Dance, nearly lost and not performed since the 1930s, was reconstructed in 1982 and performed at the Nome Elders' conference. The community house (*karigi*) was traditionally the place for music and dance performance. Even by 1938, however, the *karigi* was supplanted by the church basement (fig. 181). With all

181 BOTH OF THESE DANCES WERE PERFORMED IN THE BASEMENT OF THE KING ISLAND CHURCH, 1938. ON THE LEFT IS THE WOLF DANCE, ON THE RIGHT THE HALF-MASKED DANCE. HUBBARD COLLECTION, SANTA CLARA UNIVERSITY ARCHIVES

the regalia and hunting implements hung on the wall, the basement adequately served the purpose.[8] Today, most performances throughout Alaska take place in the local village school gymnasium — the new community house.

The Wolf Dance — performed before an audience of more than two thousand at the 1991 Alaska Federation of Natives Convention in Anchorage — is another example of a modern adaptation. In spite of changes, the core of the event — the music and dance itself — is culturally intact. The King Island people illustrate highly adaptive strategies. The elders of King Island have ensured that succeeding generations, including those not even born on the island, will know their songs and dances and be actively involved in performance activities.[9] Paul Tiulana feels that his investment in teaching the younger generations the songs and dances of King Island is his most important legacy: "Sometimes I feel discouraged that I have not done all that I should have, but when I saw my grandchildren dance the Wolf Dance I knew.... This gives me hope that our people will continue."[10]

Typical Inupiat-style dancing/singing is usually fairly stationary. The important motions of the hands, arms, head, and legs define the Inupiat style. Women dance with their feet very close together and knees slightly bent; arm gestures and the use of hands are graceful and specifically choreographed to each particular song. The male dancers keep their feet more widely apart and bend their knees more than the women. The beat of the drum, along with a slight stomping action of the feet, emphasizes the rhythm of the dance. All dancers must wear gloves and proper dancing attire (fig. 182) — usually special boots made of caribou, wolf, and seal skin, and *kuspuqs*, a dresslike over-garment.

I n the southwestern part of Alaska, the Yupik people, with their high level of language retention, also have a rich and complex culture. Many active dance groups gather in village festivals or for major regional cultural activities. Hooper Bay, Alaska, a village located on the Bering Sea coast, is home to many Yupik people. Recently, the elders of Hooper Bay have worked in cooperation with the local village corporation, Sea Lion, Inc., to revive the masked dances and songs of the Bladder Feast.[11]

The Bladder Feast encompasses a series, or cycle, of songs that portrays the village's most recent year; the songs, dances, and masks change to reflect annual successes and failures. The ceremonial is a renewal, deeply tied to subsistence activities. Subject to suppression by Christian missionaries since the late 1920s, the Bladder Feast honors the spirits of the animals that have been hunted the previous year. The bladders are all saved, ritually treated, and returned to the sea during the climax of the feast, assuring the rebirth of the animal and renewal of the subsistence or hunting cycle.

Countless examples of the traditional art and utilitarian objects of Yupik culture, especially those associated with dance, are in distant museums and private collections. Many of the Hooper Bay people have not had firsthand exposure to the rich patrimony of their own material culture. Artists and carvers must often sell their masks to private collectors and museums in order to eke out a living. Sea Lion Corporation, responding to requests from the elders, has been commissioning local carvers, drum makers, and other artists to make masks and regalia for the traditional dance group. Sea Lion's goal is to retain these objects for the village of Hooper Bay, so that the young people can understand and appreciate their aesthetic and cultural legacy. Master carver George Smart has been working with the elders who remember the Bladder Feast, last performed in the late 1920s (fig. 183). This attempt to revive an important part of the Hooper Bay heritage reflects ANCSA's influence in the preservation and remodeling of traditional performing events.

182 THESE LATE 19TH-CENTURY DANCE MITTENS ARE ADORNED WITH PUFFIN BEAKS, WHICH RATTLE SOFTLY WITH EACH MOTION. INUPIAT ESKIMO. CAPE PRINCE OF WALES, ALASKA. NATIONAL MUSEUM OF THE AMERICAN INDIAN, SMITHSONIAN INSTITUTION, NO. 8.6758

183 THIS MASK
CARVED BY GEORGE
SMART (YUPIK,
B. 1953) OF
HOOPER BAY,
ALASKA, IS WORN
BY A DANCER IN
THE BLADDER
FEAST.

Yupik dancing/singing style contrasts in many ways with Inupiat styles. Yupik songs/dances are longer, often repeated three or four times, whereas Inupiat ones are usually only several minutes in length and are rarely repeated more than twice. Yupik men and women use special dance fans — the women's dance fans are made of the beard of caribou, while the men's are carved from wood and hooped in a circle (usually a double hoop), with feathers around the hoop. Women wear elaborate headdresses, made of the long guard hairs of the wolf, with beaded headbands. The men dance sitting down, facing the audience. The women dance behind the men, standing upright. The women have a more subtle or graceful style of moving than the men. The stylized movements of the head and neck are key elements in the Yupik dance style. There are songs/dances in which the men also stand. The drum is usually smaller than the Inupiat drum and dance fans are used instead of gloves to accentuate the arm movements (figs. 184, 185). Songs and dances last about five minutes.

The Nunamta Yupik Singers and Dancers in many ways contrast with their Yupik counterparts of Hooper Bay. The Nunamta group is a small yet successful performing group, led by Chuna McIntyre (fig. 186). Not affiliated directly with any ANCSA organization, the group consists of several performers, mostly from different villages in south-

western Alaska. Chuna and the other members (Vernon Chimelgalrea, Marie Mead, and Theresa John) are highly educated in both the Western sense (degrees from colleges and universities) and Yupik sense (they speak their native language and know their culture). The group often performs in Anchorage at the Anchorage Museum of History and Art, primarily for visiting tourists. They have also performed in the Washington, D.C., area and in other parts of the United States and the former Soviet Union. They have specialized in making their

performances educational for the audience — yet the repertoire is strictly Yupik. The group came together when its members were students in the late 1970s at the University of Alaska in Fairbanks. Performing together to ease their homesickness, they ultimately became one of the most professional of Alaska's touring native groups.

T he Inupiat people of the northern regions have revived the Kivguq, or Messenger Feast. The Athabascan people of the interior involve themselves in traditional village exchanges. Many Athabascan people continue to practice important religious events, such as potlatches, that feature music. One of the largest statewide gatherings is the World Eskimo Indian Olympics (WEIO), held every July in Fairbanks. After the daytime Native Olympic events, different dance groups perform late into the night. There are competitions among the dance groups that generate a high degree of energy and excitement.

Music and dance are visible symbols of identification. They form a complex that incorporates several dynamic elements: the human body in motion, ritual significance of song/choreography/regalia, and the reinforcement of social relationships and sharing of values on a community level. Although there was a time when many of these cultural practices were beginning to fade out, and in some areas were no longer practiced, through creative adaptation and a strong underlying cultural fabric, music and dance have been renewed to accommodate the dynamics of the modern Native Alaskan world.

The identity of a cultural group is in essence acted out in music/dance performances, and because the dance/music complex is a physical and aural phenomenon, it can embody traditional expressions of self. The survival of music and dance is dependent upon the flexibility of groups to adapt to changes while keeping cultural integrity intact; the ability to remodel music and dance events has insured a place for these traditional practices in the modern world.

Native Alaskans, like all indigenous people of the world, have faced, and continue to face, tremendous challenges. The increasing demands of the Western world have had a great impact; changes have occurred and tragedies have been experienced, yet the spirit of tradition lives on.

1   Music and dance are considered synonymous — similar to many West African societies in which there is only one word to convey the complex of music/dance.

2   There are twenty different languages spoken in Alaska — eleven Athabascan languages, Sugpiaq, Aleut, Central Yupik, Siberian Yupik, Inupiaq, Tsimshian, Haida, Tlingit (distantly related to one of the Athabascan languages), and Eyak (now an extinct language).

3   Duane Champagne, *American Indian Societies: Strategies and Conditions of Political and Cultural Survival* (Cambridge, Mass.: Cultural Survival, 1989), p. 5.

4   In the 1990 U.S. Census, Alaska's population was reported at 493,000, of which Native Alaskans number almost 90,000.

5   Twelve regions were formed (later a thirteenth region was added). The twelve corporations received ten percent of the entire land mass of Alaska and 900 million dollars.

6   There are other on-going ceremonial activities occurring, but these are somewhat private and exclusive and will not be covered in this article.

7   David Katzeek, "Introduction," *Celebration of Tlingit, Haida, and Tsimshian Culture* (Juneau: Sealaska Heritage Foundation, 1992), p. 4.

8   Father Hubbard, a Jesuit priest, lived on King Island and documented many events during his time there. His entire collection of manuscripts is at Santa Clara University.

9   According to Paul Tiulana, many of the young people who performed in the 1991 Wolf Dance learned the choreography and songs by studying the videotape of the 1982 performance — an interesting example of how a modern technology has aided a geographically fragmented group in retaining a vital cultural expression. Interview with author, Anchorage, Alaska, 8 May 1992.

10 Ibid.

11 Sea Lion, Inc., was formed under ANCSA.

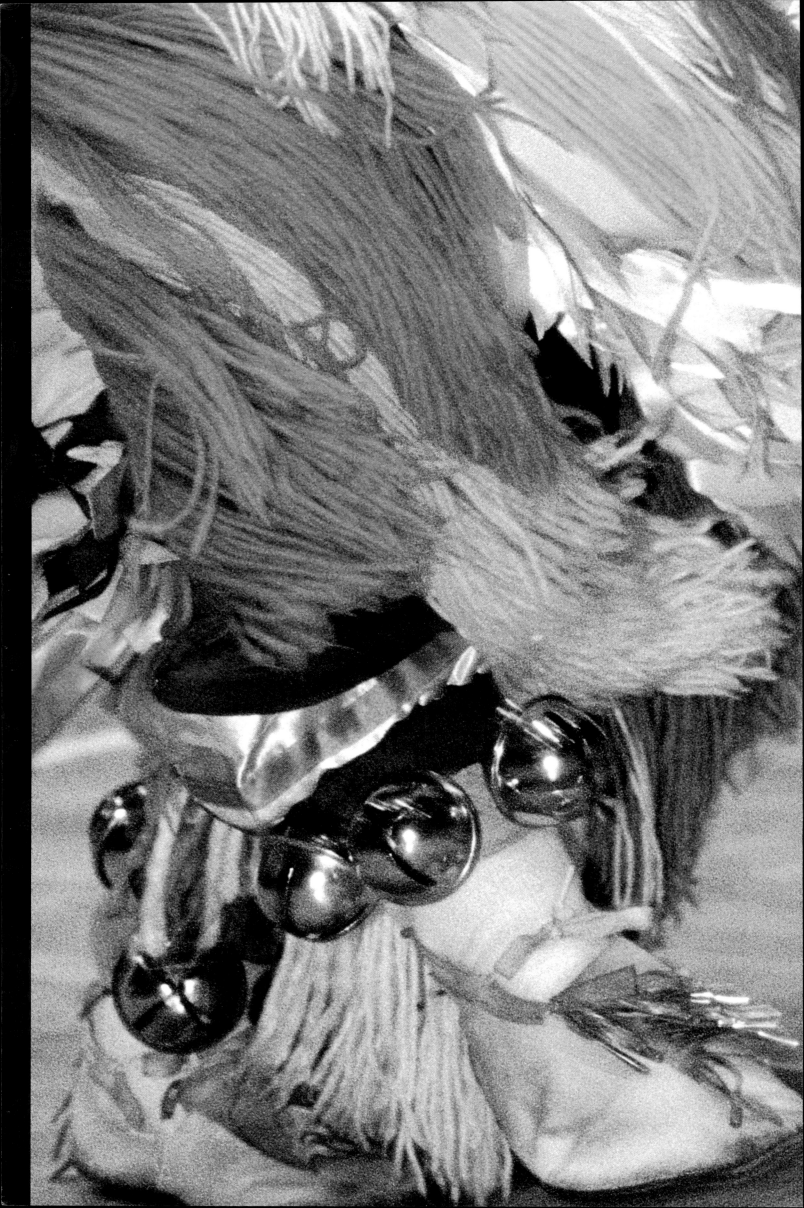

MODERN NATIVE DANCE: BEYOND TRIBE AND TRADITION

ROSALIE M. JONES

T he history of Native Americans is one of a people steeped in lessons of survival handed down through generations. While the achievement of survival can be manifest in a people's material culture, it is in their songs, dances, and oratories that the testament of their enduring spirit is truly found.

The song and dance traditions of the several hundred tribes and nations in the United States alone constitute a monumental tribute to the communal and individual strength and continuity of native cultures. Native American peoples have a tradition of preserving tradition. At the same time, viable, expanding cultures change, with usable concepts and materials retained and unwanted or unworkable elements discarded.

Interest in Native American tribal dances has been ongoing from the first moment the Europeans glimpsed what many called "the savage and primitive beauty" of the first Americans. The early exponents of modern dance in America were searching for a return to "basic" dance, to natural and "authentic" movement. Where better to turn than to the dances of the American Indian?

Ted Shawn, a pioneer of American modern dance, "interpreted" Native American dances largely on the basis of spectator observations and published photographs of the day. Shawn choreographed nearly two hundred dances during his career, including "Invocation to the Thunderbird" (1921), "Hopi Eagle Dance" (1934), "Ponca Indian Dance" (1934), and "Osage-Pawnee Dance of Greeting" (1930; fig. 187). The first three

This essay is in memory of Juan Valenzuela—dancer, educator, friend.

of these were performed on a regular basis on the "Ted Shawn and His Men Dancers" concert program, which toured nationally from 1933 to 1940. During those seven years, the Shawn dancers introduced American audiences to "American themes" — i.e., the American Indian ("aboriginal"), the American pioneer, the Spanish conquistador, the American Negro, and the American folk dancer, as well as characterizations of American farmers and laborers. A 1936 review paints a vivid image of the public level of understanding of these dances: "The [primitive] dances were marked by perfection of synchronization in rhythm that was at times little short of amazing, and served to reveal the perfection of the training, for these rhythms follow no set form. . . .   Mr. Shawn in a Hopi Indian eagle dance was a poem of grace."[1] Though perhaps not authentic Native American dance, Shawn's work offered an artist's interpretation of Indian dance. To Shawn, vigorous male dancing in America was the dance of the American Indian. The American public to whom he introduced it saw an indigenous dance form that had become not extinct, but invisible in America of the 1930s.

Other modern dancers have been inspired by the nonballetic naturalness and contained energy of tribal dancing. Martha Graham gave us a choreographer's insight into the inner nature of native dancing when she observed:

> America's great gift to the arts is rhythm: rich, full, unabashed, virile. Our two forms of indigenous
> dance, the Negro and the Indian, are as dramatically contrasted rhythmically as the land in which they
> root. The Negro dance is a dance toward freedom, a dance to forgetfulness. . . . The Indian dance,
> however, is not for freedom, or forgetfulness, or escape, but for awareness of life, complete relationship
> with that world in which he finds himself: it is a dance for power, a rhythm of integration.[2]

On the other end of the spectrum, some native dancers have chosen to perform in a Western idiom. Two of America's preeminent ballerinas, for example, are the sisters Maria and Marjorie Tallchief (figs. 188, 189). Both of Osage descent, they were trained by Bronislava Nijinska and went on to become remarkable technicians as well as noted interpreters of certain classical roles. Marjorie danced briefly with the American company Ballet Theatre and went on to make her mark with the Grand Ballet du Marquis de Cuevas (formerly the Nouveau Ballet de Monte Carlo) from 1947 to 1956; from then until 1962, she was the premiere *danseuse étiole* — the star — of the Paris Opera Ballet. Marjorie Tallchief was a skilled and dramatic interpreter of the ballets of her husband, George Skibine. Maria Tallchief, who danced with the Ballet Russe de Monte Carlo from 1942 to 1947, became a leading ballerina with New York City Ballet, dancing many roles under her choreographer-husband, George Balanchine. In 1965, she received the Capezio Dance Award, the citation of which reads:

> To Maria Tallchief. Her artistry, which encompasses superb technical discipline, command of style, and
> arresting individuality, is admired, respected, and applauded around the world. Thus, as an American
> ballerina, she has brought luster to American ballet itself, contributing immeasurably in placing it on an
> equal esthetic footing with the ballet standards of those European cultures which first nurtured the art
> of ballet.[3]

Both balletic and modern companies have utilized Native American subject matter as the basis of their choreography. While no ballets on a recognized professional level have been choreographed by a Native American with tribal affiliations, many performing companies are now availing themselves of Native American consultants. In taking this step in the direction of authenticity, they are also furthering the renewal of Native American dance traditions.

187 TED SHAWN IN "OSAGE-PAWNEE DANCE OF GREETING," 1930. THE NEW YORK PUBLIC LIBRARY

188 MARIA TALLCHIEF IN "THE FIREBIRD," CHOREOGRAPHED BY GEORGE BALANCHINE, 1949. THE NEW YORK PUBLIC LIBRARY

189 MARJORIE TALLCHIEF. THE NEW YORK PUBLIC LIBRARY

The production that has received the most public attention for its Native American element is "A Song for Dead Warriors" (1979), produced by the San Francisco Ballet (fig. 190). Choreographer Michael Smuin derived the scenario of the ballet from his personal experience growing up in Montana's Indian Country and from his perception of the occupation of Alcatraz by Native Americans from 1969 to 1971. The dance becomes a vehicle through which a "modern" Indian story is told, and a number of highly successful choreographic and theatrical effects are used to intensify the dramaturgy. Of particular interest is the performance of a Plains-style men's Fancy Dance toward the closing moments of the ballet. While the presentation of this "authentic" dance is dramatically appropriate, native people could perceive that these ballet-trained dancers do not capture the subtle and refined movements of seasoned Indian powwow dancers.

A major step forward in the utilization of Native American creative and performing artists was the development of "Maid of the Mist" (1990), a ballet choreographed by Raoul Trujillo for the Repertory Dance Theatre of Utah (fig. 191). Dr. Louis Ballard, an internationally known composer of Cherokee/Quapaw descent, wrote the musical score; and Bruce King, an Oneida painter, writer, actor, and director, wrote the story for the ballet. Consulting on the project was Elwood Green, executive director of the Native American Center of the Living Arts, in Niagara Falls, New York. This ambitious and noteworthy project was conceived through Buffalo State College, in collaboration with the Repertory Dance Theatre of Utah during the summer of 1991. During work on the project, Buffalo State offered a workshop course for college students, a teacher-training institute, and an exhibition at the Burchfield Art Center, all coordinated to the study and promotion of "Maid of the Mist."[4]

Because of the project's educational nature, the production was able to circumvent the commercial considerations that often prevent freshness of purpose within the theatrical marketplace. "Maid of the Mist" represents a significant step in recognizing that there are qualified, creative Native American musicians, writers, and choreographers available to work not only with each other, but with the best of America's dance and theater companies.

Less successful was the 1992 offering by the Joffrey Ballet in San Francisco. Among eight new works premiered was Peter Pucci's "Moon of the Falling Leaves." The *Los Angeles Times* review sketches an unfortunate picture:

> The ballet itself resembled nothing so much as a '90s male sensitivity training session: four guys wearing red paint on their faces and buckskin fringe on their pants, grimly working through exercises designed to promote trust, group identity and bonding.... Pucci substituted endless fist-clenching, arm-pumping, ritualized combat and other joyless celebrations of manhood.[5]

It should be noted that the recorded score was composed by Brent Michael Davids, who is Mohican; the music and text were based on Mohican oral tradition. Perhaps a future, more "native inspired" choreographic rendering of this "richly textured" music (as the *Times* reviewer called it) will prove more successful and aesthetically satisfying.

The high-water mark of Native American tribal dancing performed on stage must be credited to a company formed in 1987, the American Indian Dance Theatre. The brainchild of Barbara Schwei, a New York–based producer, and Hanay Geiogamah (Kiowa), a theater director and writer based at the University of California at Los Angeles, the company has assembled the cream of the crop of native dancers nationwide. Although the troupe could easily be thought of as a "glorified powwow," it does combine staged — and often extremely abridged — versions of traditional powwow dance forms with a rotating selection of tribal dances not regularly seen on the powwow circuit. These include the Zuñi Buffalo Dance, the Eagle Dance, and the

190 EVELYN CISNEROS AND
ANTONIO LOPEZ IN MICHAEL
SMUIN'S "A SONG FOR DEAD
WARRIORS," PERFORMED BY
THE SAN FRANCISCO BALLET
COMPANY

191 RAOUL TRUJILLO'S
"MAID OF THE MIST,"
PERFORMED BY THE
REPERTORY DANCE
THEATRE OF UTAH.
BUFFALO STATE
COLLEGE

Apache Crown Dance (fig. 192). The highlight of the repertoire is a spectacular triple-speed Hoop Dance (originated by Eddie Swimmer, Cherokee) that culminates in the weaving and holding aloft of a globe, or "earth" sphere, fashioned with twenty or so hoops.

Hanay Geiogamah made his mark in American theater when he created the Native American Theatre Ensemble (NATE) in the early 1970s. NATE was the first truly Indian theater company in America to tour on a national and international scope. New plays and theater dances were created and performed by native people, which meant that not only were young Native Americans being given a place to train and work in the theater profession, but also that the non-native public could experience a small, but authentic aspect of Indian life in America.

192 THE EAGLE DANCE PERFORMED BY THE AMERICAN INDIAN DANCE THEATRE

The American Indian Dance Theatre represents an overdue recognition of the true national dance of America: Native American tribal dance (figs. 193, 194). It is this kind of company that should have reached the American, as well as a world audience, much earlier in this century. Almost every other country worldwide has supported the creation and continuing development of a national dance company: among them the Moiseyev Folk Dance Ensemble of the former Soviet Union, the Philippine National Dance Company, and the Ballet Folklorico de Mexico. Not so in the United States. Only now is the American public being presented with its own true dance heritage, and it is being received as it should be: with thunderous applause and standing ovations.

If the American Indian Dance Theatre represents an artistic pinnacle of so-called traditional tribal dance, then what of the new, experimental native "modern dance" expressions that go beyond the strictly tribal and traditional?

In order to understand the comparatively small world of the modern native dancer, one must understand the societal and cultural context in which the contemporary Native American lives and works. First of all, the

193 IN RECENT YEARS, NATIVE AMERICAN TRIBAL DANCE HAS INCREASED DRAMATICALLY IN POPULARITY, AS EVIDENCED BY THE LARGE NUMBER OF POWWOWS HELD THROUGHOUT NORTH AMERICA EACH WEEKEND. THE HIGH REGARD THAT NATIVE PEOPLE HAVE FOR DANCE IS SEEN IN THE ARTISTRY OF DANCERS' CLOTHING. KEEPERS OF THE WESTERN DOOR POWWOW, ST. BONAVENTURE UNIVERSITY, NEW YORK, JULY 1992

194 ONE OF THE FOUNDATIONS OF NATIVE AMERICAN CULTURAL CONTINUITY IS COMMUNITY-BASED EVENTS AND CEREMONIES, SUCH AS THIS TRIBAL DANCE CELEBRATION IN OKLAHOMA, JULY 1992.

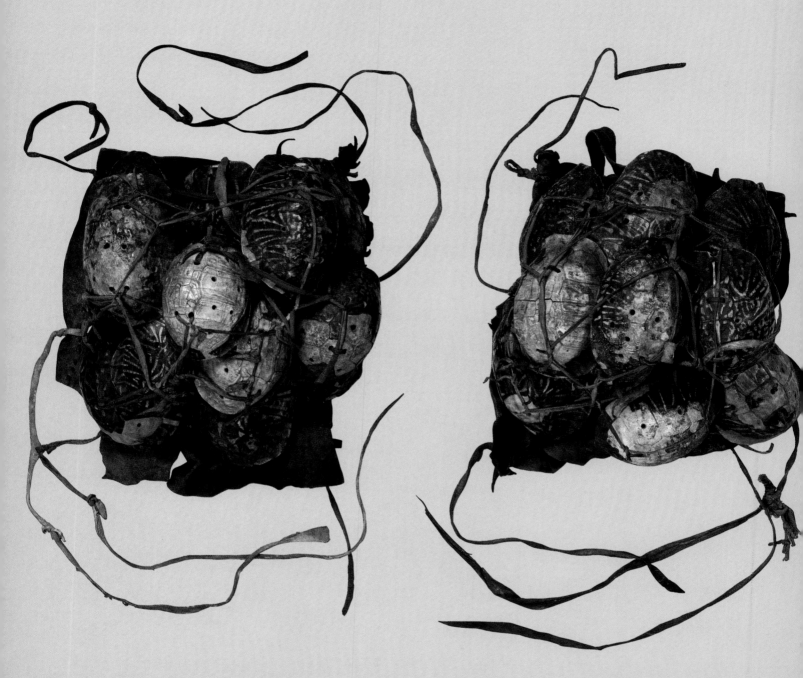

195 PAIR OF TURTLE-SHELL
DANCE LEGGINGS, SEMINOLE
(FLORIDA). NATIONAL
MUSEUM OF THE AMERICAN
INDIAN, SMITHSONIAN
INSTITUTION, NO. 1.8239

CHEROKEE STOMP DANCE: LAUGHTER RISES UP

Here's the scene. Night. A fire. A circle. Indians dancing around it. But something is wrong. Where are the beads? Only an occasional feather on a man's hat. Hats, jeans, overalls, cowboy boots. Calico dresses, regular clothes, even some from K-Mart. The music doesn't sound right either. No *dum-dum-dum-dum* drum. Just a high-pitched small drum. One man's voice calls out a line. The others respond in chorus. Sounds more African than Indian — that is, if you think all Indian music sounds like the tom-toms in the Hollywood movies. Even Sioux music doesn't sound like that, but this stuff doesn't for sure. A small drum, the water drum, small enough to fit in one hand, makes the beat for this music. Creek songs are fast and crazy; Cherokees like Creek singing. But if you don't watch it, the Creek men will charm you with that singing. Moving feet and rattles tied to the women's legs make the rest of the percussion for the call-and-response of the men's songs (fig. 195). The women make the rattles, called shackles, out of box turtles — sometimes condensed milk tins — sewn onto pieces of leather. Nowadays, they're just as likely to be sewn on the top parts of old cowboy boots. I told a friend who was making a pair that she must have had to mesmerize that cowboy so she could skin him out like that! The shackles are heavy and the people dance all night, but the shell-shakers keep the beat. Linda Hogan, a Chickasaw writer, told it this way in a poem called "Calling Myself Home":

> There were old women
> who lived in amber. Their dark hands
> laced the shells of turtles
> together, pebbles inside
> and they danced
> with rattles strong on their legs

The members of the Keetoowah Society keep the stompgrounds because they keep the Sacred Fire, including the Principal Fire and all those fires taken to other places in Oklahoma. The Keetoowahs help the Aniyunwiya remember. The people who belong to the stompgrounds sit under their seven brush arbors. Things begin when they are all represented, and everybody else rings around that huge circle. At particular celebrations, the people might play stickball and make a speech telling the history of the People and this stompground. After playing ball and sharing food, they dance. Some go back and forth to their arbors or trucks and cars and to lawn chairs and benches sitting with friends. People come from the outside rings and inside to join the counterclockwise movement of a particular dance. They dance all night. There are lots of stomp dances; some are about animals, others about friendship, even love. These are always happy dances. Sometimes the song tells a funny story and laughter rises up in the middle of the dance. You should hear what Rabbit sang when he taught the wolves a new dance. Iroquois people do dances like these too. Maybe a long time ago, they were the same dances. But for now, the Stomp Dance belongs to the Southeastern peoples. You will not see it at a powwow, scarcely even when just Indians are gathering with each other, because this music and dance haven't been widely shared with other people. Only those who know the songs, summer after summer, sing them. That's why you don't need to know too much. At the end, Cherokees might say *wado, wado*, thank you, thank you, because they have so appreciated the song and the dance. So that's what I'll say because it made me happy to tell about the Stomp Dance.

Rayna Green

196 BELINDA JAMES

178

native person is usually raised in an atmosphere of group solidarity, with the orientation primarily on communal interests rather than individual pursuits. Individual expression usually finds its outlet in the more solitary visual arts: pottery, drawing, painting, or sculpture. Second, exposure to contemporary forms of music, dance, or theater is limited on most reservations and is often unaffordable to Native Americans living in urban areas. Training in the performing arts is also limited for native peoples: few teachers of these disciplines devote themselves to Native American education and few Native Americans seek to study these forms on either a beginning or advanced level.

On the other hand, Native Americans have always been performing artists: dancers, singers, orators, musicians. Furthermore, we are witnessing in this country a reconnection of native people with their own cultures — and interestingly enough, at the same time, with the best of what is new and different outside the tribal context. It is this new sense of self, of being "native" as well as "modern," that bears the most creative potential for the Native American performing artist.

A number of Native American individuals and companies have chosen to work specifically within the idioms of contemporary American dance. All have, in varying degrees, a connection with tribal or traditional roots; all have a deliberate intent in being native; and all might well be considered in the vanguard of modern native dance. The author of this essay is of Blackfeet/Pembina Chippewa descent and counts herself among those dancer/choreographers who are in the forefront of this field, along with Juan Valenzuela (Yaqui), Belinda James (San Juan Pueblo), and Rene Highway (Canadian Cree).

Juan Valenzuela (1919–1986), to whom this article is dedicated, was of Spanish and Aztec-Yaqui parentage. During his early years, he studied primarily with Elizabeth Waters and Katherine Dunham, José Limón, and Martha Graham. Following several years of professional performance, Valenzuela returned to the West in the late 1960s to teach at the Institute of American Indian Arts in Santa Fe and with Virginia Tanner in Salt Lake City. In 1974, Valenzuela was selected as a movement specialist with the Artists in the Schools program of the National Endowment for the Arts. In this position, which he held until 1980, Valenzuela endeavored to promote interest in modern dance among Native Americans by conducting workshops and giving lectures on modern dance on reservations and in urban areas with significant Indian populations. Particularly during his later years, he was acutely aware of how few Native Americans were involved in modern dance and of the contribution they could make if more young people became active in the field. His last years were spent at Stanford University as a teaching specialist in dance and drama.

In a 1972 address to the Arizona National Conference of the Congress on Research in Dance (CORD), Valenzuela commented on the possibilities of modern dance for Native Americans:

> The Indian has been superior in the oral traditions of his culture.... In this tradition of our ancestors,
> I would like to see a new form of Indian Theater dance-drama given birth, to be created and performed
> in all aspects by our young people in the reservations.... [This] would add a new dimension to that life
> of education.[6]

An Indian woman working largely within the classical technique is Belinda James (fig. 196). James has been studying and performing in New York City since the early 1980s. This young Pueblo woman is ballet and Horton (modern) trained, and her choreographic credits include: "Stringling" (1984), "Chinook" (1985), and "Metamorphoses" (1985), the latter based on the San Juan Pueblo Deer Dance. James's fledgling company is called Divi Shadende, which means "they are dancing" in the San Juan dialect. She has described her work in the following way:

With my drive towards classical ballet, and a passion for contemporary art forms, I wish to present
choreography influenced by the mythology and history of the Native American. Utilizing concepts from
Horton technique, a modern dance method, but placing the dancer "en pointe," I am aspiring to add a
spark to the evolution of dance.[7]

A young modern dance performer who was beginning to have a significant impact on both the American and Canadian dance fields was Rene Highway (1954–1990; fig. 197). He studied at the Martha Graham and Alvin Ailey schools in New York, as well as at the Toronto Dance Theatre. Highway was a free-lance choreographer, as well as a guest teacher and dancer with the Toronto Dance Theatre, Denmark's Tukak Theatre, and the Native Canadian Centre of Toronto. With his brother Tomson Highway, a musician and playwright, Rene collaborated on a number of productions. Rene Highway created the role of Nanabush in his brother's play *The Rez Sisters* (1986), and was the choreographer for Tomson's *Dry Lips Oughta Move to Kapauskasing* (1989). Tomson's 1989 dance-drama "The Sage, The Dancer, and The Fool" was choreographed and performed by Rene. Tomson Highway wrote the music for one of Rene's most successful choreographies, "New Song, New Dance" (1987).[8]

Rene developed one of his most ambitious choreographies, however, as an independent artist. "There Is My People Sleeping" (1985) — a forty-five-minute, multimedia, quasi-autobiographical work — received excellent reviews and toured western Canada and Ontario. "Prism, Mirror, Lens," Highway's last piece, was choreographed in December 1989, ten months before his death of AIDS at age thirty-six. In this dance, a multimedia piece partially inspired by the work of science-fiction novelist Samuel Delany, Highway places his hero, who has undertaken a vision quest, not in the traditional setting of an isolated mountaintop, but in the mechanized desolation of a modern city.[9]

In his short lifetime, Rene Highway also choreographed, taught, and performed in the United States — from working with young Native Americans on the Navajo Reservation to presenting the Rene Highway Dancers at the Kennedy Center's "Night of the First Americans," thereby making Native American dance a national theatrical event.

His message to us can be gleaned from his statement at the premiere of "New Song, New Dance":

The theme is exploring Indian experience . . . and how growing up in a foreign environment affected all
our lives. . . . It's about assimilating. It shows that we are able to survive, and we have survived. . . .
Natives have already learned to express themselves in visual arts, through painting and sculpture. Now
they're starting to express themselves through the performing arts. . . . The message is to use what we've
learned and experienced and to come up with a way of expressing ourselves.[10]

A dancer, choreographer, and teacher, the author of this essay is known professionally as Daystar (fig. 198). I received a master's degree in dance from the University of Utah, and also studied with José Limón at the Juilliard School and with a master teacher, Barry Lynn, for the past twenty years. In 1980, I founded Daystar: Classical Dance-Drama of Indian America, to provide a vehicle for the promotion of Native American talent and to develop a troupe of dancers with whom I could create new choreographic work. Daystar is affiliated with the Institute of American Indian Arts, where I am also professor of dance.

The most recent production of Daystar is "Sacred Woman, Sacred Earth," a full-evening dance-drama that represents a culminating point in the company's work. The piece brings together stories from several tribal oral traditions by means of a narrator/storyteller and the use of both traditional and contemporary dance movement. The native stories featured during the course of the production range from an Iroquois creation legend ("The Woman Who Fell from the Sky") to the Cherokee story of the origin of corn ("The Corn Mother"), a Coyote "trickster" story, and the company's signature piece, "Sacred Woman, Sacred Earth."

197 RENE HIGHWAY
IN "NEW SONG,
NEW DANCE," 1987

198 ROSALIE JONES
AS SKY WOMAN IN
"THE WOMAN WHO FELL
FROM THE SKY,"
A PRODUCTION OF THE
DAYSTAR CONTEMPORARY
DANCE COMPANY

In the signature piece, the final section of the drama, the Lakota story of White Buffalo Calf Pipe Woman is simply told, using sign language, music, and narrative, without embellishment. The entering steps of the Buffalo Woman are the same as a woman's dance step in Northern Plains intertribal dancing. She enters from stage left and moves to the left in a circular pattern, as would be done in the traditional Women's Dance. The two warriors who see her move stage right and left around her, making use of the dramatic qualities of the stage. When "the Warrior with Bad Thoughts" is reduced to bones, that character emerges from a cloud of smoke, writhing in pain, his face now changed — using a mask — into the hideous skull of death (fig. 199). Dramatically speaking, this would normally conclude the story.

199 ROSALIE JONES AS WHITE BUFFALO CALF PIPE WOMAN IN "SACRED WOMAN, SACRED EARTH," A PRODUCTION OF DAYSTAR CONTEMPORARY DANCE COMPANY. TO HER LEFT IS ROSS POND AS "THE GOOD WARRIOR" MANY HORSES; TO HER RIGHT, NATHAN ROMERO AS "THE WARRIOR WITH BAD THOUGHTS."

In the Daystar rendering, however, the tale continues into the historical present. The Coyote storyteller puts on a white lab coat and safety helmet and goggles, then begins hustling the audience for "some loose change" in exchange for irradiated clothing from waste dumps in the New Mexico desert. A young Indian woman, a metaphor for Earth Mother, rises from the floor. The woman manipulates her shawl, which becomes a baby. A land surveyor enters, builds a fence (in mime) around her, and snatches the baby when it is momentarily unprotected. The mother grieves.

During the course of the mother's lament, the Buffalo Woman reappears as in a vision and silently watches. At the moment the woman falls into despair, the visionary Buffalo Woman, in traditional dress, re-enters the scene. The two then dance a duet that combines the ancient and historical. Much of the movement is built upon the psychological intensity of the characters — the falling, rolling, stretching, and collapsing movements of Earth Mother are contrasted and intermingled with the pulling and lifting movements of the Buffalo Woman. Both come into harmony with the synchronized movements of the Two-step — a Plains couple's dance normally done by a man-woman pair.

This climactic piece illustrates the premise that it is possible to build choreographic sequences by using both traditional and contemporary movement. It is also possible to imagine new dance forms in which traditional elements — posture, steps, and gesture — can be identified in terms of space, time, and energy, and subsequently synthesized into contemporary structures, in much the same way that the melody of a folk song can become the basis for a symphony.

Other names of contemporary native dancers are now coming to the fore: Michael Meyers (Blackfeet/Yokut), Ann Roberts Khalsa (Cherokee), Leilani Taliaferro (Cherokee), and Aurorah Allain (Choctaw). Some of these individuals are listed in the American Indian Registry of the Performing Arts (an organization in Los Angeles established to promote the advancement of American Indian performing artists). These artists will no doubt define the future of modern Native American dance.

The future of contemporary dance for Native Americans, however, will depend on many factors. Will the resources be available, both educational and artistic, to aid the development of emerging Native American performing artists? Will the audience, Indian and non-Indian alike, give these artists the appreciation and financial support they deserve by attending their performances? If the answer is yes on all counts, we will all reap the cultural and artistic benefits of contemporary native dance in the twenty-first century.

1   Christina L. Schlundt, *The Professional Appearance of Ted Shawn and His Men Dancers: A Chronology and an Index of Dances 1933–1940* (New York: New York Public Library, 1967), p. 41.
2   Quoted in Merle Armitage, *Martha Graham* (New York: Dance Horizons, 1968).
3   Anatole Chujoy and P. W. Manchester, *The Dance Encyclopedia* (New York: Simon and Schuster, 1967), p. 886.
4   Personal correspondence between the author and Steve Scott-Martin (director of the Performing Arts Center, Buffalo State College, Buffalo, N.Y.), May 1990.
5   "L.A. Loss of Joffrey Is S.F. Gain," *Los Angeles Times*, 14 July 1992. Entertainment section.
6   "New Dimensions in Dance Research, Anthropology and Dance — The American Indian," Cord Research Annual VI, p. 302.
7   Belinda James, curriculum vitae, June 1992. Lester Horton, modern dancer and choreographer who established his own school of dance in Los Angeles, created the first racially integrated modern-dance company in the U.S.
8   Rene Highway, curriculum vitae (courtesy of Tomson Highway), June 1992.
9   See the *Toronto Star* (Canada), 15 August 1985 and 1 December 1989.
10 Ibid., 18 March 1988.

SELECT BIBLIOGRAPHY, DISCOGRAPHY, AND VIDEOGRAPHY

The bibliography, discography, and videography that follow are intended as guides for further study on Native American dance, music, and culture. Notes following the individual articles in this book contain additional, specific references.

BIBLIOGRAPHY

ANTHOLOGIES, COLLECTIONS, AND REFERENCES

Collaer, Paul, ed. *Music of the Americas: An Illustrated Music Ethnology of the Eskimo and American Indian Peoples.* New York: Praeger Publishers, 1973.

Comstock, Tamara, ed. *New Dimensions in Dance Research, Anthropology and Dance—The American Indian,* CORD Research Annual VI. New York: CORD, 1974.

Geiogamah, Hanay. *New Native American Drama: Three Plays.* Norman: University of Oklahoma Press, 1980.

Heth, Charlotte, ed. *Sharing a Heritage: American Indian Arts.* Vol. 5, Contemporary American Indian Issues Series. Los Angeles: UCLA, American Indian Studies Center, 1984.

Huenemann, Lynn F. *Songs and Dances of Native America: A Resource Text for Teachers and Students* (book and tapes). Tsaile, Ariz.: Education House, 1978.

Izikowitz, Karl Gustav. *Musical and Other Sound Instruments of the South American Indians.* 1935. Reprint. Göteberg, Sweden: Elanders Boktryckeri Aktieb, 1970.

Kurath, Gertrude Prokosch. *Half a Century of Dance Research.* Flagstaff, Ariz.: Cross-Cultural Dance Resources, 1986.

Powers, William K. *War Dance: Plains Indian Musical Performance.* Tucson: University of Arizona Press, 1990.

Smyth, Willie, ed. *Songs of Indian Territory: Native American Music Traditions of Oklahoma* (books and tapes). Oklahoma City: Center of the American Indian, 1989.

Weatherford, Jack. *Indian Givers.* New York: Crown Publishers, 1988.

NORTH AMERICAN PLAINS

Blish, Helen H., ed. *A Pictographic History of the Oglala Sioux: Drawings by Amos Bad Heart Bull.* Lincoln: University of Nebraska Press, 1967.

Callahan, Alice A. *The Osage Ceremonial Dance I'n-Lon-Schka.* Norman: University of Oklahoma Press, 1990.

Grobsmith, Elizabeth S. *Lakota of Rosebud: A Contemporary Ethnography.* New York: Holt, Rinehart and Winston, 1981.

Horse Capture, George P. *Powwow.* Cody, Wyo.: Buffalo Bill Historical Center, 1989.

Huenemann, Lynn F. "Dakota/Lakota Music and Dance: An Introduction." In *The Arts of South Dakota.* Edited by R. McIntyre and R.L. Bell. Sioux Falls: Center for Western Studies, 1988.

Mails, Thomas E. *Dog Soldiers, Bear Men and Buffalo Women: A Study of the Societies and Cults of the Plains Indians.* Englewood Cliffs: Prentice-Hall, 1973.

——— *The Mystic Warriors of the Plains.* New York: Doubleday and Co., 1972.

Merriam, Alan P. *Ethnomusicology of the Flathead Indians.* Chicago: Aldine, 1967.

Nurge, Ethel, ed. *The Modern Sioux.* Lincoln: University of Nebraska Press, 1970.

Snow, John. *These Mountains Are Our Sacred Places: The Story of the Stoney People.* Toronto: Samuel Stevens, 1977.

Theisz, R.D., and Ben Black Bear, Sr. *Songs and Dances of the Lakota.* Rosebud, S. Dak.: Sinte Gleska College, 1976.

Vennum, Thomas. "The Ojibwa Dance Drum: Its History and Construction." Washington, D.C.: *Smithsonian Institution Folklife Studies,* no. 1 (1982).

SOUTHWESTERN UNITED STATES

Basso, Keith H. "The Gift of Changing Woman." Anthropological Papers no. 76. Bureau of American Ethnology Bulletin no. 196 (Washington, D.C., 1966): 113–73.

——— *The Cibecue Apache: Case Studies in Cultural Anthropology.* 1970. Reprint. Prospect Heights, Ill.: Waveland Press, 1986.

Frisbie, Charlotte J., ed. *New Perspectives on the Pueblos.* Albuquerque: University of New Mexico Press, 1972.

——— *Southwestern Indian Ritual Drama.* Albuquerque: University of New Mexico Press, 1980.

Goseyun, Anna Early. "Carla's Sunrise." *Native Peoples* 4, no. 2 (1991): 8-16.

Kurath, Gertrude P., with Antonio Garcia. *Music and Dance of the Tewa Pueblos.* Santa Fe: Museum of New Mexico, 1970.

Laski, Vera. *Seeking Life.* Memoirs of the American Folklore Society, no. 50 (1959).

Ortiz, Alfonso. *The Tewa World: Space, Time, Being and Becoming in a Pueblo Society.* Chicago: University of Chicago Press, 1969.

Ortiz, Alfonso, ed. *Handbook of North American Indians.* Vols. 9 and 10, "Southwest." Washington, D.C.: Smithsonian Institution, 1979, 1983.

Quintero, Nita. "Coming of Age the Apache Way." *National Geographic*. 157, no. 2 (1980): 262–71.

Roediger, Virginia. *Ceremonial Costumes of the Pueblo Indians*. Berkeley: University of California Press, 1961.

Sweet, Jill D. *Dances of the Tewa Pueblo Indians: Expressions of New Life*. Santa Fe: School of American Research, 1985.

EASTERN UNITED STATES AND CANADA

Barreiro, José, and Carol Cornelius. *Knowledge of the Elders*. Ithaca: Cornell University, Akwe:kon Press, 1991.

Cornelius, Carol. *The Six Nation Series*. Ithaca: Cornell University, Akwe:kon Press, 1990.

Hertzberg, Hazel W. *The Great Tree and the Longhouse*. New York: Macmillan Co., 1966.

Howard, James. "The Southeastern Ceremonial Complex and Its Interpretation." *Memoir: Missouri Archaeological Society* (December 1968).

Hudson, Charles. *The Southeastern Indians*. Knoxville: University of Tennessee Press, 1976.

Kurath, Gertrude P. *Dance and Song Rituals of the Six Nations Reserve, Ontario*. Ottawa: National Museum of Canada, *Bulletin* 220, 1968.

Speck, Frank G., Leonard Broom, and Will West Long. *Cherokee Dance and Drama*. 1951. Reprint. Norman: University of Oklahoma Press, 1983.

Trigger, Bruce, ed. *Handbook of North American Indians*. Vol. 15, "Northeast." Washington, D.C.: Smithsonian Institution, 1978.

NORTHWEST COAST AND ARCTIC (U.S. AND CANADA)

Damas, David, ed. *Handbook of North American Indians*. Vol. 5, "Arctic." Washington, D.C.: Smithsonian Institution, 1984.

Fane, Diana, Ira Jacknis, and Lise M. Breen. *Objects of Myth and Memory: American Indian Art at the Brooklyn Museum*. New York: The Brooklyn Museum, 1991.

Helm, June, ed. *Handbook of North American Indians*. Vol. 6, "Subarctic." Washington, D.C.: Smithsonian Institution, 1981.

Holm, Bill. *Spirit and Ancestor*. Seattle: University of Washington Press and Thomas Burke Memorial Washington State Museum, 1987.

Katzeek, David. "Introduction." In *Celebration of Tlingit, Haida, and Tsimshian Culture*. Juneau: Sealaska Heritage Foundation, 1992.

Langdon, Steven J. *The Native People of Alaska*. Anchorage: Greatland Graphics, 1987.

Marr, Helen Hubbard. *Voices of the Ancestors: Music in the Life of the Northwest Coast Indians*. Greenwich, Conn.: The Bruce Museum, 1986.

Tiulana, Paul. *A Place for Winter: Paul Tiulana's Story*. Anchorage: CIRI Foundation, 1988.

MEXICO AND SOUTH AMERICA

Altamirano, León, et al. *Trajes y danzas de México*. Mexico: Joaquín Porrúa, 1984.

Bouysse-Cassgne, Thérèse. *La identidad aymara*. La Paz, Bolivia: Hisbol, 1987.

Brandes, Stanley. *Power and Persuasion: Fiestas and Social Control in Rural Mexico*. Philadelphia: University of Pennsylvania Press, 1988.

Bricker, Victoria Reifler. *Ritual Humor in Highland Chiapas*. Austin: University of Texas Press, 1973.

Buechler, Hans C. *The Masked Media: Aymara Fiestas and Social Interaction in the Bolivian Highlands*. The Hague: Mouton Publishers, 1980.

Buechler, Hans C., and Judith-Maria Buechler. *The Bolivian Aymara*. New York: Holt, Rinehart and Winston, 1971.

Fonapas-Ini. *50 encuentros de música indígenas*. Mexico: Instituto Nacional Indigenista, 1980.

Guiteras Holmes, C. *Los peligros del alma: Visión del mundo de un Tzotzil*. Translated by Carlo Antonio Castro. Mexico: Fondo de Cultura Económica, 1986.

Jordá, A. Enrique. *Fiesta en el mundo aymara*. Cochabamba, Bolivia: Revista Yachay, 1, no. 2 (1984).

Monast, J. *Los indios aimaraes*. Buenos Aires: Cuadernos Latinoamericanos, 1972.

Morris, Walter F., Jr. *Mil años del tejido en Chiapas*. Chiapas, Mexico: Instituto de la Artesanía Chiapaneca, 1984.

Olivera B., Mercedes. *Catálogo nacional de danzas*. Vol. I. Mexico: Fonadan, 1974.

Paredes Candia, Antonio. *La Danza folklórica en Bolivia*. La Paz: Isla, 1966.

———— *Fiestas populares de Bolivia*. Vols. 1 and 2. La Paz: Isla, 1976.

Pérez Lópe, Enrique. *Chamula: Un pueblo indígena tzotzil*.

Chiapas, Mexico: Gobierno del Estado de Chiapas, 1990.

Ramos Smith, Maya. *La danza en México durante la época colonial*. Mexico: CNCA-Alianza Editorial Mexicana, 1990.

Ríos Morales, Manuel. *Los Zapotecos de la Sierra Norte de Oaxaca*. Mexico: in press, 1992.

Warman, Arturo. *La danza de moros y cristianos*. Mexico: Instituto Nacional de Antropología e Historia, 1972.

Wauchope, Robert, ed. *Handbook of Middle American Indians*. Austin: University of Texas Press, 1969.

DISCOGRAPHY

NORTH AMERICA

Apache Music of the American Indian. Library of Congress AFS L42.

Cloud Dance Songs of San Juan Pueblo. Indian House IH 1102.

Crow Celebration. Ten Great Drums at Crow Fair. Canyon 6089.

The Eskimos of Hudson Bay and Alaska. Folkways FE 4444.

Honor the Earth Powwow: Songs of the Great Lakes Indians. Rykodisc RCD 10199.

Indian Music of the Pacific Northwest Coast. Folkways FE 4523.

Iroquois Social Dance Songs. Iroqrafts Q.C. 727, 728, 729.

Love Songs of the Lakota. Indian House IH 4315.

Music from San Juan Pueblo, Featuring the Garcia Brothers. Tribal Music International.

Music of the Kutchin Indians of Alaska. Folkways FE 4253.

Oku Shareh: Turtle Dance Songs of San Juan Pueblo. New World Records NW 301 (80301).

Powwow Songs: Music of the Plains Indians. New World Records NW 301.

Pueblo Indian Songs from San Juan. Canyon Records 6065.

Seneca Social Dance Music. Folkways FE 4072.

Sioux Favorites. Canyon Records 6059.

Songs and Dances of the Eastern Indians from Medicine Spring and Allegany. New World Records NW 337 (80337).

Songs and Dances of the Flathead Indians. Ethnic Folkways Library LP P445.

Songs from the Blood Reserve. Kai-Spai Singers. Canyon Records 6133.

Songs of Earth, Water, Fire, and Sky: Music of the American Indian. New World Records NW 246 (80246).

Songs of the Arizona Apache. Canyon Records 705.

Songs of the Sioux. Library of Congress AFS L40.

Songs of the Sioux: Ironwood Singers Live at Rosebud Fair. Indian House IH 4321.

Songs of the White Mountain Apache. Canyon Records 6165.

Stomp Dance. Vols. 1–4. Indian House IH 3003, 3004, 3005, 3006.

MEXICO AND SOUTH AMERICA

Aliriña, Grupo Aymara. Flying Fish Records FF 70535.

Banda Mixe de Oaxaca. Mariano Escobedo, Mexico: Peerless Records 89/238.

Folk Music of Mexico. Library of Congress AFS L19.

Guelaguetza Oaxaqueña. Mariano Escobedo, Mexico: Peerless Records ADP-516-4.

Indian Music of Mexico. Folkways 4413.

Indian Music of Mexico. Folkways 8851 (collected by Laura Bolton).

Modern Maya: The Indian Music of Chiapas. Folkways 4379.

Música tradicional de Bolivia. Cochabamba, Bolivia: Lauro Records, BLRL 1464.

Sol del Ande. Cochabamba, Bolivia: Lauro Records, BLRL 1464.

VIDEORECORDINGS

A Box of Daylight. Juneau: Sealaska Heritage Foundation, 1990.

A Dancing People. Bethel, Alaska: KYUK, 1983.

American Indian Dance Theatre: Finding the Circle. Great Performances, Public Television. Available from Canyon Records.

Celebration '88. Juneau: Sealaska Heritage Foundation, 1989.

Eyes of the Spirit. Bethel, Alaska: KYUK, 1983.

Keet Shagoon. Juneau: Sealaska Heritage Foundation, 1989.

Old Dances, New Dancers. Bethel, Alaska: KYUK, 1984.

We of the River. Bethel, Alaska: KYUK, 1985.

C O N T R I B U T O R S

ARTHUR AMIOTTE (OGLALA LAKOTA), a prominent Native American artist, has shown his work in numerous solo and group exhibitions. An adjunct professor of native studies and art at Brandon University in Manitoba, Canada, Amiotte is also artist, writer, and consultant on Indian cultures of the Northern Plains for White Horse Creek, Ltd. in Custer, South Dakota. Amiotte, who holds a master's degree in interdisciplinary studies from the University of Montana, has won many awards for his work.

JAIME TORRES BURGUETE (TZOTZIL) is a Tzotzil ethnolinguist at the Department of Ethnic Cultures of the Chiapanec Institute of Culture in Chiapas, Mexico. He has taught courses in anthropology and social sciences and collaborated in the development of curriculum for bilingual and bicultural education in Chiapas. He has been actively involved in the organization of state and regional music and dance festivals. Burguete is co-author of the "Memoria," a documentary on the first Maya Zoque Festival, and editor of the journal *Nuestra Sabiduria* (Our Knowledge), written in eight native languages. Burguete conducted fieldwork research for the National Museum of the American Indian's dance program.

OLIVIA CADAVAL, folklore specialist and curator of the Smithsonian Center for Folklife Programs and Cultural Studies' Quincentenary Program, has conducted research and collaborated in public programming with the Washington, D.C. Latino, Caribbean, and Latin American communities for over a decade. She has curated several programs—including "Cultural Encounters in the Caribbean," "U.S. Virgin Islands," and "Land in Native American Cultures"—for the Festival of American Folklife Program. Cadaval, who received her doctorate in American Studies/Folklife from the George Washington University, has written for a number of publications, including *Urban Odyssey, Creative Ethnicity*, and the *Journal of Folklore Research.*

CÉCILE R. GANTEAUME, an assistant curator at the National Museum of the American Indian, is completing her M.A. in anthropology at New York University. Her main areas of interest include North American Indian ethnology, especially Apachean ethnology, and material culture studies. She recently directed a collections documentation project that involved consolidating and improving the documentation of the Apachean collections of the National Museum of the American Indian.

RAYNA GREEN, of European and Cherokee ancestry, is Director of the American Indian Program for the Smithsonian's National Museum of American History. Green earned her doctorate in folklore and American studies from Indiana University. Her publications include three books on Native American women—*Native American Women: A Contextual Bibliography*; *That's What She Said: Fiction and Poetry by Native American Women*; and *Women in American Indian Society*—and numerous scholarly essays. Widely known as a writer, researcher, and lecturer in several areas (including Native American studies, folklife, women's studies, and ethnoscience), Green has also won acclaim for her work in film, television, and museum exhibitions. Green's poetry and fiction have appeared in many literary publications as well.

CHARLOTTE HETH (CHEROKEE) is the Chairperson of the Department of Ethnomusicology and Systematic Musicology at the University of California, Los Angeles. Heth, former director of the American Indian Studies Center at UCLA, and of the American Indian Program at Cornell University, holds a doctorate in music from UCLA and is regarded as a leading specialist on American Indian music and dance. She has produced eight videotapes for a series called "Interviews with American Indian Musicians" and six record albums for the *Recorded Anthology of American Music* (New World Records). In addition, she has written extensively on Indian music and dance for a wide variety of scholarly publications, including the *American Indian Culture and Research Journal*, *Selected Reports in Ethnomusicology*, *Journal of Cherokee Studies* and the *Handbook of North American Indians*.

TOMÁS HUANCA LAURA (AYMARA), an anthropologist and professor at the University of La Paz, Bolivia, has conducted fieldwork and research for the National Museum of the American Indian's dance program and is one of the selectors for the museum's *Points of View* exhibition. He is a founding member of the Instituciones del Taller de Historia Oral Andina, THOA (Office of Oral Andean History) and Comunidad PACHA, where he has been director, dedicating his efforts to the investigation, strengthening, publishing, and reporting of Aymara cultural values. As an investigator, he is renowned in academic and grassroots organizations, and his publications include numerous articles on education and political-cultural problems. Currently he assists community organizations and Aymara institutions, and does research on ecological, environmental, and health problems from a native perspective.

LYNN HUENEMANN, Director of the Office of Indian Education for the Sioux City, Iowa, Community Schools, holds a B.F.A. in music education from the University of South Dakota and an M.A. in cultural anthropology from Indiana University. Former coordinator of American Indian Studies at Dakota Wesleyan University, and a faculty member of the Navajo Community College and the Oglala Lakota College, Huenemann has written and lectured widely on Native American music and dance. He was a contributor to *The Arts of South Dakota* (Center for Western Studies, 1988) and has written for such journals as *Ethnomusicology*.

ROSALIE M. JONES, of Blackfeet/Pembina Chippewa ancestry, is the founder and artistic director of Daystar: Classical Dance-Drama of Indian America, a performing arts company dedicated to the development of contemporary Native American theatrical forms based on native oral tradition. Performer, teacher, and choreographer, Jones has created many solo and ensemble dance/dramas. Professor of dance at the Institute of American Indian Arts in Santa Fe, she has taught and lectured widely. Jones's work in film and television production includes *American Indian Music and Dance*, six half-hour video programs that she wrote, edited, and produced for the University of Minnesota and the Wisconsin Arts Council.

THOMAS WHITNEY KAVANAGH is curator of collections at the Mathers Museum of Anthropology at Indiana University. He received his Ph.D. in anthropology from the University of New Mexico, Albuquerque, focusing his scholarly work on the Comanche Indians of Oklahoma. Kavanagh, who has worked on the artifact research for the Smithsonian's *Handbook of North American Indians*, has lectured and published widely on Native American culture and politics. He is the former director of the Hopi Tricentennial Project at the Hopi Cultural Center-Museum in Second Mesa, Arizona.

RON LAFRANCE (MOHAWK), a Ph.D. candidate in education at Cornell University, is director of Cornell's American Indian Program. LaFrance was also director and founder of the Akwesasne Freedom School, Mohawk Nation at Akwesasne. In addition to his work as a consultant, lecturer, and speaker on Native American issues, LaFrance is also a poet and fiction writer.

MARY JANE LENZ, associate curator at the National Museum of the American Indian, is a Ph.D. candidate in anthropology at the City University of New York. She has curated several exhibitions, including shows on Northwest Coast art and Alaskan Eskimo masks. She was curator, and exhibition catalogue author, for *The Stuff of Dreams: Native American Dolls* (Heye Foundation, 1987).

LINLEY B. LOGAN (SENECA) is an artist who was educated at the Rochester Institute of Technology, where he received a B.F.A. in industrial design, and the Institute of American Indian Arts, from which he holds an associate degree in fine arts. Logan, who has held internships at both the Smithsonian and the Schoharie Museum of the Iroquois, has shown his work in numerous exhibitions. He is currently on the staff of the National Museum of the American Indian, as Program Assistant for Exhibitions.

WILLIAM C. MEADOWS, a doctoral candidate in anthropology at the University of Oklahoma, Norman, wrote his master's thesis on the Kiowa Tonkonga (or Black Legs Society). Meadows has done fieldwork among the Kiowa, Kiowa-Apache, and Comanche tribes of Oklahoma. He is currently working on a dissertation that focuses on the role of military societies in the social organization of Southern Plains Indians. Meadows was given the name Koi-hayn-tay-k'i (Kiowa History Man) by the Kiowa.

FRED NAHWOOKSY (COMANCHE), Exhibitions Coordinator for the National Museum of the American Indian, attended the University of Oklahoma and has a B.A. degree in government and politics from the University of Maryland. Nahwooksy, who competed successfully in Fancy Dance contests as a teenager, continues to be involved in organizing Native American events. Formerly technical director at the Smithsonian's Office of Folklife Programs, he is project coordinator for the Native American dance program held in conjunction with NMAI's *Pathways of Tradition* exhibition at the Alexander Hamilton U.S. Custom House in New York.

GUS PALMER, SR. (KIOWA), a World War II Air Force veteran, is a prominent cultural leader in the Kiowa tribe of Oklahoma. In addition to reviving the Tonkonga, or Black Legs Society, in 1958, Palmer has served as Kiowa Tribal Chairman, Kiowa tribal director for the American Indian Exposition, and president of the Kiowa chapter of the Native American Church. Palmer, whose Kiowa name is My-yah-paw-dah (The Enemy Bounces When You Hit Them), is the *pawtok'i* (leader) of the Kiowa Polaiyi, or Rabbit Society. He is also a member of the Kiowa Ohoma Society and the Kiowa Gourd Clan.

EDGAR PERRY (WHITE MOUNTAIN APACHE) is the director of the White Mountain Apache Cultural Center. As director, Perry has compiled a White Mountain Apache dictionary; conducted and recorded more than 400 oral histories; and lectures extensively on White Mountain Apache history and culture. Perry also teaches the White Mountain Apache language to non-Indians living on his reservation. In addition, Perry heads a Crown Dance group and has danced in Europe as well as throughout the United States. Edgar Perry uses dance to educate people about White Mountain Apache culture and tradition.

MANUEL RÍOS MORALES (ZAPOTEC) is a Zapotec anthropologist, currently a professor/research associate of the Centro de Investigaciones y Estudios Superiores en Antropologia Social in Oaxaca, Mexico. As a migrant Zapotec to Mexico City, Ríos has been involved in the organization of the Zapotec Union Fraternal Zoogo-chense and directed and played clarinet for its band. Ríos has taught elementary school in different Indian communities and conducted research on the Mixtecs, Tlapanecs, and Nahuas in the mountain regions of Guerrero in Mexico. A selector for the National Museum of the American Indian's *Points of View* exhibition, Ríos has conducted fieldwork research for the National Museum of the American Indian's dance program.

NANCY B. ROSOFF, assistant curator at the National Museum of the American Indian, has worked on collaborative projects between the museum and Native Americans and has lectured on native peoples of the Amazonian rain forest. Rosoff, who is working toward her Ph.D. in anthropology at the City University of New York, is currently working on a documentation project with the Shuar and Achuar peoples of Ecuador.

JILL DRAYSON SWEET, associate professor of anthropology at Skidmore College in Saratoga Springs, New York, is the author of *Dances of the Tewa Pueblo Indians: Expressions of New Life* (Santa Fe: School of American Research Press, 1985) and numerous essays on Indian dance and culture. A former Weatherhead Fellow at the School of American Research in Santa Fe, Sweet spent more than two years at the Rio Grande Pueblos as part of her anthropological fieldwork. Sweet, who has lectured and taught widely, holds a B.A. and M.F.A. in dance from the University of California, Irvine, and a Ph.D. in anthropology from the University of New Mexico.

RINA SWENTZELL (TEWA, SANTA CLARA PUEBLO) received her M.A. in architecture and Ph.D. in American studies from the University of New Mexico. Swentzell, from the Santa Clara Pueblo, writes and lectures on the philosophical basis of the Pueblo world and its educational, artistic, and architectural expressions.

DAVE WARREN (TEWA, SANTA CLARA PUEBLO) is special assistant with the Smithsonian's Office of the Assistant Secretary for Public Service. A former director of the Cultural Research Center, Institute of American Indian Arts, in Santa Fe, Warren has helped organize programs of cultural resources training, study and research for Native Americans at a number of major research institutions. Warren, who holds advanced degrees in colonial Latin American history from the University of New Mexico, is the author of numerous articles on American Indian history, education, and culture. Dr. Warren is former deputy director of the National Museum of the American Indian.

MARIA WILLIAMS (TLINGIT/COOK INLET REGION, INC. SHAREHOLDER) is the Native Folk Arts Director for the Alaska State Council on the Arts. Currently enrolled in a Ph.D. program, with a specialization in ethnomusicology, at the University of California, Los Angeles, Williams has been extensively involved with Indian music and dance. In addition to her academic contributions, Williams's "hands-on" experience includes her work with such artists as the King Island Dance Group and various Alaskan Native dance groups.

I N D E X

Note: Numbers in boldface refer to pages featuring illustrations.

A

African influences, 4
Agricultural ritual
    Aymara, 54, 58–62
    Mayan, 44, 48, 49, 51
    prehistoric, 4
    Tewa Pueblo Indian, 84, **86**, 93
    Zapotec, 34
Akwesasne Singers, **22**
Alaska Native Claims Settlement Act, 156,
    157, 164
Alaskan Native dance
    biennial Celebration, 157, **157**, 159, **159**,
    160
    dance rattle in, **154**, 155
    evolution of, 150–52, 156
    Haida people, **150**, **151**, **154**, 156, 157,
    159, **161**
    Inupiat people, **162**, **163**, 163–64
    role of, 167
    suppression of, 149
    Tlingit people, **150**, 156, 157, **157**, **158**,
    159, **159**, **160**
    Tsimshian people, **150**, 154, 156, 157,
    159
    Wolf Dance, **162**, **163**, 163
    Yupik people, 164, **165**, **166**, 166–67
Aleut Indians. *see* Alutiiq Indians
Allain, Aurorah, 183
Alligator Dance, **28**, 29, 30
Alutiiq Indians, **152**, **153**, 156
American Indian Dance Theatre, 14, 172,
    174, **174**
American Indian Registry of the Performing
    Arts, 183
Amiotte, Arthur, 136, 188
Apache
    clown dancer, **15**
    music, 12
Apache, White Mountain
    Crown Dance, 66–67, 72–79, **72–79**
    history of, 65
    Hoop Dance, 80
    role of dance to, 65–67
    Sunrise Dance, 67–72, **67–72**
    War Dance, 79
Arapaho, 105, 127
    Crow Dance, **106**
    Sun Dance, **106**
Arizona, Navajo Nation Fair, **128**, **132**, **138**,
    139, **140**
Assiniboine Indians, 127
Athabascan Indians, 156, 167
Aymara
    Carnival celebrations, **52**, 53, **53**, **56**, **57**,
    58, 58
    cosmology, 52, 56–58
    demographics, 52
    Devil Dance, 54, **54**, **55**
    fiesta, 56–61
    music, 53, **57**, 60–61
    role of dance, 52, 56–58

Aztecs
    drum, **8**
    influences on Zincantán Maya, 43
    in Zapotec Malinche Dance, 37

B

Balanchine, George, 170, **171**
Ballard, Louis, 172
Ballet, 170
Basket Dance, 13, **95**
Bautista López, Salvador, 46
Bean Dance, 134
Bird Dance, 12
Black Bear, Ben, Sr., 129
Black Legs Society, **116**, 116–117
Blackfeet, 127
Blackstar, Linda, **114**
Bladder Feast, 164, **165**
Blood Indians, 127
Bolivia. *See* Aymara
Bread Dance, **27**
Brush Dance, 121
Buffalo Dance, **87**, **89**
Burguete, Jaime Torres, 43, 51, 62, 188
Butterfly Dance, **87**, **111**

C

Cadaval, Olivia, 188
Canada
    British Columbia, **4**
    potlatch ban, 7
    Stoney Reserve, 142–43
Cant Tinza Society, 127
Carnival celebrations
    Aymara, **52**, 53, **53**, **56**, **57**, **58**, 58, 62
    Mayan, **5**, 44–46, **47**, **49**, 49–51, **50**, **51**
Ceremonies. *See also* Carnival celebrations;
    Fiesta dances; Powwows; Sun Dance
    Aymara, 52–54, 56–62
    Catholic influences on, 4, 7, 33–34, 34–
    37, 44, 60
    Gallup Ceremonial, New Mexico (1990),
    vii, **126**, **130**, **132**
    Haudenosaunee, 25–30
    Kiowa Black Legs Society, 116–17
    Mayan, 44, **45**, 46, **47**, 48, 49–51
    name–giving, 19
    Native Alaskan, **150**, **151**
    San Ildefonso Pueblo patron saint feast
    day, **99–102**, 99–103
    Tewa Pueblos, 83, 93
    White Mountain Apache, 65–68, 72, 80
    Yupik, 164
    Zapotec, 38
Cherokee, 177
    Stomp Dance, 13
Cheyenne, 127, **136**
    Dog Soldiers, **136**
Chiapas, Mexico, 43
Chicken Dance, **143**
Chicken Scratch dance, 17
Chimelgalrea, Vernon, 166
Choreography
    Apache Crown Dance, 67, 75–76
    Aymara ceremonial, 57, 58–60

Aymara *Qhashwa* dance, 60–62
Gourd Dance, 107, **107**
Grass Dance, 111, 138
Hoop Dance, 80
Inupiat dances, 163–64
modern, Native American influence on,
    169–70, 172–73, 179–80, 182–83
Northern Plains Indians, 138, 146
Omaha/Grass/Crow Dance, 111
Pick–up Dance, 127
Straight Dance, 111
Tewa Indian, 83, 94
Yupik dance, 166
Zapotec traditional dances, 37, 40
Cisneros, Evelyn, **173**
Cloud Dance, 13, **95**
Cocopelli, **6**
Coffey, Wallace, **114**
Comanche
    Buffalo Dance, 106
    Homecoming celebration, **11**, **112**, **114**,
    115, **119**, **120**, 121–23, **122**
    societies within, 107
    in Tewa Indian parodies, 96, **97**, **100**
Competitions, dance, 14
    Southern Plains Indian powwows, 118,
    121
Concha, Benito, **145**
Corn Dance, 30
Corn Maiden Dance, **95**
Cortés, Hernando, 37, **90**
Cosmology
    Aymara Indian, 52, 56–58
    Haudenosaunee, 20, 25
    Mayan, 43, 44
    Northwest Coast Indians, 155
    role in dance, 12
    of Sun Dance, 135–36
    Tewa Pueblo Indian, 93
    White Mountain Apache, 66, 80
    Zapotec Indian, 37, 38
Coyote Dance, **3**
Cree Indians, 127
Creek Indians
    Stomp Dance, 13
Crow Dance, **106**, 109–12, **110**
Crow Indians, 127
Crown Dance, 66–67, 72–79, **72–79**

D

Dakota Indians. *See* Lakota/Dakota Sioux
Dance clothes
    Alutiiq Indians, **153**
    Aymara, 53, 54, 56, 62
    Cherokee Stomp Dance, 177
    Comanche buckskin, **120**
    Corn Dance, **86**
    Crown Dance, **73**, **74**, 75, 79
    Dance of the Black Men, 40, **40**
    eagle–feather bustle, Plains Indian, **129**
    Fancy Dance, **viii**, **xi**, 138
    Fancy–Shawl Dance, 138, **139**
    fingerweaving, **3**

Gourd Dance, 118
Grass Dance, 115, 138, **139**
hair "roach" headdress, Plains Indian, **128**
Haudenosaunee, **26**
Inupiat dance, 164, **164**
Jingle Dress, **120**, **140**, 140
Kiowa Black Leg(gin)s Society, 117
mass–manufactured items in, 8
Mayas of highland Chiapas, 43–44, 46
Native Alaskan, 159, **160**
Navajo powwow, **132**
Northern Plains tribes, 127, 131
Omaha/Grass/Crow Dance, 111–12, **112**
Seminole dance leggings, **176**
Southern Plains powwow dances, 118
Straight Dance, 111
Sunrise Ceremony, White Mountain Apache, 68
Tewa Pueblo Indian, **92**, 93, **99**
White Mountain Apache, **68**, 68
Yupik people's, **165**, **166**, 166
Zapotec Indian, 37, 40
Dance for the World, 135
Dance of the Black Men, 40, **40**, 44
Dance of the Chinas of Oaxaca, **36**
Dance rattle, **154**, 155
Dances. *See also* Choreography; Fiesta dances; Modern Native American dance; Role of dance; Tewa Pueblo dances
Alligator Dance, **28**, 29, 30
Alutiiq Indian, **152**, **153**
Basket Dance, 13
Bean Dance, 134
Bird Dance, 12
Bread Dance, **27**
Brush Dance, 121
Buffalo Dance, **87**, **89**
Butterfly Dance, **87**, **111**
Chicken Dance, **143**
Chicken Scratch dance, 17
Cloud Dance, 13
contemporary occasions for, 14, 79
Corn Dance, 30
Coyote, **3**
Crow Dance, **106**, 109–12, **110**
Crown Dance, 66–67, 72–79, **72–79**
Dance for the World, 135
Dance of the Black Men, 40, **40**, 44
Dance of the Chinas of Oaxaca, **36**
Deer Dance, **88**, **100**
Delaware Skin Dance, 29
Devil Dance, 54, **54**, 55
Dream Dance, 111
Drum Dance, 111
Eagle Dance, **11**, **107**, 107, 172, **173**
evolution of, 13–14, 17
Fancy Dance, **viii**, **xi**, 118, **130**, 138, 172
Fancy–Shawl Dance, 14, **16**, 134, 138, **139**, **144**
Fish Dance, 30
Forty–Nine Dance, 122

Geese Dance, 93
general features of, 10–13
Ghost Dance, 7, 109–12, **110**, 129
Gourd Dance, 8, **107**, 107, 118, **119**, 121
Grass Dance, 109–12, **114**, 115, 134, **139**
Great Feather Dance, **25**, 25
Haudenosaunee Women's, 25, 29–30, **31**
Hoop Dance, 10–12, 80, 107, **145**, 146, 174
Hopi Corn Dance, **85**, 86
Horn Dance, 106
intertribal, 134
Jingle–Dress Dance, 14, **15**, 115, **120**, **140**, 140
Malinche Dance, **36**, 37, **40**
Matachines' Dance, **90**, 91
Mayan Carnival, 44–46, **47**
Medicine Lodge Dance, 135
Moccasin Dance, **21**
Negrito Dance, **40**
Northern Plains Indians, general features, 138–39, 145–46
Old Man's Cane Dance, 29
Omaha Dance, 109, **109**, 111, 134
Owl Dance, 106, 134, **134**
performance space, 10–12
Pick–up Dance, 127, 134
Pine Tree Dance, 30
Qhashwa Dance, Aymara, **59**, 60–62
Rabbit Dance, 29, 131, 134
Rain Dance, **9**, 93, **93**
Reverse Dance, 117
Robin Dance, 30
Round Dance, 106, **119**, 122, **132**, 134, **142**
Shaking Bottle Dance, 30
Shaking the Bush Dance, 30
Shawl Dance, **114**, 115, **126**
Shuffle Dance, 25
Skin Dance, 29
Snake–and–Buffalo Dance, 106
Snake Dance, 30, 134
Sneak–up Dance, 127, 133, **143**
Spear–and–Shield Dance, 107
Standing Quiver Dance, 29
Stomp Dance, 13, 29, 177
Straight Dance, **110**, 111, 118
Sun Dance, 7, **106**, 116, 121, 125, 127, 129, 135–36, 142
Sunrise Dance, 67–72, **67–72**
Swaying Dance, 122
Thirst Dance, 135
Tiger Dance, **39**
Turn Around Dance, 117
Turtle Dance, 13
War Dance, 79, 109, **109**, 118, **119**, **126**, 134, 145
Wolf Dance, **162**, **163**, 163
Woman's Dance, Southern Plains Indians, 115
Yupik people's, 164, **165**, **166**, 166–67
Davids, Brent Michael, 172
Daystar Contemporary Dance Company, 180–83, **181**, **182**

Deer Dance, **88**, **100**
Deities. *See also* Cosmology
Aymara Indian, 52, 53, 58
Haudenosaunee, 25
in Mayan traditions, 44, 46–48, 49, 51
White Mountain Apache, 66, 67, 72
Delaware Indians, 29
Devil Dance, 54, **54**, 55
Dream Dance, 111
Drum Dance, 111
Drums
Aztec, **8**
Haudenosaunee water, **22**, 23
Inupiat box, **162**
in Native Alaskan ceremonies, **150**
in Northern Plains Indian powwows, 140, **141**
Southern Plains Indian ceremonial, **132**
Tlingit box, **158**
White Mountain Apache, **74**
Yupik, 166, **166**
Dunham, Katherine, 179

E

Eagle Dance, **11**, **107**, 107, 172, **173**
Earl Medicine, **2**
Eight Northern Indian Arts and Craft Fair (1989), **13**, **99**, **131**
Encarnación Peña, José (Soqueen/Soqween), **9**
Entrada parade (Bolivia), 53, **53**
European influence, 4, 33
in Aymara culture, 52–53
in Mayan costume, 44
in Zapotec music, 42

F

Fancy Dance, **viii**, **xi**, 118, **130**, 138, 172
Fancy–Shawl Dance, 14, **16**, 134, 138, **139**, **144**
Fiesta dances
Aymara, 54–61
Mayan traditions, 43–51
role of, 33–34, 44, 54–58, 61–62
sponsorship of, 33–34
Zapotec traditions, 34–42
Fingerweaving, **3**
Fish Dance, 30
Flag songs, 133
Flathead Indians, 127
Forty–Nine Dance, 122

G

Ganteaume, Cécile, 188
Garcia Gómez, Agustin, 44
Geese Dance, 93
Geiogamah, Hanay, 172, 174
Ghost Dance, 109–12, **110**, 129
government ban on, 7
Goddard, Pliny, 66
Gourd Dance, 8, **107**, 107, 118, **119**, 121

Graham, Martha, 170, 179, 180
Grass Dance, 109–12, **114**, 115, 134, **139**
Great Feather Dance, **25**, 25
Green, Elwood, 172
Green, Rayna, 177, 188
Gros Ventre Indians, 127
Guatemala, 40

H

Haida people, **4**, **150**, **151**, **154**, 156, 157, 159, **161**
Haudenosaunee
    adopted dances of, 29
    Alligator Dance, **28**, 29, 30
    Bread Dance, **27**
    ceremonial dances, 25–31
    cosmology, 20, 25
    dance clothes, **26**
    Great Feather Dance, **25**, 25
    name–giving ceremony, 19
    Onondaga tribe, **22**
    social dances, 19–23, 29–30
    Stomp Dance, 29
    Tonawanda Longhouse, **20**
Hernández Bautista, Mauro, 44
Heth, Charlotte, 188–89
Highway, Rene, 179, 180, **181**
Highway, Tomson, 180
Hogan, Linda, 177
Honor songs, 140
Hoop Dance, 10–12, 80, 107, **145**, 146, 174
Hopi Corn Dance, **85**, 86
Hopi Indians, 146
Horn Dance, 106
Houle, Vern, **143**
Huanca Laura, Tomás, 52, 53, 189
Huenemann, Lynn, 189

I

Inloshka Society, 111
Inupiat people, 156, **162**, **163**, 163–64, 167
Iowa Indians, **110**
Iroquois. *See* Haudenosaunee

J

James, Belinda, 179–80
Jim Skye Dancers, **23**, **28**
Jingle–Dress Dance, 14, **15**, 115, **120**, **140**, 140
John, Theresa, 168
Jones, Rosalie, 180, **181**, 189

K

Kansa Indians, 109
Kansas, 105
Katzeek, David, 157
Kavanagh, Thomas Whitney, 189
Kealiinohomoku, Joanne W., 14
Keel, John, iv, **113**

Keepers of the Western Door Powwow, **6**, **15**, **16**, **22**, **112**, **114**, **141**, **144**, **175**
Keetoowah Society, 177
Khalsa, Ann Roberts, 183
King, Bruce, 172
King Island Inupiat Dancers, **162**, 163
Kiowa
    Black Legs Society, **116**, 116–17
    contemporary dances, 14
    Gourd Clan, 107
Koweonarre (Little Chief), **136**
Kurath, Gertrude P., 14
KuuJaw, **4**

L

LaFrance, Ron, 189
Lakota/Dakota Sioux
    dance practices, 127–31, 134
    features of dance, 145–46
    flag songs, 133
    powwows, 133–34
    range, 127
    warrior societies within, 127–29
Lenz, Mary Jane, 155, 189
Limón, José, 179, 180
Little Chief (Koweonarre), **136**
Little Pony society, 107
Logan, Linley, 190
Lopez, Antonio, **173**
López Ruiz, Pascual, 46
Lupe, Ronnie, 66, 80
Lynn, Barry, 179

M

Malinche Dance, **36**, 37, **40**
    Malinche character in Tewa Pueblo dance, **90**
Martinez, Julian, **10**
Masks
    Aymara Devil Dance, 54, **55**
    Yupik, **165**, **166**
    Zapotec, 40–42, **41**
Matachines' Dance, **90**, 91
Mayac, Earl, **162**
Mayas, 34
    black–men personages, 46, **46**
    Carnival celebrations, 5, 44–46, **47**, **49**, 49–51, **50**, **51**
    ceremonial drinking horn, 44, **45**
    cosmology, 43, 44
    costume, 43–44, 46
    Dance of the Negritos, 40, **40**, 44
    dances commemorating wars, 46
    fiesta dances, 44–46
    of highland Chiapas, 43
    music of, 46–48, **48**
McIntyre, Chuna, 166
McNaughton, Franklyn E., **22**
Mead, Marie, 168
Meadows, William, 117, 190
Medicine Lodge Dance, 135
Mexico. *See also* Mayas; Zapotecs
    Chamula, 43, 46, 48, **48**, 50–51
    indigenous peoples of, 34
    music/musicians in ancient art, **5**, **7**, **8**

San Cristóbal de las Casas, 43
San Pedro Chenalhó, 43, 44, 46, **46**, **47**, 48, 51
    Tenejapa, 43, **47**, 48, **49**, **50**
    Tenejapa weavers' cooperative, **4**
    Zincantán, 43, 44, **45**, 48
Meyers, Michael, 183
Miccasukee Indians, 29
Michigan State University Powwow, **130**, **134**, **139**
Moccasin Dance, **21**
Moctezuma, 37, 40, **90**
Modern Native American dance, 169–70, **171**, 172, **174**, 174, **175**, **176**, **178**, 179–80, **181**, **182**, 182–83
Mohican Indians, 172
Montezuma. *See* Moctezuma
Mopope, Stephen, **107**
Mountain Spirit Dance. *See* Crown Dance
Music
    Aymara, 56, **57**, 60–63
    Bolivian Carnival, 53, **56**, **57**
    Cocopelli petroglyph, **6**
    general features, 12
    Haudenosaunee singing, 29
    Mayan, 44, 46–48, **48**, **49**, 49–50, 49–51, **50**
    Plains Indian, 118, 145
    powwow singing, 29, 118, 145
    Tewa Pueblo songs, 94
    White Mountain Apache ceremonial songs, 66, 68
    Zapotec, 42
Musical instruments. *See also* Drums
    Aymara Indian, 60–61, **61**, 62
    ceramic rattles, **7**
    evolution of, 7–8
    flute, ancient Mexican, **8**
    general features, 12
    Haudenosaunee, **22**, 23
    Mayan, 46–48
    pinkillu, **61**
    White Mountain Apache, **74**
    Zapotec, 38, **39**, **42**, 42

N

Nahuas, 34
Nahwooksy, Fred, 143, 190
Native American Theatre Ensemble, 174
Navajo, 146
    powwow dress, **132**
    Tewa Indian parody of, 96
Navajo Nation Fair, **128**, **132**, **138**, **139**, **140**
Nebraska, 105, 111
New Mexico
    Cocopelli petroglyph, **6**
    Gallup Ceremonial, **126**, **130**, **132**
    Tewa Indian villages, 83–84
New York
    Border Crossing Event, **21**
    intertribal powwow, **2**

Keepers of the Western Door Powwow (1992), **6**, **15**, **16**, **21**, **112**, **114**, **141**, **144**, **175**
Nijinska, Bronislava, 170
Nunamta Yupik Singers and Dancers, 166, **166**

O

Ojibwa Indians, 127
Oklahoma, 105, 109, 111, 115, 121
   Comanche Homecoming celebration (1992), **11**, **112**, **114**, 115, **119**, **120**, 121–23, **122**
Old Man's Cane Dance, 29
Omaha Dance, 109, **109**, 111, 129, 134
Omaha Indians, 109, 111, 129, 134
Omaha Warrior Society, 129
Onondaga, **22**
Oqwa Pi (Red Cloud; Abel Sánchez), iv
Osage Indians, 111
Owl Dance, 106, 134, **134**

P

Paiute Indians, 109
Palmer, Gus, Sr., 116, 117, 190
Pawnee, 109, 111
Pérez López, José, 48
Perry, Edgar, 66, 78, 190
Persian Gulf War, 14, 79
Pick–up Dance, 127, 134
Pine Tree Dance, 30
Ponca Indians, 109, 111
Poolaw, Pascal C., 117
Potlatch, Canadian government ban on, 7
Powwows
   dance contests at, 118, 121
   etymology, 105
   Indian Ecumenical Conference, 1992, 142–43, **143**
   intertribal, **2**, 115, 145, 146
   Keepers of the Western Door, **viii**, **xi**, **6**, **15**, **16**, **22**, **112**, **114**, **141**, **144**, **175**
   Lewiston, New York (1992), **2**
   Michigan State University (1992), **130**, **134**, **139**
   New Jersey (1992), **3**
   Northern Plains Indians practices at, 125, 127, 129, 131, 133–34, 142–43, 145, 146
   Red Earth, 115
   singing style of, 29, 145
   Southern Plains Indian practices, 105–09, 115, 118, 121–22
Prehistoric dance, 4
   musical instruments, **5**, 7, **7**, **8**
Pucci, Peter, 172
Pueblo Indians. *See also* Tewa Pueblo dances
   dance style, 10
   revolt of 1680, 7
   Spanish persecution of, 89

Q

Qhashwa Dance, **59**, 60–62
Quintero, Canyon Z., 79
Quispe Fernandez, Bonificia, **56**

R

Rabbit Dance, 29, 131, 134
Rain Dance, **9**
   Tewa Pueblo, 93, **93**
Ramos, George, **159**
Red Cloud (Oqwa Pi; Abel Sánchez), iv
Reverse Dance, 117
Riley, Ramon, 76
Ríos Morales, Manuel, 34, 37, 38, 190
Robin Dance, 30
Role of dance, 8, 65, 169
   in Aymara culture, 52, 56–58
   fiesta dances, 33–34, 44, 54–58, 61–62
   Lakota/Dakota Sioux, 131
   to Native Alaskan peoples, 167
   to Northern Plains Indians, 125, 129, 136, 146
   to Tewa Pueblo Indians, 84, 89, 93, 96, 98, 103
   to White Mountain Apache, 65–67, 80
Roman Catholic Church, 4, 7, 33–34, 34–37, 44
   influence in Aymara culture, 54, 58
   influence on Tewa Pueblo Indians, 89, 91
   in Tewa Indian parodies, 96
Rosoff, Nancy, 191
Round Dance, 106, **119**, 122, **132**, 134, **142**

S

Sánchez, Abel (Oqwa Pi; Red Cloud), iv
Schwei, Barbara, 172
Scott, H. L., 116
Sea Lion Corporation, 164
Sealaska Heritage Foundation, 157
Seminoles, 29
Shaking Bottle Dance, 30
Shaking the Bush Dance, 30
Shawl Dance, **114**, 115, **126**
Shawn, Ted, 169–70, **171**
Shoshone, 127
Shuffle Dance, 25
   New Women's, 29
Sioux. *See* Lakota/Dakota Sioux
Six Nations, 29
Skibine, George, 170
Skin Dance, 29
Skye, Jim, **23**, **28**
Smart, George, 164, **165**
Smith, Ernest, **24**, **25**, **26**, **27**
Smuin, Michael, 172, **173**
Snake–and–Buffalo Dance, 106
Snake Dance, 30, 134
Sneak–up Dance, 127, 133, **143**
Socialization, role of dance in, 80
   in fiestas, 33–34, 57
   Haudenosaunee traditions, 19–23, 25–27, 29
   Tewa Pueblo dances, 98, 103

Soqueen/Soqween (José Encarnación Peña), **9**
Spear–and–Shield Dance, 107
Standing Quiver Dance, 29
Stomp Dance, 13, 29, 177
Stoney Reserve, 142–43
Straight Dance, **110**, 111, 118
Sun Dance, **106**, 116, 121, 127, 129, 135–36
   government ban on, 7, 116, 125
   Stoney Reserve Sioux practices, 142
Sunrise Dance, 67–72, **67–72**
Suppression of native practices, 7, 116, 125, 149, 164
Swaying Dance, 122
Sweet, Jill Drayson, 191
Swentzell, Rina, 93, 191
Swimmer, Eddie, 174

T

Taliaferro, Leilani, 183
Tallchief, Maria, 170, **171**
Tallchief, Marjorie, 170, **171**
Tanner, Virginia, 179
Taos Pueblo Indians, 127
Tewa Pueblo dances
   Basket Dance, **95**
   Buffalo Dance, **87**, **89**
   Butterfly Dance, **87**
   choreography, 94
   Cloud Dance, **95**
   cultural empowerment and, 98, 103
   Deer Dance, **88**, **100**
   Hopi Corn Dance, **85**, **86**
   humor in, 96
   for non–Indian audiences, 91
   patron saint feast days, 89–91, **90**
   Rain Dance, 93, **93**
   San Ildefonso patron saint feast day, 98–103, **99–102**
   seasonal themes, 84, 93
   secrecy in, 89
Theatrical performance of traditional dance, 1, 14, 91, 115, 172. *See also* Modern Native American dance
   Inupiat people, 163
   Yupik, 166–67
They Dance Staring at the Sun. *See* Sun Dance
Thirst Dance. *See* Sun Dance
Tiger Dance, **39**
Tiulana, Charles, **162**
Tiulana, Paul, 163
Tlingit Indians, **150**, 156, 157, **157**, **158**, 159, **159**, **160**
Tokala Society, 127
Tonkonga, 116–17
Tonawanda Longhouse, **20**
Traditional, defining, 17
Training, 1
   Tewa Pueblo dancers, 94
   White Mountain Apache Crown dancers, 76
Tribes/indigenous peoples. *See also* Apache, White Mountain; Haudenosaunee

Alutiiq, **152**, **153**, 156
Apache, 12, **15**
Arapaho, 105, **106**, 127
Assiniboine, 127
Athabascan, 156, 167
Aymara, 33–34, 52–62
Blackfeet, 127
Blood Indians, 127
Cherokee, 13, 177
Cheyenne, 105, 127, **136**
Comanche, **11**, 106, 107, **112**, **114**, 115, **119**, **120**, 121–23, **122**
Cree, 127
Creek, 13
Crow, 127
Dakota, 127–31
Delaware, 29
Flathead, 127
Gros Ventre, 127
Haida, **4**, **150**, **151**, **154**, 156, 157, 159, **161**
Hopi, 146
intertribal cultural exchange, **2**, 2, 7, 29, 109, 115, **126**, 129, 134, 145, 146
Inupiat, 156, **162**, **163**, 163–64, 167
Iowa, **110**
Kansa, 109
Kiowa, 14, 107, 116–117
Lakota, 127–131
Mayas, 33–34, 34, 43–51, 61–62
Miccasukee, 29
Mohican, 172
Nahuas, 34
Navajo, **128**, **132**, **138**, **139**, **140**, 146
Ojibwa, 127
Omaha, 109, 111, 129, 134
Onondaga, **22**
Osage, 111
Paiute, 109
Pawnee, 109, 111
Ponca, 109, 111
Pueblo, 7, 10
Seminole, 29
Shoshone, 127
Sioux, 127–31, 142–43
Stoney Reserve Sioux, 142–43
Taos, 127
Tewa Pueblo, 83
Tlingit, **150**, 156, 157, **157**, **158**, 159, **159**, **160**
Tsimshian, **150**, **154**, 156, 157, 159
Ute, 127
Winnebago, 127, 134
Yuchi, 13
Yupik, 156, 164, **165**, **166**, 166–67
Zapotec, 33–42, 61–62
Zuñi, 89
Trujillo, Raoul, 172, **173**
Tsimshian Indians, **150**, **154**, 156, 157, 159
Turn Around Dance, 117
Turtle Dance, 13
Tzeltal. *See* Mayas
Tzotzil. *See* Mayas

U

United States government
    dances banned by, 7, 116, 125
    Native Alaskans and, 156
    White Mountain Apache and, 65
Ute Indians, 127

V

Valenzuela, Juan, 179
Venezuela, 12
Vietnam Veterans Annual Powwow
    (Anadarko, Oklahoma), **109**, **113**, **118**, **119**, **120**

W

War Dance, 118, **119**
    Dakota, **126**
    Plains Indian songs, 145
    Sioux–speaking tribes, 134
    Southern Plains Indians, 109, **109**
    White Mountain Apache, 79
Ware, Lehman, **110**
Warren, Dave, 93, 191
Waters, Elizabeth, 179
Wauahdooah, Nicholas, **114**
West, W. Richard, Jr., x
White Eagle, Lance Quiver, **3**
White Eagle, Brenda, **3**
Wildcat, Darrell, **110**
Williams, Maria, 191
Winnebago Indians, 127, 134
Wolf Dance, **162**, **163**, 163
Women in dance
    Bread Dance, **27**
    dance contests, 121
    Fancy–Shawl Dance, 14, **16**, 138, **139**
    Haudenosaunee traditions, 25, 29–30, **31**
    Jingle–Dress Dance, 14, **15**, 115, **140**, 140
    Northern Plains Indian tradition, 145
    Shawl Dance, 115
    Southern Plains Indian, 115
Woodring, Carl, **110**

Y

Yuchi Indians, 13
Yupik Indians, 156, 164, **165**, **166**, 166–67

Z

Zapotec, 34, 38
    bailes tradicionales, 37
    dance masks, 40–42, **41**
    Dance of the Black Men, 40, **40**
    Dance of the Chinas of Oaxaca, **36**
    danzas tradicionales, 37, 42
    Malinche Dance, **36**, 37, **40**
    music, 38, **39**, **42**, 42
    Negrito Dance, **40**
    role of fiesta dances, 33–34, 61–62
    Tiger Dance, **39**

PHOTOGRAPHY CREDITS

The photographers and the sources of photographic material are as follows. Copyright is in the name of the photographer, unless otherwise indicated.

Chris Arend: figs. 179, 180, 184; Jacinto Arias: figs. 53, 55; Christian Barthelmess: fig. 119, © Smithsonian Institution; Bert Bell: fig. 141; Walter Bigbee: figs. 16, 124, 127, 129, 134–36, 138, 143, 194, © Smithsonian Institution; Pam Dewey: p. ii, figs. 6, 10–14, 47, 51, 65, 103, 116, 121, 123, 151, 167, 168, 172, 182, 195 © Smithsonian Institution; Jeffrey Jay Foxx: pp. vii, viii, xi, 184, figs. 5, 7–9, 15, 17–20, 22, 23, 25, 36, 49, 50, 52, 54, 56–60, 90, 93, 95–99, 101, 104, 107, 109, 113, 115, 125, 128, 139, 140, 142, 145–49, 152, 154–56, 193; Karen Furth: figs. 30, 102, 177, © Smithsonian Institution; Kim Garnick: fig. 3; Murrae Haynes: fig. 199; Richard Hill, Sr.: figs. 1–2, 4; Fred Hirschmann: p. i, figs. 74, 76–80, 82, 164–66; Mark Kelley: figs. 162, 170–71, 173–76; Kevin King: figs. 27, 33–35, © Smithsonian Institution; Barbara Lau: fig. 161, © Smithsonian Institution; Kitty Leaken: fig. 196; Scott Logan: fig. 21; William C. Meadows: figs. 130–31; James Mooney: figs. 114, 120; Michael Moore: figs. 75, 81, 83, 84, 87; Fred Nahwooksy: figs. 144, 150, 153, 157–159; Norm Regniér: fig. 198; Robertson: fig. 187; Nancy Rosoff: figs. 38–46, 48, 61–64, 66–73, © Smithsonian Institution; Sea Lion Corporation: fig. 183; Izzy Seidman: figs. 24, 160; Marty Sohl: fig. 190; Roger Sweet: figs. 91, 92, 94, 100, 105, 106, 108, 110–12; Jeff Tinsley: fig. 185; Harry Tonemah: figs. 117, 118, 122, 126, 132, 133, 137, © Smithsonian Institution; Joe Travers: fig. 191; Ch. Vandamme: fig. 189; Cylla von Tiedemann: fig. 197; Maria Williams: figs. 169, 178, 186; Winter and Pond: fig. 163.